BISON
BOOKS

Theodore Roosevelt

PRESIDENTIAL EDITION

THE WINNING OF THE WEST

BY

THEODORE ROOSEVELT

VOLUME ONE

FROM THE ALLEGHANIES TO THE MISSISSIPPI
1769–1776

WITH MAP

Introduction to the Bison Book Edition by
John Milton Cooper Jr.

University of Nebraska Press
Lincoln and London

Introduction to the Bison Book Edition © 1995
by the University of Nebraska Press
Manufactured in the United States of America

♾ The paper in this book meets the minimum requirements of
American National Standard for Information Sciences—Perma-
nence of Paper for Printed Library Materials, ANSI
Z39.48-1984.

First Bison Book printing: 1995
Most recent printing indicated by the last digit below:
10   9   8   7   6   5   4   3   2   1

Library of Congress Cataloging-in-Publication Data
Roosevelt, Theodore, 1858–1919.
The winning of the West / by Theodore Roosevelt—Presidential
ed.
p. cm.
Includes index.
Originally published: New York: G. P. Putnam's Sons, 1894.
Contents: v. 1. From the Alleghanies to the Mississippi, 1769–
1776—v. 2. From the Alleghanies to the Mississippi, 1777–
1783—v. 3. The founding of the trans-Alleghany common-
wealths, 1784–1790—v. 4. Louisiana and the Northwest, 1791–
1807.
ISBN 0-8032-8958-8 (set)—ISBN 0-8032-8954-5 (v. 1)—
ISBN 0-8032-8955-3 (v. 2)—ISBN 0-8032-8956-1 (v. 3)—
ISBN 0-8032-8957-X (v. 4)
1. United States—Territorial expansion. 2. Northwest, Old—
History. 3. West (U.S.)—History. I. Title.
E179.5.R66   1995
976—dc20
94-46645   CIP

The four-volume set of *The Winning of the West* was copyrighted
and published between 1889 and 1896 by G. P. Putnam's Sons,
New York. This Bison Book is a reprint of volume 1, © 1889,
which includes Theodore Roosevelt's 1900 foreword and was
later designated as the Presidential Edition. The index for volume 1 is found at the end of volume 2.

THIS BOOK IS DEDICATED, WITH HIS PERMISSION

TO

FRANCIS PARKMAN

TO WHOM AMERICANS WHO FEEL A PRIDE IN THE PIONEER HISTORY OF
THEIR COUNTRY ARE SO GREATLY INDEBTED

' O strange New World that yit wast never young,
  Whose youth from thee by gripin' need was wrung,
  Brown foundlin' o' the woods, whose baby-bed
  Was prowled roun' by the Injun's cracklin' tread,
  And who grew'st strong thru shifts an' wants an' pains,
  Nursed by stern men with empires in their brains,
  Who saw in vision their young Ishmel strain
  With each hard hand a vassal ocean's mane ;
  Thou skilled by Freedom and by gret events
  To pitch new states ez Old World men pitch tents,
  Thou taught by fate to know Jehovah's plan,
  Thet man's devices can't unmake a man.
      .   .   .   .

Oh, my friends, thank your God, if you have one, that he
'Twixt the Old World and you set the gulf of a sea,
Be strong-backed, brown-handed, upright as your pines,
By the scale of a hemisphere shape your designs."

—LOWELL.

INTRODUCTION

John Milton Cooper Jr.

No American president has enjoyed stronger associations with the West than Theodore Roosevelt. Of all his physical characteristics, only his teeth and eyeglasses identified him better than his broad-brimmed rancher's hat. His cavalry regiment in the Spanish-American War drew heavily, though not exclusively, on men from the Great Plains and Rocky Mountains, who proudly bore the press-spawned sobriquet of "Rough Riders." Political friends and foes alike dubbed Roosevelt a "cowboy." Nor did these western associations end with experiences and imagery. Roosevelt also wrote several books about the West. One of those books was a brief, hastily done biography of Thomas Hart Benton, while others collected his 1880s magazine articles recounting his exploits as a hunter and rancher. But the West also furnished the subject of the most substantial and scholarly writing that he ever did. Between 1889 and 1897, Roosevelt published four volumes analyzing the expansion of Euro-Americans from the British colonies (and later the United States) from 1763 to 1807. The work was entitled *The Winning of the West.*

Strong as those personal and literary associations were, however, much remained odd about Theodore Roosevelt as a westerner. No other president has been more of an urbanite than this native of New York City (the only one to gain the White House), where he ran for mayor and served as police commissioner—or more of an "easterner" than this blueblooded descendant of Knickerbockers and *Mayflower* voyagers, this Harvard graduate and member of Porcellian, who had lived and traveled extensively in Europe be-

fore he ever ventured beyond the Appalachians. Never a
permanent resident of the West, Roosevelt spent only a few
discontinuous months in the Dakota Territory, and there
he often hobnobbed with British gentlemen and European
aristocrats. Despite the Rough Riders, his engagement
with things military involved naval affairs far more than
land fighting, and the subject that initially attracted his
attention as a historian and occasioned his first book was
naval warfare. Inasmuch as Roosevelt was always a westerner with a difference, he wrote a special kind of history in
The Winning of the West.[1]

The most revealing and misleading clue to the character
of the work comes in its dedication:

To
Francis Parkman
To Whom Americans Who Feel a Pride in the
Pioneer History of Their Country
Are So Greatly Indebted

On one level, Roosevelt was expressing nothing more than
heartfelt admiration and wishes to emulate a heroic master. "I suppose that every American who cares at all for the
history of his own country feels a certain personal pride in
your work————," he wrote to Parkman, asking permission to dedicate the work to him, "but those of us who have
a taste for history, and yet have spent much of our time on
the frontier, perhaps realize even more keenly than our fellows, that your works stand alone, and that they must be
models for all historical treatment of the founding of new
communities and the growth of the frontier here in the wilderness."[2]

On a slightly deeper level, Roosevelt was expressing a
legitimate personal and literary identification with Parkman. Like the older Bostonian, the New Yorker had strug-
gled against physical weaknesses and ailments and sought
out dangerous, physically trying first-hand experiences in
the wilderness and on the edges of Euro-American settle-

ment. Like his Brahmin predecessor, the patrician fol-
lower was an amateur who pursued history from the position of old-fashioned gentlemanly leisure rather than the
new-fangled professionalism of trained academics. In succeeding years, Roosevelt would repeatedly denounce what
he regarded as mindless pedantry and arid specialization
among "scientific" historians in universities. Yet he also
wished to emulate both Parkman and the professors in the
depth and extent of his research in original sources. Just
before he began *The Winning of the West,* Roosevelt told his
friend Henry Cabot Lodge, "If I write another historical
work of any kind—and my dream is to make one such that
will be my *magnum opus*—I shall certainly take more
time and do it carefully and thoroughly, so as to avoid the
roughness and interruption of the Benton [biography]."[3]

On all those grounds, the dedication to Parkman offered
an accurate foretaste of the ensuing volumes. But that dedication was also misleading in two respects. First, as Roosevelt must have regretted often to himself, anyone who approached *The Winning of the West* with expectations of a
great historical narrative on the order of Parkman's
France and England in the New World was in for a disap-
pointment. Narrative—artful telling of stories, evocative
depictions of personalities in action, dramatic rendering of
events—was the weakest aspect of this work of history,
and narrative would remain a signal shortcoming in Roosevelt's writing throughout his career. Why he fell short as
a narrator is an interesting question that has several possible answers.

The most readily apparent explanation is the one Roosevelt himself mentioned to Lodge. He was able to do almost
no uninterrupted work on these volumes. Between the
time when he began the project in 1888 and finished it in
1896, he took part in three presidential campaigns, served
for five years on the United States Civil Service Commis-
sion, and became New York's police commissioner—all
while he had a growing young family, pursued vigorous
sports and outdoor pastimes, and read voraciously and

spoke and wrote frequently on a variety of other topics besides western history, especially foreign and naval affairs. The wonder of these volumes is not their shortcomings or, conversely, their excellent features apart from the narrative. The wonder of them is that they got written at all. If nothing else, *The Winning of the West* stands as another monument to Roosevelt's preternatural energy and powers of concentration. No other active statesman in the English-speaking world, not even Winston Churchill, produced such a solidly scholarly work of history while he was, as the Romans said, *in medias res*—in the midst of things.[4]

By invoking Parkman's aegis, Roosevelt set an impossibly high standard for himself. Among American narrative historians Parkman stands on the same summit of eminence as Macaulay does among their British counterparts. Since Parkman's time, only two of his countrymen have approached him as masters of this literary art. One was his slightly younger compatriot from the Harvard-trained New England elite, Henry Adams, who also published the first two volumes of his *History of the United States of America during the Administrations of Thomas Jefferson and James Madison* in 1889. The only other claimaint to this mantle has been another Harvard historian, Arthur M. Schlesinger Jr., whose three-volume *Age of Roosevelt* remains the finest narrative history done by an American in the twentieth century. In such exalted company, *The Winning of the West* does not come off too badly.

A final explanation cuts deeper into Roosevelt's character and the gifts required of different kinds of historians. Of all the varieties of historical writing, narrative most resembles the novel, and the narrator must write more like a novelist than the rest of his fellow practitioners. In the context of western literature, the successful novelist Wallace Stegner once observed about his friend, the accomplished critic and historian Bernard DeVoto, "His fictions failed because he never got the hang of ventriloquism, of disguising his own voice." To a lesser degree, Stegner's observation holds true for the narrative historian. This form of historical writing requires a measure of self-effacement, a willingness to surrender to the story being told. Roosevelt, in common with most other politicians who have turned historian and critics who have turned novelist, lacked that faculty. His own voice and views were too important to him, perhaps simply too irrepressible, to be subordinated to the narrative.[5]

The invocation of Parkman raises expectations of an identity of views and intepretations between him and Roosevelt. Similarities certainly abound to link the pair spiritually and intellectually. Both men produced works that were strikingly Eurocentric, racist, male-dominated, and environmentally obtuse from a late-twentieth-century point of view. Moreover, each man openly played favorites within his preferred categories, with the English and later the Americans standing taller and morally better than the French and Spanish and, later, the British. Above all, Parkman and Roosevelt wrote ethnocentrically triumphalist histories that either ignored alternative arguments or contemptuously dismissed them, as Roosevelt did early in *The Winning of the West,* when he scorned "sentimental historians [who] speak as if the blame had all been ours. . . . [T]heir utterances are as shallow as they are untruthful. Unless we were willing that the whole continent west of the Alleghanies should remain an unpeopled waste, the hunting-ground of savages, war was inevitable. . . ." And so was the American white man's triumph.[6]

Yet for all the echoes of Parkman in that statement and scores of others in *The Winning of the West,* Roosevelt revealed a different sensibility, informed by a radically altered intellectual environment and divergent scholarly background. Where Parkman breathed the spirit of full-blown mid-nineteenth century American romanticism, albeit chastened and enriched by latter-day New England Federalism and Calvinism, Roosevelt swam in the seas of European and American imperialism, fed and strengthened by the scientific revolutions of his age, especially but

not only the pervasive influence of Darwinism. The shift of
sensibilities jumps out in the opening sentence of *The Winning of the West,* where Roosevelt asserts, "During the past
three centuries the spread of the English-speaking peoples
over the world's waste places has been not only the most
striking feature in the world's history, but also the event of
all others most far-reaching in its effects and in its importance." He then immediately launches into a disquisition
on "great periods of race-expansion—as distinguished
from mere conquest" going back to the movements of peoples in Europe during Roman times and coming forward
through the overseas spread of Europeans since the sixteenth century. "All of this is not foreign to American history," Roosevelt observed just four pages into the text. "The
vast movement by which this continent was conquered and
peopled cannot be rightly understood if considered solely
by itself."[7]

That opening salvo best distinguishes Roosevelt's viewpoint from Parkman's. Whereas the great Brahmin had de-
picted the Anglo-French struggle over North America on
the grand scale of cultures and societies that produced
heroes and social advantages, with perhaps a bit of divine
favor involved, the New Yorker saw world historical forces
at work, at least in some measure propelled by imperatives
of the physical, natural world. At bottom, despite his disdain for academic specialists, Roosevelt was much more of
a "scientific" historian than he acknowledged and wrote
much more like that breed than he realized. The affinity
sprang from more specific influences than merely living in
the same era and sharing an intellectual environment. As
a boy and well into his college years, Roosevelt had wanted
to be a scientist, specifically a biologist, and he had abandoned those youthful ambitions for both personal and intellectual reasons. Even after he had turned definitely to
politics and history, however, he maintained a passionate
interest in all the natural sciences, especially the biolog-
ical ones, and he later became the most scientifically liter-
ate president since Thomas Jefferson. Small wonder, then,

that he wrote a different, more "scientific" history than his predecessor.[8]

The clearest indication of this new approach came in a chapter in the third volume, published in 1894, entitled "Kentucky's Struggle for Statehood, 1784–1790." Before he launched into an account of the political activities of such men as George Rogers Clark, Benjamin Logan, and others, Roosevelt described the physical conditions of life for settlers as a prelude to this generalization: "In all new-settled regions in the United States, so long as there was frontier at all, the changes in the pioneer population proceeded in a certain definite order, and Kentucky furnished an example of the process. . . . Nowhere else on the continent has so sharply defined and distinctively American a type been produced as on the frontier, and a single generation has always been more than enough for its production. The influence of the wild country upon the man is almost as great as the effect of the man upon the country." Those sentences have a familiar ring to readers in the succeeding century, and their author at once disclosed his intellectual debt with a footnote: "Frederick Jackson Turner: 'The Significance of the Frontier in American History.' A suggestive pamphlet published by the State Historical Society of Wisconsin."[9]

Roosevelt was among the first to grasp the significance of Turner's frontier thesis. The young assistant professor at the University of Wisconsin had delivered his paper at the American Historical Association's meeting in Chicago less than a year earlier, and, as indicated, the essay had seen the light of publication only as a pamphlet issued by his home state's historical society. Yet Roosevelt wrote to Turner on 10 February 1894, "I have been greatly interested in your pamphlet on the Frontier. It come at *the* right time for me, for I intend to make use of it in writing the third volume of my 'Winning of the West,' of course making full acknowledgment. I think you have struck some first class ideas, and have put into definite shape a good deal of thought that has been floating around rather loosely."

Within a short time, the published volume made good on the promise, and this exchange between the amateur and the professor illuminated the complicated workings of intellectual influence.[10]

In one way, Roosevelt was simply acknowledging his openness to new ideas and exhibiting his catholicity of taste by seizing upon an exciting insight that emanated from the camp of the "scientific" academic professionals. But he was doing more than borrowing. Roosevelt's reference to "a good deal of thought that has been floating around rather loosely" included his own expressions. Repeatedly in the first two volumes of *The Winning of the West,* published four years before Turner delivered his paper, Roosevelt had characterized frontier people as types who had undergone processes that had left lasting effect. In an early chapter he had praised "the daring and resolute courage of men and the patient endurance of women," while condemning their "deeds of the foulest and most wanton aggression, the darkest treachery, the most wanton cruelty. . . ." But he had also insisted, "in spite of their many failings, they were of all men the best fitted to conquer the wilderness and hold it against all comers." In short, in their good deeds and bad, America's frontiersmen and frontierswomen were instruments of great historical forces.[11]

The most interesting question that can be asked about the Roosevelt-Turner exchange is who influenced whom. The answer seems to be that the amateur helped to shape the professor's thinking much more than the other way around. Although Turner's interest in the West and speculations about the frontier began in his youth, reviewing the first two volumes of *The Winning of the West* in 1889 had offered him one of his earliest opportunities to express some of his ideas. In the review, Turner had asserted that the West, not New England, had early on formed the nation's "center of gravity," where "a new composite nationality is being produced, a distinct American people, speaking the English language, but not English." That last point merely recapitulated Roosevelt's observation that "the backwoodsmen, whatever their blood, had become Americans, one in speech, thought, and character. . . . They had lost all remembrance of Europe, and all sympathy with things European. . . . They resembled one another, and differed from the rest of the world—even the world of America, and infinitely more the world of Europe—in dress, in customs, and in mode of life." Roosevelt's volumes had clearly provided grist for the mill of the aspiring thesis-builder, just as Turner's essay subsequently lent theoretical respectability to the researcher's earlier findings.[12]

But Roosevelt's influence over Turner ran deeper than mutual utility and admiration. In *The Winning of the West,* Roosevelt practiced what Turner never more than preached. As William Cronon recently observed, the frontier essay and its later counterpart on sectionalism offered a stark contrast to all the rest of Turner's research and writing. He never followed up these daring early think-pieces with the labors necessary to test their validity and refine their application for specific times and places. Readers must look elsewhere for the actual history of the frontier, and one of the first places they can look is *The Winning of the West.* Although the four volumes contain various elements, the bulk of the work and nearly all the serious interpretive sections treat the frontier of Euro-American settlement between the Appalachians and the Mississippi and between the Great Lakes and the Gulf of Mexico during the three decades from the late 1760s to the late 1790s. Subsequent studies have amplified or modified or even sometimes overturned Roosevelt's accounts, but no one has supplanted *The Winning of the West* as a detailed, comprehensive treatment of the white American frontier over a comparable period.[13]

Yet, as Cronon also argues, Turner's frontier was not the same as Roosevelt's. Whereas Roosevelt celebrated and concentrated on hunters, scouts, woodsmen, and militiamen—the whites who first penetrated the forests and confronted the Indians as would-be displacers—Turner gave primacy to settled agriculturists and town builders as the most important shapers of the Western and American character. Cronon is correct to draw this contrast, but only up to a point. Indeed, the frontier story that Roosevelt tells in *The Winning of the West* is primarily a military story. The traits that he saw the frontier environment drawing forth and reinforcing in these white intruders were those which lent themselves to fighting. In this regard, Roosevelt's vision of the frontier is closer to the more recent works of Richard Slotkin and others who have stressed the strains of violence in American culture than to Turner's more bucolic, middlewestern-derived vision. This stress on the military aspects of Euro-American settlement further explains, beyond that era's largely unchallenged, usually unconscious gender biases, why *The Winning of the West* recounts almost exclusively male history. This is not to say that the volumes' military emphasis is entirely misplaced, because this episode in the history of the American frontier was bloody and violent and witnessed virtually unremitting warfare between Indians and whites.[14]

Valid though Cronon's distinction is between the two men's frontiers, it creates a partially misleading impression about Roosevelt's viewpoint. The ex-rancher admitted "that it has been a labor of love to write about the great deeds of the border people. . . . The men who have shared in the fast-vanishing frontier life of the present feel a peculiar sympathy with the already vanished frontier life of the past." Still, sentimental regard notwithstanding, Roosevelt never viewed these people's historical roles as anything but a transitory phase in the relentless march of civilization. Directly following his generalization of the frontier thesis and his acknowledgment of Turner, he delineated four "different types of settlers [who] appeared successively on the frontier"; first, the trappers and hunters; second, "the rude hunter-settler"; third, settlers "who were thrifty as well as adventurous" and therefore came to form "the backbone and body of the State"; and, finally and sometimes alongside the true settlers, "men of means," lawyers, merchants, planters, who came from well-to-do families in the seaboard states. With the predominance of the last two types "came the corresponding change in intellectual interests and in material pursuits," principally because "farms became thick, and towns throve, and life became more complex, [and] chances for variety in life and work and thought increased likewise." Roosevelt might have shed some tears for the freedom and physical challenges of the woods and plains, but his ideal society did not really differ from Turner's.[15]

Furthermore, Roosevelt not only bent his backwoodsman beneath the lash of his stern moral judgments, as already noted, but he also condemned their lack of organization and perseverance from a military standpoint. For example, although he praised the fighting prowess of the Carolina mountaineers at the battle of King's Mountain in 1780, he roundly condemned their lack of follow through. Comparing these Carolinians to Andreas Hofer's Tyroleans against Napoleon and to Highland Scots against British regulars, Roosevelt judged them all "tumultuous gatherings of hardy and warlike men, greatly to be dreaded under certain circumstances, but incapable of a long campaign and almost as much demoralized by a victory as by a defeat." Likewise, late in the fourth volume, Roosevelt bid farewell to one of the few individual heroes in *The Winning of the West,* Daniel Boone, with a mixed assessment. Although he praised Boone's "fierce impatience of restraint" and his "frontiersman's wonderful capacity to shift for himself," Roosevelt regretted his incapacity "of acting in combination with others of his kind." Boone and his fellow pioneers "were so restless and so intolerant of the pressure of their kind, that as neighbors came in they moved ever westward. They could not act with their fellows."[16]

This ambivalence about the frontiersmen went to the heart of *The Winning of the West.* Standing as he did between Parkman and Turner, Roosevelt shared the tastes of both the romantic and the devotee of science. Such mixed sentiments were characteristic of the late-nineteenth-century generation of imperialists, of whom Roosevelt became such an outstanding exemplar. These Europeans and Americans celebrated the scientific, technological, and economic advances of their time and yet railed against them. In the non-white world, they wished either to expand into and settle "waste places" or to conquer and uplift "backward" peoples, while at the same time enjoying for themselves some of the lawlessness, violence, and irrationalism that their "civilization" seemed to be eradicating. This divided attitude of Roosevelt's gave *The Winning of the West* both its greatest weaknesses and greatest strengths as a work of history. The flaws are easy to find and some have already been noted, especially the near total inattention toward women. In addition, and oddly for a person of his scientific interests and training, Roosevelt paid scant attention to geography, except as it affected settlement routes and military operations, or to the environment, particularly neglecting agriculture. As with his gender bias, these neglects sprang from obsessive attention to the frontier as a theater of war and frontiersmen as warriors.[17]

But the most surprising weakness of all to stem from that skewed perspective was Roosevelt's failure to deal with the westward extension of sectional differences. Slavery and African Americans merited only two paragraphs in the four volumes. Commenting on the introduction of slavery into the southwestern territories (the area below the Ohio River), he bemoaned its "baleful influence upon any slaveholding people, and especially upon those members of the master caste who do not own slaves. Moreover, the negro, unlike so many of the inferior races, does not dwindle away in the presence of the white man." Citing Haiti as the extreme example of slavery's consequences, Roosevelt argued that "it invariably in the end threatens the existence of the master caste. From this point of view, the presence of the negro is the real problem; slavery is merely the worst possible way of solving the problem." After a few more sentences, African Americans disappeared from *The Winning of the West,* and their absence left a large gap in the story of the settlement of the area that became Kentucky, Tennessee, Alabama, and Mississippi.[18]

Roosevelt's fumbling with sectional differences extended further. His focus on frontiersmen as fighters led him unconsciously to narrow his coverage of the frontier mainly to Kentucky and Tennessee. Not only did that area witness the greatest settlement and most fighting in this period, but it also best fitted the frontier typology that he set forth. Roosevelt devoted far less attention and coverage to the Old Northwest (the area above the Ohio). The difference sprang, in part, from slower settlement and less fighting there before the 1790s, although "Mad Anthony" Wayne's escapade at Fallen Timbers affords Roosevelt his only other great battle scene besides King's Mountain. He also admitted that the federal government and regular army units played much larger roles in Ohio and elsewhere in the Northwest, while the settlers there "were almost all soldiers of the Revolutionary armies; they were hard-working orderly men of trained courage and intellect." These people belonged more on Turner's frontier than on Roosevelt's, and they earned his neglect because they did not fit his case so well.[19]

Despite such weaknesses, *The Winning of the West* remains one of the greatest works of Western history. Roosevelt's implicit definition of the frontier as the initial stage of Euro-American intrusion saved him from the conceptual ambiguities that beset Turner and his successors. Roosevelt's militaristic priorities spared him, compared to his contemporaries and many later practitioners, from excessive denigration of the Indians. Such formidable foes deserved attention, even praise, and the three early chapters of the first volume on the native peoples showed understanding and sympathy. Presentism sneaked into the later volumes, particularly when this nationalistic post–Civil War Republican politician denigrated Thomas Jefferson and his political legacies, but he also condemned the shortsighted provincialism of New England Federalists and eschewed their disdain for democracy. Above all, Roosevelt highlighted his work with his cosmopolitanism, as he invoked comparisons with different fighting forces and colonial regimes across two millenia of time and from every part of the globe. In sum, *The Winning of the West* reflects the character of its author. It is sometimes quirky and full of prejudices and blind spots, but it is cultivated and sweeping in its learning and encompassing in its judgments. Just as Theodore Roosevelt was such an unusual American politician and president, so his western history stands in its own special class.

NOTES

1. Roosevelt was not the last New Yorker to adopt a western hat as his symbol. Fiorello LaGuardia, also a native of the city, did the same during his years in Congress and as mayor, partly as a reminder of his boyhood in Arizona as an Army bandmaster's son and partly as a token of his admiration for Roosevelt.

2. Roosevelt to Francis Parkman, 23 Apr. 1888, in Elting E. Morison, ed., *The Letters of Theodore Roosevelt* (Cambridge MA: 1951), 139.

3. Roosevelt to Henry Cabot Lodge, 15 Feb. 1887, ibid., 122. For Roosevelt's views on "scientific" history, see especially his presidential address to the American Historical Association, delivered on 27 December 1912 in Hermann Hagedorn, ed., *The Works of Theodore Roosevelt* (New York, 1926), National Edition, vol. 12, 3–24; and also John Milton Cooper Jr., "Theodore Roosevelt: On Clio's Active Service," *Virginia Quarterly Review* 62 (winter, 1986): 21–37. For expressions of Roosevelt's concern for original sources, see both Roosevelt to Parkman, 23 April 1888, in *Letters of Roosevelt,* vol. 1, 140, and his preface to *The Winning of the West.*

4. Churchill, who was awarded the Nobel Prize for Literature for his historical writings, did most of them while he was out of office. In Roosevelt's case, the pull of affairs explains even less of the flaws of *The Winning of the West* when it is noted that in 1899 he wrote his best book, *Oliver Cromwell,* while serving as gover-

nor of New York. The story that he dictated that book while being shaved in the morning is evidently apocryphal, but it highlights Roosevelt's ability to cast aside distractions.

5. Wallace Stegner, *The Uneasy Chair: A Biography of Bernard DeVoto* (Garden City NY, 1974), 325. For further discussion of critics' failures as novelists, see John Milton Cooper Jr., *Walter Hines Page: The Southerner as American, 1856–1918* (Chapel Hill NC, 1977), 201–2. Two possible exceptions to the unwillingness of political figures to abandon their own voices in order to write narrative history may be Churchill and Roosevelt's contemporary and political cohort, Albert J. Beveridge. In the cases of both these men, however, much of their historical writing flowed from such strongly held viewpoints and personal identification with their subjects (often biographical for both men) that no suppression of self was required in their narratives. In the 1920s, one English critic allegedly dismissed Churchill's *The World Crisis* as "personal memoirs disguised as the history of the world." Roosevelt might have done better as a narrator than he did, but the point about self-abnegation seems to remain valid.

6. Roosevelt, *The Winning of the West,* in Hagedorn, ed., *Works of Roosevelt,* vol. 8, 69.

7. Ibid., 3, 7. On Parkman, see especially David Levin, *History as Romantic Art: Bancroft, Prescott, Motley, and Parkman* (Stanford CA, pub. 1959), esp. 210–28, and Howard Doughty, *Francis Parkman* (New York, pub. 1962).

8. On these early interests and their abandonment, see Cooper, *Virginia Quarterly Review* 62: 23–24.

9. Roosevelt, *Winning of the West,* in Hagedorn, ed., *Works of Roosevelt,* vol. 9, 180–81.

10. Roosevelt to Turner, Feb. 10, 1894, in Morison, ed., *Letters of Roosevelt,* vol. 1, 363.

11. Roosevelt, *Winning of the West,* in Hagedorn, ed., *Works of Roosevelt,* vol. 8, 76–77, 108.

12. Turner review in *The Dial,* Aug. 1889, quoted in Ray Allen Billington, *Frederick Jackson Turner: Historian, Scholar, Teacher* (New York, 1973), 83; Roosevelt, *Winning of the West,* in Hagedorn, ed., *Works of Roosevelt,* vol. 8, 89.

13. Cronon, Merle Curti lecture, University of Wisconsin–Madison, 12 Nov. 1993. This is one of three lectures in which Professor Cronon offers a centennial evaluation of the frontier thesis, which will be published by the University of Wisconsin Press. I

am indebted to Professor Cronon for discussing these matters with me. The final two chapters of the fourth volume, which treat a few events after 1800, namely the Louisiana Purchase, Burr's conspiracy, and the Lewis and Clark and Pike expeditions, are derivative and almost perfunctory.

14. Cronon, Curti lecture, 12 Nov. 1993. See Slotkin, *Gunfighter Nation: The Myth of the Frontier in Twentieth Century America* (New York, pub. 1992).

15. Roosevelt, *Winning of the West,* in Hagedorn, ed., *Works of Roosevelt,* vol. 8, xliv, 181–84.

16. Ibid., 504, vol. 9, 448–49.

17. On Roosevelt's imperialism see John Milton Cooper Jr., *The Warrior and the Priest: Woodrow Wilson and Theodore Roosevelt* (Cambridge MA, 1983), 33–36.

18. Roosevelt, *Winning of the West,* in Hagedorn, ed., *Works of Roosevelt,* vol. 9, 44–45.

19. Ibid., 244.

PREFACE.

Much of the material on which this work is based is to be found in the archives of the American Government, which date back to 1774, when the first Continental Congress assembled. The earliest sets have been published complete up to 1777, under the title of " American Archives," and will be hereafter designated by this name. These early volumes contain an immense amount of material, because in them are to be found memoranda of private individuals and many of the public papers of the various colonial and State governments, as well as those of the Confederation. The documents from 1789 on—no longer containing any papers of the separate States—have also been gathered and printed under the heading of " American State Papers "; by which term they will be hereafter referred to.

The mass of public papers coming in between these two series, and covering the period extending from 1776 to 1789, have never been published, and in great part have either never been examined or else have been examined in the most cursory manner. The original documents are all in the Department of State at Washington, and for convenience will be referred to as " State Department MSS." They are bound in two or three hundred large volumes;

exactly how many I cannot say, because, though they are numbered, yet several of the numbers themselves contain from two or three to ten or fifteen volumes apiece. The volumes to which reference will most often be made are the following:

No. 15. Letters of Huntington.

No. 16. Letters of the Presidents of Congress.

No. 18. Letter-Book B.

No. 20. Vol 1. Reports of Committees on State Papers.

No. 27. Reports of Committees on the War Office. 1776 to 1778.

No. 30. Reports of Committees.

No. 32. Reports of Committees of the States and of the Week.

No. 41. Vol. 3. Memorials E. F. G. 1776–1788.

No. 41. Vol. 5. Memorials K. L. 1777–1789.

No. 50. Letters and Papers of Oliver Pollock. 1777–1792.

No. 51. Vol. 2 Intercepted Letters. 1779–1782.

No. 56. Indian Affairs.

No. 71. Vol. 1. Virginia State Papers.

No. 73. Georgia State Papers.

No. 81. Vol. 2. Reports of Secretary John Jay.

No. 120. Vol. 2. American Letters.

No. 124. Vol. 3. Reports of Jay.

No. 125. Negotiation Book.

No. 136. Vol. 1. Reports of Board of Treasury.

No. 136. Vol. 2. Reports of Board of Treasury.

No. 147. Vol. 2. Reports of Board of War.

No. 147. Vol. 5. Reports of Board of War.

No. 147. Vol. 6. Reports of Board of War.

No. 148. Vol. 1. Letters from Board of War.

No. 149. Vol. 1. Letters and Reports from B. Lincoln, Secretary at War.

No. 149. Vol. 2. Letters and Reports from B. Lincoln, Secretary at War.

No. 149. Vol. 3. Letters and Reports from B. Lincoln, Secretary at War.

No. 150. Vol. 1. Letters of H. Knox, Secretary at War.
No. 150. Vol. 2. Letters of H. Knox, Secretary at War.
No. 150. Vol. 3. Letters of H. Knox, Secretary at War.
No. 152. Vol. 11. Letters of General Washington.
No. 163. Letters of Generals Clinton, Nixon, Nicola, Morgan, Harmar, Muhlenburg.
No. 169. Vol. 9. Washington's Letters.
No. 180. Reports of Secretary of Congress.

Besides these numbered volumes, the State Department contains others, such as Washington's letter-book, marked War Department 1792, '3, '4, '5. There are also a series of numbered volumes of "Letters to Washington," Nos. 33 and 49 containing reports from Geo. Rogers Clark. The Jefferson papers, which are likewise preserved here, are bound in several series, each containing a number of volumes. The Madison and Monroe papers, also kept here, are not yet bound; I quote them as the Madison MSS. and the Monroe MSS.

My thanks are due to Mr. W. C. Hamilton, Asst. Librarian, for giving me every facility to examine the material.

At Nashville, Tennessee, I had access to a mass of original matter in the shape of files of old newspapers, of unpublished letters, diaries, reports, and other manuscripts. I was given every opportunity to examine these at my leisure, and indeed to take such as were most valuable to my own home. For this my thanks are especially due to Judge John M. Lea, to whom, as well as to my many other friends in Nashville, I shall always feel under a debt on account of the unfailing courtesy with which I was treated. I must express my particular acknowledgments to Mr. Lemuel R. Campbell. The Nashville manuscripts, etc. of which I have made most use are the following:

The Robertson MSS., comprising two large volumes, entitled the "Correspondence, etc., of Gen'l James Robertson," from 1784 to 1814. They belong to the library of Nashville University; I had some difficulty in finding the second volume but finally succeeded.

The Campbell MSS., consisting of letters and memoranda to and from different members of the Campbell family who were prominent in the Revolution; dealing for the most part with Lord Dunmore's war, the Cherokee wars, the battle of King's Mountain, land speculations, etc. They are in the possession of Mr. Lemuel R. Campbell, who most kindly had copies of all the important ones sent me, at great personal trouble.

Some of the Sevier and Jackson papers, the original MS. diaries of Donelson on the famous voyage down the Tennessee and up the Cumberland, and of Benj. Hawkins while surveying the Tennessee boundary, memoranda of Thos. Washington, Overton and Dunham, the earliest files of the Knoxville *Gazette*, from 1791 to 1795, etc. These are all in the library of the Tennessee Historical Society.

For original matter connected with Kentucky, I am greatly indebted to Col. Reuben T. Durrett, of Louisville, the founder of the "Filson Club," which has done such admirable historical work of late years. He allowed me to work at my leisure in his library, the most complete in the world on all sub-

jects connected with Kentucky history. Among
other matter, he possesses the Shelby MSS., containing a number of letters to and from, and a dictated
autobiography of, Isaac Shelby; MS. journals of
Rev. James Smith, during two tours in the western
country in 1785 and '95; early files of the "Kentucke
Gazette"; books owned by the early settlers; papers
of Boon, and George Rogers Clark; MS. notes on
Kentucky by George Bradford, who settled there in
1779; MS. copy of the record book of Col. John
Todd, the first governor of the Illinois country after
Clark's conquest; the McAfee MSS., consisting of
an Account of the First Settlement of Salt River,
the Autobiography of Robert McAfee, and a Brief
Memorandum of the Civil and Natural History of
Kentucky; MS. autobiography of Rev. William
Hickman, who visited Kentucky in 1776, etc., etc.

I am also under great obligations to Col. John
Mason Brown of Louisville, another member of the
Filson Club, for assistance rendered me; particularly
for having sent me six bound volumes of MSS., con-
taining the correspondence of the Spanish Minister
Gardoqui, copied from the Spanish archives.

At Lexington I had access to the Breckenridge
MSS., through the kindness of Mr. Ethelbert D.
Warfield; and to the Clay MSS. through the kindness of Miss Lucretia Hart Clay. I am particularly
indebted to Miss Clay for her courtesy in sending
me many of the most valuable old Hart and Benton
letters, depositions, accounts, and the like.

The Blount MSS. were sent to me from California
by the Hon. W. D. Stephens of Los Angeles,

although I was not personally known to him; an instance of courtesy and generosity, in return for which I could do nothing save express my sincere appreciation and gratitude, which I take this opportunity of publicly repeating.

The Gates MSS., from which I drew some important facts not hitherto known concerning the King's Mountain campaign, are in the library of the New York Historical Society.

The Virginia State Papers have recently been published, and are now accessible to all.

Among the most valuable of the hitherto untouched manuscripts which I have obtained are the Haldimand papers, preserved in the Canadian archives at Ottawa. They give, for the first time, the British and Indian side of all the northwestern fighting; including Clark's campaigns, the siege of Boonsborough, the battle of the Blue Licks, Crawford's defeat, etc. The Canadian archivist, Mr. Douglass Brymner, furnished me copies of all I needed with a prompt courtesy for which I am more indebted than I can well express.

I have been obliged to rely mainly on these collections of early documents as my authorities, especially for that portion of western history prior to 1783. Excluding the valuable, but very brief, and often very inaccurate, sketch which Filson wrote down as coming from Boon, there are no printed histories of Kentucky earlier than Marshall's, in 1812; while the first Tennessee history was Haywood's, in 1822. Both Marshall and Haywood did excellent work; the former was an able writer, the latter was a student, and (like the Kentucky historian Mann Butler) a sound political thinker, devoted to the Union, and prompt to stand up for the right. But both of them, in dealing with the early history of the country beyond the Alleghanies, wrote about matters that had happened from thirty to fifty years before, and were obliged to base most of their statements on tradition or on what the pioneers remembered in their old age. The later historians, for the most part, merely follow these two. In consequence, the mass of original material, in the shape of official reports and contemporary letters, contained in the Haldimand MSS., the Campbell MSS., the McAfee MSS., the Gardoqui MSS., the State Department MSS., the Virginia State Papers, etc., not only cast a flood of new light upon this early history, but necessitate its being entirely re-written. For instance, they give an absolutely new aspect to, and in many cases completely reverse, the current accounts of all the Indian fighting, both against the Cherokees and the Northwestern tribes; they give for the first time a clear view of frontier diplomacy, of the intrigues with the Spaniards, and even of the mode of life in the backwoods, and of the workings of the civil government. It may be mentioned that the various proper names are spelt in so many different ways that it is difficult to know which to choose. Even Clark is sometimes spelt Clarke, while Boon was apparently indifferent as to whether his name should or should not contain the final silent *e*. As for the original Indian titles, it is often quite impossible to give them even approximately; the early writers often wrote the same Indian words in such different ways that they bear no resemblance whatever to one another.

In conclusion I would say that it has been to me emphatically a labor of love to write of the great deeds of the border people. I am not blind to their manifold shortcomings, nor yet am I ignorant of their many strong and good qualities. For a number of years I spent most of my time on the frontier, and lived and worked like any other frontiersman. The wild country in which we dwelt and across which we wandered was in the far west; and there were of course many features in which the life of a cattle-man on the Great Plains and among the Rockies differed from that led by a backwoodsman in the Alleghany forests a century before. Yet the points of resemblance were far more numerous and striking. We guarded our herds of branded cattle and shaggy horses, hunted bear, bison, elk, and deer, established civil government, and put down evil-doers, white and red, on the banks of the Little Missouri and among the wooded, precipitous foot-hills of the Bighorn, exactly as did the pioneers who a hundred years previously built their log-cabins beside the Kentucky or in the valleys of the Great Smokies. The men who have shared in the fast vanishing frontier life of the present feel a peculiar sympathy with the already long-vanished frontier life of the past.

THEODORE ROOSEVELT.

SAGAMORE HILL, *May*, 1889.

FOREWORD.

In the year 1898 the United States finished the work begun over a century before by the backwoodsman, and drove the Spaniard outright from the western world. During the march of our people from the crests of the Alleghanies to the Pacific, the Spaniard was for a long period our chief white opponent; and after an interval his place among our antagonists was taken by his Spanish-American heir. Although during the Revolution the Spaniard at one time became America's friend in the sense that he was England's foe, he almost from the outset hated and dreaded his new ally more than his old enemy. In the peace negotiations at the close of the contest he was jealously eager to restrict our boundaries to the line of the Alleghanies; while even during the concluding years of the war the Spanish soldiers on the upper Mississippi were regarded by the Americans in Illinois as a menace no less serious than the British troops at Detroit.

In the opening years of our national life the Western backwoodsman found the Spanish ownership of the mouth of the Mississippi even more hurtful and irksome than the retention by the Britisn king of the posts on the Great Lakes. After years of tedi-ous public negotiations, under and through which ran a dark woof of private intrigue, the sinewy western hands so loosened the Spanish grip that in despair Spain surrendered to France the mouth of the river and the vast territories stretching thence into the dim Northwest. She hoped thereby to establish a strong barrier between her remaining provinces and her most dreaded foe. But France in her turn grew to understand that America's posi-tion as regards Louisiana, thanks to the steady west-ward movement of the backwoodsman, was such as to render it on the one hand certain that the retention of the province by France would mean an armed clash with the United States, and on the other hand no less certain that in the long run such a conflict would result to France's disadvantage. Louisiana thus passed from the hands of Spain, after a brief interval, into those of the young Republic. There remained to Spain, Mexico and Florida; and forthwith the pressure of the stark forest riflemen began to be felt on the outskirts of these two prov-inces. Florida was the first to fall. After a por-tion of it had been forcibly annexed, after Andrew Jackson had marched at will through part of the remainder, and after the increasing difficulty of repressing the American filibustering efforts had shown the imminence of some serious catastrophe, Spain ceded the peninsula to the United States. Texas, New Mexico, and California did not fall into American hands until they had passed from the Spaniard to his half-Indian sons.

Many decades went by after Spain had lost her foothold on the American continent, and she still held her West Indian empire. She misgoverned the islands as she had misgoverned the continent; and in the islands, as once upon the continent, her own children became her deadliest foes. But generation succeeded generation, and the prophecies of those far-seeing statesmen who foretold that she would lose to the northern Republic her West Indian possessions remained unfulfilled. At last, at the close of one of the bloodiest and most brutal wars that even Spain ever waged with her own colonists, the United States intervened, and in a brief summer campaign destroyed the last vestiges of the mediæval Spanish domain in the tropic seas alike of the West and the remote East.

We of this generation were but carrying to completion the work of our fathers and of our fathers' fathers. It is moreover a matter for just pride that while there was no falling off in the vigor and prowess shown by our fighting men, there was a marked change for the better in the spirit with which the deed was done. The backwoodsmen had pushed the Spaniards from the Mississippi, had set up a slave-holding republic in Texas, and had conquered the Californian gold-fields, in the sheer masterful exercise of might. It is true that they won great triumphs for civilization no less than for their own people; yet they won them unwittingly, for they were merely doing as countless other strong young races had done in the long contest carried on for so many thousands of years between the fit and the unfit. But in 1898 the United States, while having gained in strength, showed that there had likewise been gain in justice, in mercy, in sense of responsibility. Our conquest of the Southwest has been justified by the result. The Latin peoples in the lands we won and settled have prospered like our own stock. The sons and grandsons of those who had been our foes in Louisiana and New Mexico came eagerly forward to serve in the army that was to invade Cuba. Our people as a whole went into the war, primarily, it is true, to drive out the Spaniard once for all from America; but with the fixed determination to replace his rule by a government of justice and orderly liberty.

To use the political terminology of the present day, the whole western movement of our people was simply the most vital part of that great movement of expansion which has been the central and all-important feature of our history — a feature far more important than any other since we became a nation, save only the preservation of the Union itself. It was expansion which made us a great power; and at every stage it has been bitterly antagonized, not only by the short-sighted and the timid, but even by many who were neither one nor the other. There were many men who opposed the movement west of the Alleghanies and the peopling of the lands which now form Kentucky, Tennessee, and the great States lying between the Ohio and the Lakes. Excellent persons then foretold ruin to the country from bringing into it a disorderly population of backwoodsmen, with the same solemnity that has in our own day marked the prophecies of those who have seen similar ruin in the intaking of Hawaii and Porto Rico. The annexation of Louisiana, including the entire territory between the northern Mississippi and the Pacific Ocean, aroused such frantic opposition in the old-settled regions of the country, and especially in the Northeast, as to call forth threats of disunion, the language used by the opponents of our expansion into the Far West being as violent as that sometimes used in denouncing our acquisition of the Philippines. The taking of Texas and of California was complicated by the slave question, but much of the opposition to both was simply the general opposition to expansion — that is, to national growth and national greatness. In our long-settled communities there have always been people who opposed every war which marked the advance of American civilization at the cost of savagery. The opposition was fundamentally the same, whether these wars were campaigns in the old West against the Shawnees and the Miamis, in the new West against the Sioux and the Apaches, or in Luzon against the Tagals. In each case, in the end, the believers in the historic American policy of expansion have triumphed. Hitherto America has gone steadily forward along the path of greatness, and has remained true to the policy of her early leaders who felt within them the lift towards mighty things. Like every really strong people, ours is stirred by the generous ardor for daring strife and mighty deeds, and now with eyes undimmed looks far into the misty future.

At bottom the question of expansion in 1898 was but a variant of the problem we had to solve at every stage of the great western movement. Whether the prize of the moment was Louisiana or Florida, Oregon or Alaska, mattered little. The same forces, the same types of men, stood for and against the cause of national growth, of national greatness, at the end of the century as at the beginning.

My non-literary work has been so engrossing

during the years that have elapsed since my fourth volume was published, that I have been unable to go on with " The Winning of the West " ; but my design is to continue the narrative as soon as I can get leisure, carrying it through the stages which marked the taking of Florida and Oregon, the upbuilding of the republic of Texas, and the acquisition of New Mexico and California as the result of the Mexican war.

Theodore Roosevelt

EXECUTIVE CHAMBER, ALBANY, N. Y.
    January 1, 1900.

CONTENTS.

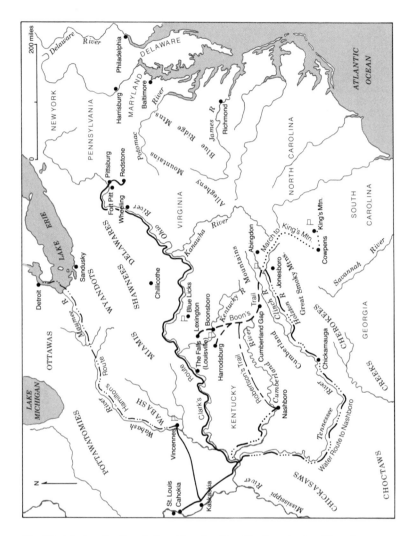

The West during the Revolution. Showing Hamilton's route from Detroit to Vincennes; Clark's route from Redstone to the Illinois, and thence to Vincennes; Boon's trail, on the Wilderness Road to Kentucky; Robertson's trail to the settlement he founded on the Cumberland; the water route from the Watauga to Nashboro, that taken by the *Adventure;* the march of the backwoodsmen from the Sycamore Shoals to King's Mountain. The flags denote the battles of the Great Kanawha, the Blue Licks, the Island Flats of the Holston, and King's Mountain; and the assaults on Boonsboro and Vincennes. Based on a map by G. P. Putnam's Sons, New York and London.

THE WINNING OF THE WEST.

CHAPTER I.

THE SPREAD OF THE ENGLISH-SPEAKING PEOPLES.

DURING the past three centuries the spread of the English-speaking peoples over the world's waste spaces has been not only the most striking feature in the world's history, but also the event of all others most far-reaching in its effects and its importance.

Spread of the Modern English Race.

The tongue which Bacon feared to use in his writings, lest they should remain forever unknown to all but the inhabitants of a relatively unimportant insular kingdom, is now the speech of two continents. The Common Law which Coke jealously upheld in the southern half of a single European island, is now the law of the land throughout the vast regions of Australasia, and of America north of the Rio Grande. The names of the plays that Shakespeare wrote are household words in the mouths of mighty nations, whose wide domains were to him more unreal than the realm of Prester John. Over half the descendants of their fellow countrymen of that day now dwell in lands which, when these three Englishmen were born, held not a single white inhabitant; the race which, when they were in their prime, was hemmed in between the North and the Irish seas, to-day holds sway over worlds, whose endless coasts are washed by the waves of the three great oceans.

There have been many other races that at one time or another had their great periods of race expansion— as distinguished from mere conquest,—but there has never been another whose expansion has been either so broad or so rapid.

At one time, many centuries ago, it seemed as if the Germanic peoples, like their Celtic foes and neighbors, would be absorbed into the all-conquering Roman power, and, merging their identity in that of the victors, would accept their law, their speech, and their habits of thought. But this danger vanished forever on the day of the slaughter by the Teuto-burger Wald, when the legions of Varus were broken by the rush of Hermann's wild warriors.

Two or three hundred years later the Germans, no longer on the defensive, themselves went forth from their marshy forests conquering and to **First Overflow of the Germanic Peoples.** conquer. For century after century they swarmed out of the dark woodland east of the Rhine, and north of the Danube; and as their force spent itself, the move-ment was taken up by their brethren who dwelt along the coasts of the Baltic and the North At-lantic. From the Volga to the Pillars of Hercules, from Sicily to Britain, every land in turn bowed to the warlike prowess of the stalwart sons of Odin.

Rome and Novgorod, the imperial city of Italy as well as the squalid capital of Muscovy, acknowledged the sway of kings of Teutonic or Scandinavian blood.

In most cases, however, the victorious invaders merely intruded themselves among the original and far more numerous owners of the land, ruled over them, and were absorbed by them. This happened to both Teuton and Scandinavian ; to the descendants of Alaric, as well as to the children of Rurik. The Dane in Ireland became a Celt; the Goth of the Iberian peninsula became a Spaniard ; Frank and Norwegian alike were merged into the mass of Romance-speaking Gauls, who themselves finally grew to be called by the names of their masters. Thus it came about that though the German tribes conquered Europe they did not extend the limits of Germany nor the sway of the German race. On the contrary, they strengthened the hands of the rivals of the people from whom they sprang. They gave rulers —kaisers, kings, barons, and knights—to all the lands they overran; here and there they imposed their own names on kingdoms and principalities—as in France, Normandy, Burgundy, and Lombardy ; they grafted the feudal system on the Roman jurisprudence, and interpolated a few Teutonic words in the Latin dialects of the peoples they had conquered ; but, hopelessly outnumbered, they were soon lost in the mass of their subjects, and adopted from them their laws, their culture, and their language. As a result, the mixed races of the south—the Latin nations as they are sometimes called—strengthened

Fails Greatly to Extend Germany.

by the infusion of northern blood, sprang anew into vigorous life, and became for the time being the leaders of the European world.

There was but one land whereof the winning made a lasting addition to Germanic soil; but this **The Win-** land was destined to be of more im- **ning of Eng-** portance in the future of the Germanic **land Stands** peoples than all their continental posses- **by Itself.** sions, original and acquired, put together.

The day when the keels of the low-Dutch sea-thieves first grated on the British coast was big with the doom of many nations. There sprang up in conquered southern Britain, when its name had been significantly changed to England, that branch of the Germanic stock which was in the end to grasp almost literally world-wide power, and by its over-shadowing growth to dwarf into comparative insignificance all its kindred folk. At the time, in the general wreck of the civilized world, the making of England attracted but little attention. Men's eyes were riveted on the empires conquered by the hosts of Alaric, Theodoric, and Clovis, not on the swarm of little kingdoms and earldoms founded by the nameless chiefs who led each his band of hard-rowing, hard-fighting henchmen across the stormy waters of the German Ocean. Yet the rule and the race of Goth, Frank, and Burgund have vanished from off the earth; while the sons of the unknown Saxon, Anglian, and Friesic warriors now hold in their hands the fate of the coming years.

After the great Teutonic wanderings were over, there came a long lull, until, with the discovery of

America, a new period of even vaster race expansion began. During this lull the nations of Europe took on their present shapes. Indeed, the so-called Latin nations—the French and Spaniards, for instance—may be said to have been born after the first set of migrations ceased. Their national history, as such, does not really begin until about that time, whereas that of the Germanic peoples stretches back unbroken to the days when we first hear of their existence. It would be hard to say which one of half a dozen races that existed in Europe during the early centuries of the present era should be considered as especially the ancestor of the modern Frenchman or Spaniard. When the Romans conquered Gaul and Iberia they did not in any place drive out the ancient owners of the soil; they simply Romanized them, and left them as the base of the population. By the Frankish and Visigothic invasions another strain of blood was added, to be speedily absorbed ; while the invaders took the language of the conquered people, and established themselves as the ruling class. Thus the modern nations who sprang from this mixture derive portions of their governmental system and general policy from one race, most of their blood from another, and their language, law, and culture from a third.

The English race, on the contrary, has a perfectly continuous history. When Alfred reigned, the English already had a distinct national being; when Charlemagne reigned, the French, as we use the term to-day, had no national being whatever. The Ger-

Marginal note: Formation of the Nations ; Races of Mixed Blood.

mans of the mainland merely overran the countries that lay in their path; but the sea-rovers who won England to a great extent actually **Peculiarity of English History.** displaced the native Britons. The former were absorbed by the subject-races; the latter, on the contrary, slew or drove off or assimilated the original inhabitants. Unlike all the other Germanic swarms, the English took neither creed nor custom, neither law nor speech, from their beaten foes. At the time when the dynasty of the Capets had become firmly established at Paris, France was merely part of a country where Latinized Gauls and Basques were ruled by Latinized Franks, Goths, Burgunds, and Normans; but the people across the Channel then showed little trace of Celtic or Romance influence. It would be hard to say whether Vercingetorix or Cæsar, Clovis or Syagrius, has the better right to stand as the prototype of a modern French general. There is no such doubt in the other case. The average Englishman, American, or Australian of to-day who wishes to recall the feats of power with which his race should be credited in the shadowy dawn of its history, may go back to the half-mythical glories of Hengist and Horsa, perhaps to the deeds of Civilis the Batavian, or to those of the hero of the Teutoburger fight, but certainly to the wars neither of the Silurian chief Caractacus nor of his conqueror, the after-time Emperor Vespasian.

Nevertheless, when, in the sixteenth century, the European peoples began to extend their dominions beyond Europe, England had grown to differ profoundly from the Germanic countries of the mainland. A very large Celtic element had been introduced into the English blood, and, in addition, there had been a considerable Scandinavian admixture. More important still were the radical changes brought by the Norman conquest; chief among them the transformation of the old English tongue into the magnificent language which is now the common inheritance of so many widespread peoples. England's insular position, moreover, permitted it to work out its own fate comparatively unhampered by the presence of outside powers; so that it developed a type of nationality totally distinct from the types of the European mainland.

England's Separate Position.

All this is not foreign to American history. The vast movement by which this continent was conquered and peopled cannot be rightly understood if considered solely by itself. It was the crowning and greatest achievement of a series of mighty movements, and it must be taken in connection with them. Its true significance will be lost unless we grasp, however roughly, the past race-history of the nations who took part therein.

When, with the voyages of Columbus and his successors, the great period of extra-European colonization began, various nations strove to share in the work. Most of them had to plant their colonies in lands across the sea; Russia alone was by her geographical position enabled to extend her frontiers by land, and in consequence her comparatively recent coloni-

Period of Extra-European Colonization.

zation of Siberia bears some resemblance to our own
work in the western United States. The other
countries of Europe were forced to find their outlets
for conquest and emigration beyond the ocean, and,
until the colonists had taken firm root in their new
homes the mastery of the seas thus became a matter
of vital consequence.

Among the lands beyond the ocean America was
the first reached and the most important. It was
conquered by different European races, and shoals
of European settlers were thrust forth upon its
shores. These sometimes displaced and sometimes
merely overcame and lived among the natives.
They also, to their own lasting harm, committed a
crime whose shortsighted folly was worse than its
guilt, for they brought hordes of African slaves,
whose descendants now form immense populations
in certain portions of the land. Throughout the
continent we therefore find the white, red, and black
races in every stage of purity and intermixture. One
result of this great turmoil of conquest and immigration has been that, in certain parts of America,
the lines of cleavage of race are so far from coinciding
with the lines of cleavage of speech that they run at
right angles to them—as in the four communities of
Ontario, Quebec, Hayti, and Jamaica.

Each intruding European power, in winning for
itself new realms beyond the seas, had to wage a
twofold war, overcoming the original inhabitants
with one hand, and with the other warding off the
assaults of the kindred nations that were bent on
the same schemes. Generally the contests of the

latter kind were much the most important. The
victories by which the struggles between the European conquerors themselves were ended   Twofold
deserve lasting commemoration. Yet, some-   Character
times, even the most important of them,   of the
sweeping though they were, were in parts   Warfare.
less sweeping than they seemed. It would be impossible to overestimate the far-reaching effects of the overthrow of the French power in America; but Lower
Canada, where the fatal blow was given, itself suffered nothing but a political conquest, which did not
interfere in the least with the growth of a French
state along both sides of the lower St. Lawrence. In
a somewhat similiar way Dutch communities have
held their own, and indeed have sprung up in South
Africa.

All the European nations touching on the Atlantic seaboard took part in the new work, with very
varying success; Germany alone, then rent by many
feuds, having no share therein. Portugal founded a
single state, Brazil. The Scandinavian nations did
little; their chief colony fell under the control of
the Dutch. The English and the Spaniards were
the two nations to whom the bulk of the new lands
fell; the former getting much the greater   Spain's
portion. The conquests of the Spaniards   Share.
took place in the sixteenth century. The West
Indies and Mexico, Peru and the limitless grass plains
of what is now the Argentine Confederation,—all
these and the lands lying between them had been
conquered and colonized by the Spaniards before
there was a single English settlement in the New

World, and while the fleets of the Catholic king still held for him the lordship of the ocean. Then the cumbrous Spanish vessels succumbed to the attacks of the swift war-ships of Holland and England, and the sun of the Spanish world-dominion set as quickly as it had risen. Spain at once came to a standstill; it was only here and there that she even extended her rule over a few neighboring Indian tribes, while she was utterly unable to take the offensive against the French, Dutch, and English. But it is a singular thing that these vigorous and powerful new-comers, who had so quickly put a stop to her further growth, yet wrested from her very little of what was already hers. They plundered a great many Spanish cities and captured a great many Spanish galleons, but they made no great or lasting conquests of Spanish territory. Their mutual jealousies, and the fear each felt of the others, were among the main causes of this state of things; and hence it came about that after the opening of the seventeenth century the wars they waged against one another were of far more ultimate consequence than the wars they waged against the former mistress of the western world. England in the end drove both France and Holland from the field; but it was under the banner of the American Republic, not under that of the British Monarchy, that the English-speaking people first won vast stretches of land from the descendants of the Spanish conquerors.

The three most powerful of Spain's rivals waged many a long war with one another to decide which should grasp the sceptre that had slipped from

Spanish hands. The fleets of Holland fought with
stubborn obstinacy to wrest from England   The
her naval supremacy; but they failed, and   French
in the end the greater portion of the Dutch   and the
domains fell to their foes. The French   Dutch.
likewise began a course of conquest and colonization at the same time the English did, and
after a couple of centuries of rivalry, ending in pro-
longed warfare, they also succumbed. The close of
the most important colonial contest ever waged left
the French without a foot of soil on the North
American mainland; while their victorious foes had
not only obtained the lead in the race for supremacy
on that continent, but had also won the command of
the ocean. They thenceforth found themselves free
to work their will in all seagirt lands, unchecked by
hostile European influence.

Most fortunately, when England began her career
as a colonizing power in America, Spain had
already taken possession of the populous tropical
and subtropical regions, and the northern power was
thus forced to form her settlements in the sparsely
peopled temperate zone.

It is of vital importance to remember that the
English and Spanish conquests in America differed
from each other very much as did the
original conquests which gave rise to   Difference
                                          between the
the English and the Spanish nations.   Spanish and
The English had exterminated or as-   the English
similated the Celts of Britain, and they Conquests.
substantially repeated the process with the Indians of America; although of course in America

there was very little, instead of very much, assimilation. The Germanic strain is dominant in the blood of the average Englishman, exactly as the English strain is dominant in the blood of the average American. Twice a portion of the race has shifted its home, in each case undergoing a marked change, due both to outside influence and to internal development; but in the main retaining, especially in the last instance, the general race characteristics.

It was quite otherwise in the countries conquered by Cortes, Pizarro, and their successors. Instead of killing or driving off the natives as the English did, the Spaniards simply sat down in the midst of a much more numerous aboriginal population. The process by which Central and South America became Spanish bore very close resemblance to the process by which the lands of southeastern Europe were turned into Romance-speaking countries. The bulk of the original inhabitants remained unchanged in each case. There was little displacement of population. Roman soldiers and magistrates, Roman merchants and handicraftsmen were thrust in among the Celtic and Iberian peoples, exactly as the Spanish military and civil rulers, priests, traders, land-owners, and mine-owners settled down among the Indians of Peru and Mexico. By degrees, in each case, the many learnt the language and adopted the laws, religion, and governmental system of the few, although keeping certain of their own customs and habits of thought. Though the ordinary Spaniard of to-day speaks a Romance dialect, he is mainly of Celto-Iberian blood ; and though most Mexicans and Peruvians speak Spanish, yet the great majority of them trace their descent back to the subjects of Montezuma and the Incas. Moreover, exactly as in Europe little ethnic islands of Breton and Basque stock have remained unaffected by the Romance flood, so in America there are large communities where the inhabitants keep unchanged the speech and the customs of their Indian forefathers.

The English-speaking peoples now hold more and better land than any other American nationality or set of nationalities. They have in their veins less aboriginal American blood than any of their neighbors. Yet it is noteworthy that the latter have tacitly allowed them to arrogate to themselves the title of " Americans," whereby to designate their distinctive and individual nationality.

So much for the difference between the way in which the English and the way in which other European nations have conquered and colonized. But there have been likewise very great differences in the methods and courses of the English-speaking peoples themselves, at different times and in different places.

The English Settlements and Conquests.

The settlement of the United States and Canada, throughout most of their extent, bears much resemblance to the later settlement of Australia and New Zealand. The English conquest of India and even the English conquest of South Africa come in an entirely different category. The first was a mere political conquest, like the Dutch conquest of Java or the extension of the Roman Empire over parts of Asia. South Africa in some respects stands by itself, because there the English are confronted by another white race which it is as yet uncertain whether they can assimilate, and, what is infinitely more important, because they are there confronted by a very large native population with which they cannot mingle, and which neither dies out nor recedes before their advance. It is not likely, but it is at least within the bounds of possibility, that in the course of centuries the whites of South Africa will suffer a fate akin to that which befell the Greek colonists in the Tauric Chersonese, and be swallowed up in the overwhelming mass of black barbarism.

On the other hand, it may fairly be said that in America and Australia the English race has already entered into and begun the enjoyment of its great inheritance. When these continents were settled they contained the largest tracts of fertile, temperate, thinly peopled country on the face of the globe. We cannot rate too highly the importance of their acquisition. Their successful settlement was a feat which by comparison utterly dwarfs all the European wars of the last two centuries ; just as the importance of the issues at stake in the wars of Rome and Carthage completely overshadowed the interests for which the various contemporary Greek kingdoms were at the same time striving.

Australia, which was much less important than **Australia.** America, was also won and settled with far less difficulty. The natives were so few in number and of such a low type, that they practically offered no resistance at all, being but little more hindrance than an equal number of ferocious beasts.

There was no rivalry whatever by any European power, because the actual settlement—not the mere expatriation of convicts—only began when England, as a result of her struggle with Republican and Imperial France, had won the absolute control of the seas. Unknown to themselves, Nelson and his fellow admirals settled the fate of Australia, upon which they probably never wasted a thought. Trafalgar decided much more than the mere question whether Great Britain should temporarily share the fate that so soon befell Prussia; for in all probability it decided the destiny of the island-continent that lay in the South Seas.

The history of the English-speaking race in America has been widely different. In Australia there was no fighting whatever, whether with natives or with other foreigners. In America for the past two centuries and a half there has been a constant succession of contests with powerful and warlike native tribes, with rival European nations, and with American nations of European origin. But even in America there have been wide differences in the way the work has had to be done in different parts of the country, since the close of the great colonial contests between England, France, and Spain.

The extension of the English westward through Canada since the war of the Revolution has been in its essential features merely a less important repetition of what has gone on in the **Canada.** northern United States. The gold miner, the transcontinental railway, and the soldier have been the pioneers of civilization. The chief point of differ-

ence, which was but small, arose from the fact that
the whole of western Canada was for a long time
under the control of the most powerful of all the fur
companies, in whose employ were very many French
voyageurs and coureurs des bois. From these there
sprang up in the valleys of the Red River and the
Saskatchewan a singular race of half-breeds, with a
unique semi-civilization of their own. It was with
these half-breeds, and not, as in the United States,
with the Indians, that the settlers of northwestern
Canada had their main difficulties.

In what now forms the United States, taking the
country as a whole, the foes who had to be met and
overcome were very much more formidable. The
The United ground had to be not only settled but con-
States. quered, sometimes at the expense of the
natives, often at the expense of rival European races.
As already pointed out the Indians themselves formed
one of the main factors in deciding the fate of the
continent. They were never able in the end to avert
the white conquest, but they could often delay its
advance for a long spell of years. The Iroquois,
for instance, held their own against all comers for
two centuries. Many other tribes stayed for a time
the oncoming white flood, or even drove it back;
in Maine the settlers were for a hundred years confined to a narrow strip of sea-coast. Against the
Spaniards, there were even here and there Indian
nations who definitely recovered the ground they
had lost.

When the whites first landed, the superiority and,
above all, the novelty of their arms gave them a

very great advantage. But the Indians soon became accustomed to the new-comers' weapons and style of warfare. By the time the English had consolidated the Atlantic colonies under their rule, the Indians had become what they have remained ever since, the most formidable savage foes ever encountered by colonists of European stock. Relatively to their numbers, they have shown themselves far more to be dreaded than the Zulus or even the Maoris.

Their presence has caused the process of settlement to go on at unequal rates of speed in different places; the flood has been hemmed in at one point, or has been forced to flow round an island of native population at another. Had the Indians been as helpless as the native Australians were, the continent of North America would have had an altogether different history. It would not only have been settled far more rapidly, but also on very different lines. Not only have the red men themselves kept back the settlements, but they have also had a very great effect upon the outcome of the struggles between the different intrusive European peoples. Had the original inhabitants of the Mississippi valley been as numerous and unwarlike as the Aztecs, de Soto would have repeated the work of Cortes, and we would very possibly have been barred out of the greater portion of our present domain. Had it not been for their Indian allies, it would have been impossible for the French to prolong, as they did, their struggle with their much more numerous English neighbors.

The Indians have shrunk back before our advance only after fierce and dogged resistance. They were never numerous in the land, but exactly what their numbers were when the whites first appeared is impossible to tell. Probably an estimate of half a million for those within the limits of the present United States is not far wrong; but in any such calculation there is of necessity a large element of mere rough guess-work. Formerly writers greatly over-estimated their original numbers, counting them by millions. Now it is the fashion to go to the other extreme, and even to maintain that they have not decreased at all. This last is a theory that can only be upheld on the supposition that the whole does not consist of the sum of the parts; for whereas we can check off on our fingers the tribes that have slightly increased, we can enumerate scores that have died out almost before our eyes. Speaking broadly, they have mixed but little with the English (as distinguished from the French and Spanish) invaders. They are driven back, or die out, or retire to their own reservations; but they are not often assimilated. Still, on every frontier, there is always a certain amount of assimilation going on, much more than is commonly admitted [1]; and whenever a French or Span-

---

[1] To this I can testify of my own knowledge as regards Montana, Dakota, and Minnesota. The mixture usually takes place in the ranks of the population where individuals lose all trace of their ancestry after two or three generations; so it is often honestly ignored, and sometimes mention of it is suppressed, the man regarding it as a taint. But I also know many very wealthy old frontiersmen whose half-breed children are now being educated, generally at convent schools, while in the Northwestern cities I could point out some very charming men and women, in the best society, with a strain of Indian blood in their veins.

ish community has been absorbed by the energetic Americans, a certain amount of Indian blood has been absorbed also. There seems to be a chance that in one part of our country, the Indian territory, the Indians, who are continually advancing in civilization, will remain as the ground element of the population, like the Creoles in Louisiana, or the Mexicans in New Mexico.

The Americans when they became a nation continued even more successfully the work which they had begun as citizens of the several English colonies. At the outbreak of the Revolution they still all dwelt on the seaboard, either on the coast itself or along the banks of the streams flowing into the Atlantic. When the fight at Lexington took place they had no settlements beyond the mountain chain on our western border. It had taken them over a century and a half to spread from the Atlantic to the Alleghanies. In the next three quarters of a century they spread from the Alleghanies to the Pacific. In doing this they not only dispossessed the Indian tribes, but they also won the land from its European owners. Britain had to yield the territory between the Ohio and the Great Lakes. By a purchase, of which we frankly announced that the alternative would be war, we acquired from France the vast, ill-defined region known as Louisiana. From the Spaniards, or from their descendants, we won the lands of Florida, Texas, New Mexico, and California.

All these lands were conquered after we had be-

come a power, independent of every other, and one
within our own borders; when we were no longer a
loose assemblage of petty seaboard communities, each with only such relationship
to its neighbor as was implied in their
common subjection to a foreign king and a
foreign people. Moreover, it is well always to remember that at the day when we began
our career as a nation we already differed from
our kinsmen of Britain in blood as well as in name;
the word American already had more than a merely
geographical signification. Americans belong to the
English race only in the sense in which Englishmen
belong to the German. The fact that no change of
language has accompanied the second wandering of
our people, from Britain to America, as it accompanied
their first, from Germany to Britain, is due to the
further fact that when the second wandering took
place the race possessed a fixed literary language,
and, thanks to the ease of communication, was kept
in touch with the parent stock. The change of blood
was probably as great in one case as in the other.
The modern Englishman is descended from a Low-
Dutch stock, which, when it went to Britain, received
into itself an enormous infusion of Celtic, a much
smaller infusion of Norse and Danish, and also a certain infusion of Norman-French blood. When this
new English stock came to America it mingled with
and absorbed into itself immigrants from many European lands, and the process has gone on ever since.
It is to be noted that, of the new blood thus acquired,
the greatest proportion has come from Dutch and

The Ameri-cans a Dis-tinct People from the British.

German sources, and the next greatest from Irish, while the Scandinavian element comes third, and the only other of much consequence is French Huguenot. Thus it appears that no new element of importance has been added to the blood. Additions have been made to the elemental race-strains in much the same proportion as these were originally combined.

Some latter-day writers deplore the enormous immigration to our shores as making us a heterogeneous instead of a homogeneous people; but as a matter of fact we are less heterogeneous at the present day than we were at the outbreak of the Revolution. Our blood was as much mixed a century ago as it is now. No State now has a smaller proportion of English blood than New York or Pennsylvania had in 1775. Even in New England, where the English stock was purest, there was a certain French and Irish mixture; in Virginia there were Germans in addition. In the other colonies, taken as a whole, it is not probable that much over half of the blood was English; Dutch, French, German, and Gaelic communities abounded.

But all were being rapidly fused into one people. As the Celt of Cornwall and the Saxon of Wessex are now alike Englishmen, so in 1775 Hollander and Huguenot, whether in New York or South Carolina, had become Americans, undistinguishable from the New Englanders and Virginians, the descendants of the men who followed Cromwell or charged behind Rupert. When the great western movement began

Territorial Expansion.

we were already a people by ourselves. Moreover, the immense immigration from Europe that has taken place since, had little or no effect on the way in which we extended our boundaries; it only began to be important about the time that we acquired our present limits. These limits would in all probability be what they now are even if we had not received a single European colonist since the Revolution.

Thus the Americans began their work of western conquest as a separate and individual people, at the moment when they sprang into national life. It has been their great work ever since. All other questions save those of the preservation of the Union itself and of the emancipation of the blacks have been of subordinate importance when compared with the great question of how rapidly and how completely they were to subjugate that part of their continent lying between the eastern mountains and the Pacific. Yet the statesmen of the Atlantic seaboard were often unable to perceive this, and indeed frequently showed the same narrow jealousy of the communities beyond the Alleghanies that England felt for all America. Even if they were too broad-minded and far-seeing to feel thus, they yet were unable to fully appreciate the magnitude of the interests at stake in the west. They thought more of our right to the North Atlantic fisheries than of our ownership of the Mississippi valley; they were more interested in the fate of a bank or a tariff than in the settlement of the Oregon boundary. Most contemporary writers showed similar shortcomings in their sense of historic perspective. The names of Ethan Allen and Marion are probably better known than is that of George Rogers Clark; yet their deeds, as regards their effects, could no more be compared to his, than his could be compared to Washington's. So it was with Houston. During his lifetime there were probably fifty men who, east of the Mississippi, were deemed far greater than he was. Yet in most cases their names have already almost faded from remembrance, while his fame will grow steadily brighter as the importance of his deeds is more thoroughly realized. Fortunately, in the long run, the mass of easterners always backed up their western brethren.

The kind of colonizing conquest, whereby the people of the United States have extended their borders, has much in common with the similar movements in Canada and Australia, all of them standing in sharp contrast to what has gone on in Spanish-American lands. But of course each is marked out in addition by certain peculiarities of its own. Moreover, even in the United States, the movement falls naturally into two divisions, which on several points differ widely from each other.

The way in which the southern part of our western country—that is, all the land south of the Ohio, and from thence on to the Rio Grande and the Pacific—was won and settled, stands quite alone. The region north of it was filled up in a very different manner. The North-west Acquired by the Nation. The Southwest, including therein what was once called simply the West, and afterwards the Middle West, was won by the people themselves, acting as individuals, or as groups of individuals, who hewed out their own fortunes in advance of any governmental action. On the other hand, the Northwest, speaking broadly, was acquired by the government, the settlers merely taking possession of what the whole country guaranteed them. The Northwest is essentially a national domain; it is fitting that it should be, as it is, not only by position but by feeling, the heart of the nation.

North of the Ohio the regular army went first. The settlements grew up behind the shelter of the federal troops of Harmar, St. Claire, and Wayne, and of their successors even to our own day. The wars in which the borderers themselves bore any part were few and trifling compared to the contests waged by the adventurers who won Kentucky, Tennessee, and Texas.

In the Southwest the early settlers acted as their own army, and supplied both leaders and men. Sevier, Robertson, Clark, and Boon led their fellow pioneers to battle, as Jackson did afterwards, and as Houston did later still. Indeed the Southwesterners not only won their own soil for themselves, but they were the chief instruments in the original acquisition of the Northwest also. Had it not been for the conquest of the Illinois towns in 1779 we would probably never have had any Northwest to settle; and the huge tract between the upper Mississippi and the Columbia, then called Upper Louisiana, fell into our hands, only because the Kentuckians and Tennesseeans were resolutely bent on taking possession of New Orleans, either by bargain or battle. All of our territory lying beyond the Alleghanies, north and south, was first won for us by the Southwesterners, fighting for their own hand. The northern part was afterwards filled up by the thrifty, vigorous men of the Northeast, whose sons became the real rulers as well as the preservers of the Union; but these settlements of Northerners were rendered possible only by the deeds of the nation as a whole. They entered on land that the Southerners had won, and they were kept there by the strong arm of the Federal Government; whereas the Southerners owed most of their victories only to themselves.

The first-comers around Marietta did, it is true, share to a certain extent in the dangers of the existing Indian wars; but their trials are not to be mentioned beside those endured by the early settlers of Tennessee and Kentucky, and whereas these latter themselves subdued and drove out their foes, the former took but an insignificant part in the contest by which the possession of their land was secured. Besides, the strongest and most numerous Indian tribes were in the Southwest.

The Southwest developed its civilization on its own lines, for good and for ill; the Northwest was settled under the national ordinance of 1787, which absolutely determined its destiny, and thereby in the end also determined the destiny of the whole nation. Moreover, the gulf coast, as well as the interior, from the Mississippi to the Pacific, was held by foreign powers; while in the north this was only true of the country between the Ohio and the Great Lakes during the

The Southwest Won by Individual Settlers.

first years of the Revolution, until the Kentucky
backwoodsmen conquered it. Our rivals of European race had dwelt for generations along the lower
Mississippi and the Rio Grande, in Florida, and in
California, when we made them ours. Detroit,
Vincennes, St. Louis, and New Orleans, St. Augustine, San Antonio, Santa Fé, and San Francisco are
cities that were built by Frenchmen or Spaniards ;
we did not found them, but conquered them. All
but the first two are in the Southwest, and of these
two one was first taken and governed by Southwesterners. On the other hand, the Northwestern cities,
from Cincinnati and Chicago to Helena and Portland,
were founded by our own people, by the people who
now have possession of them.

The Southwest was conquered only after years of
hard fighting with the original owners. The way in
The Win- which this was done bears much less resem-
ning of the blance to the sudden filling up of Australia
West and and California by the practically unopposed
Southwest. overflow from a teeming and civilized mother
country, than it does to the original English conquest
of Britain itself. The warlike borderers who thronged
across the Alleghanies, the restless and reckless hunters, the hard, dogged, frontier farmers, by dint of
grim tenacity overcame and displaced Indians, French,
and Spaniards alike, exactly as, fourteen hundred
years before, Saxon and Angle had overcome and
displaced the Cymric and Gaelic Celts. They were
led by no one commander ; they acted under orders
from neither king nor congress ; they were not
carrying out the plans of any far-sighted leader. In

obedience to the instincts working half blindly within
their breasts, spurred ever onwards by the fierce desires of their eager hearts, they made in the wilderness homes for their children, and by so doing
wrought out the destinies of a continental nation.
They warred and settled from the high hill-valleys
of the French Broad and the Upper Cumberland to
the half-tropical basin of the Rio Grande, and to
where the Golden Gate lets through the long-heaving
waters of the Pacific. The story of how this was
done forms a compact and continuous whole. The
fathers followed Boon or fought at King's Mountain; the sons marched south with Jackson to overcome the Creeks and beat back the British; the
grandsons died at the Alamo or charged to victory
at San Jacinto. They were doing their share of a
work that began with the conquest of Britain, that
entered on its second and wider period after the
defeat of the Spanish Armada, that culminated in
the marvellous growth of the United States. The
winning of the West and Southwest is a stage in the
conquest of a continent.

CHAPTER II.

THE result of England's last great colonial struggle with France was to sever from the latter all her
American dependencies, her colonists becoming the
subjects of alien and rival powers. England won
Canada and the Ohio valley; while France ceded to
her Spanish allies Louisiana, including therein all
the territory vaguely bounded by the Mississippi
and the Pacific. As an offset to this gain Spain had
herself lost to England both Floridas, as the coast
regions between Georgia and Louisiana were then
called.

Thus the thirteen colonies, at the outset of their
struggle for independence, saw themselves surrounded north, south, and west, by lands where the
rulers and the ruled were of different races, but
where rulers and ruled alike were hostile to the new
people that was destined in the end to master them
all.

The present province of Quebec, then called Canada, was already, what she has to this day remained,
a French state acknowledging the English king as
her over-lord. Her interests did not conflict with
those of our people, nor touch them in any way, and
she has had little to do with our national history,

and nothing whatever to do with the history of the west.

In the peninsula of East Florida, in the land of the cypress, palmetto, and live oak, of open savannas, of sandy pine forests, and impenetrable, interminable morasses, a European civilization more ancient than any in the English colonies was mouldering in slow decay. Its capital city was quaint St. Augustine, the old walled town that was founded by the Spaniards long years before the keel of the *Half-Moon* furrowed the broad Hudson, or the ships of the Puritans sighted the New England coast. In times past St. Augustine had once and again seen her harbor filled with the huge, cumbrous hulls, **East Florida.** and whitened by the bellying sails, of the Spanish war vessels, when the fleets of the Catholic king gathered there, before setting out against the seaboard towns of Georgia and the Carolinas; and she had to suffer from and repulse the retaliatory inroads of the English colonists. Once her priests and soldiers had brought the Indian tribes, far and near, under subjection, and had dotted the wilderness with fort and church and plantation, the outposts of her dominion; but that was long ago, and the tide of Spanish success had turned and begun to ebb many years before the English took possession of Florida. The Seminoles, fierce and warlike, whose warriors fought on foot and on horseback, had avenged in countless bloody forays their fellow-Indian tribes, whose very names had perished under Spanish rule. The churches and forts had crumbled into nothing; only the cannon and the brazen bells, half buried in the rotting mould, remained to mark the place where once stood spire and citadel. The deserted plantations, the untravelled causeways, no longer marred the face of the tree-clad land, for even their sites had ceased to be distinguishable; the great high-road that led to Pensacola had faded away, overgrown by the rank luxuriance of the semi-tropical forest. Throughout the interior the painted savages roved at will, uncontrolled by Spaniard or Englishman, owing allegiance only to the White Chief of Tallasotchee.[1] St. Augustine, with its British garrison and its Spanish and Minorcan townsfolk,[2] was still a gathering place for a few Indian traders, and for the scattered fishermen of the coast; elsewhere there were in all not more than a hundred families.[3]

Beyond the Chattahooche and the Appalachicola, stretching thence to the Mississippi and its delta, lay the more prosperous region of West Florida.[4] Although taken by the English from Spain, there were few Spaniards among the people, who were controlled by the scanty British garrisons at Pensacola, Mobile, and Natchez. On the Gulf coast the inhabitants were mainly French creoles. They were an indolent, pleasure-loving race, fond of dancing and merriment, living at ease in their low, square, roomy houses on the straggling, rudely farmed plantations that lay along

West Florida.

---

[1] "Travels by William Bartram," Philadelphia, 1791, pp. 184, 231, 232, etc. The various Indian names are spelt in a dozen different ways.

[2] Reise, etc. (in 1783 and 84), by Johann David Schöpf, 1788, II. 362 The Minorcans were the most numerous and prosperous; then came the Spaniards, with a few creoles, English, and Germans.

[3] J. D. F. Smyth, "Tour in the United States" (1775), London, 1784, II., 35. [4] *Do.*

the river banks. Their black slaves worked for them; they themselves spent much of their time in fishing and fowling. Their favorite arm was the light fowling-piece, for they were expert wing shots [1]; unlike the American backwoodsmen, who knew nothing of shooting on the wing, and looked down on smooth-bores, caring only for the rifle, the true weapon of the freeman. In winter the creoles took their negroes to the hills, where they made tar from the pitch pine, and this they exported, as well as indigo, rice, tobacco, bear's oil, peltry, oranges, and squared timber. Cotton was grown, but only for home use. The British soldiers dwelt in stockaded forts, mounting light cannon; the governor lived in the high stone castle built of old by the Spaniards at Pensacola.[2]

In the part of west Florida lying along the east bank of the Mississippi, there were also some French creoles and a few Spaniards, with of course negroes and Indians to boot. But the population consisted mainly of Americans from the old colonies, who had come thither by sea in small sailing-vessels, or had descended the Ohio and the Tennessee in flat-boats, or, perchance, had crossed the Creek country with pack ponies, following the narrow trails of the Indian traders. With them were some English and Scotch, and the Americans themselves had little sympathy with the colonies, feeling instead a certain dread and dislike

---

[1] " Mémoire ou Coup-d'Œil Rapide sur més différentes voyages et mon sejour dans la nation Crëck, par Le Gal. Milfort, Tastanégy ou grand chef de guerre de la nation Crëck et Géneral de Brigade au service de la Republique Francaise." Paris, 1802. Writing in 1781, he said Mobile contained about forty proprietary families, and was " un petit paradis terrestre."   [2] Bartram, 407.

of the rough Carolinian mountaineers, who were their nearest white neighbors on the east.[1] They therefore, for the most part, remained loyal to the crown in the Revolutionary struggle, and suffered accordingly.

When Louisiana was ceded to Spain, most of the French creoles who formed her population **Louisiana.** were clustered together in the delta of the Mississippi; the rest were scattered out here and there, in a thin, dotted line, up the left bank of the river to the Missouri, near the mouth of which there were several small villages,—St. Louis, St. Geneviève, St. Charles.[2] A strong Spanish garrison held New Orleans, where the creoles, discontented with their new masters, had once risen in a revolt that was speedily quelled and severely punished. Small garrisons were also placed in the different villages.

Our people had little to do with either Florida or Louisiana until after the close of the Revolutionary war; but very early in that struggle, and soon after the movement west of the mountains began, we were thrown into contact with the French of the Northwestern Territory, and the result was of the utmost importance to the future welfare of the whole nation.

This northwestern land lay between the Mississippi, the Ohio, and the Great Lakes. It now constitutes five of our large States and part of **The Ohio Valley French.** a sixth. But when independence was declared it was quite as much a foreign territory, considered from the standpoint of the old

[1] *Magazine of American History*, IV., 388. Letter of a New England settler in 1773.

[2] " Annals of St. Louis." Frederic L. Billon. St. Louis, 1886. A valuable book.

thirteen colonies, as Florida or Canada; the difference was that, whereas during the war we failed in our attempts to conquer Florida and Canada, we succeeded in conquering the Northwest. The Northwest formed no part of our country as it originally stood; it had no portion in the declaration of independence. It did not revolt; it was conquered. Its inhabitants, at the outset of the Revolution, no more sympathized with us, and felt no greater inclination to share our fate, than did their kinsmen in Quebec or the Spaniards in St. Augustine. We made our first important conquest during the Revolution itself,—beginning thus early what was to be our distinguishing work for the next seventy years.

These French settlements, which had been founded about the beginning of the century, when the English still clung to the estuaries of the seaboard, were grouped in three clusters, separated by hundreds of miles of wilderness. One of these clusters, containing something like a third of the total population, was at the straits, around Detroit.[1] It was the

[1] In the Haldimand MSS., Series B, vol. 122, p. 2, is a census of Detroit itself, taken in 1773 by Philip Dejean, justice of the peace. According to this there were 1,367 souls, of whom 85 were slaves; they dwelt in 280 houses, with 157 barns, and owned 1,494 horned cattle, 628 sheep, and 1,067 hogs. Acre is used as a measure of length; their united farms had a frontage of 512, and went back from 40 to 80. Some of the people, it is specified, were not enumerated because they were out hunting or trading at the Indian villages. Besides the slaves, there were 93 servants.

This only refers to the settlers of Detroit proper, and the farms adjoining. Of the numerous other farms, and the small villages on both sides of the straits, and of the many families and individuals living as traders or trappers with the Indians, I can get no good record. Perhaps the total population, tributary to Detroit was 2,000. It may have been over this. Any attempt to estimate this creole population perforce contains much guess-work.

seat of the British power in that section, and remained in British hands for twenty years after we had become a nation.

The other two were linked together by their subsequent history, and it is only with them that we have to deal. The village of Vincennes lay on the eastern bank of the Wabash, with two or three smaller villages tributary to it in the country round about; and to the west, beside the Mississippi, far above where it is joined by the Ohio, lay the so-called Illinois towns, the villages of Kaskaskia and Cahokia, with between them the little settlements of Prairie du Rocher and St. Philip.[1]

Both these groups of old French hamlets were in the fertile prairie region of what is now southern Indiana and Illinois. We have taken into our language the word prairie, because when our backwoodsmen first reached the land and saw the great natural meadows of long grass—sights unknown to the gloomy forests wherein they had always dwelt—they knew not what to call them, and borrowed the term already in use among the French inhabitants.

The great prairies, level or rolling, stretched from north to south, separated by broad belts of high timber. Here and there copses of woodland lay like islands in the sunny seas of tall, waving grass. Where the rivers ran, their alluvial bottoms were densely covered with trees and underbrush, and were often overflowed in the spring freshets. Sometimes the prairies were long, narrow strips of

The Illinois and Vincennes.

[1] State Department MSS., No. 150, Vol. III., p. 89.

meadow land; again they were so broad as to be a day's journey across, and to the American, bred in a wooded country where the largest openings were the beaver meadows and the clearings of the frontier settlers, the stretches of grass land seemed limitless. They abounded in game. The buffalo crossed and recrossed them, wandering to and fro in long files, beating narrow trails that they followed year in and year out; while bear, elk, and deer dwelt in the groves around the borders.[1]

There were perhaps some four thousand inhabitants in these French villages, divided almost equally between those in the Illinois and those along the Wabash.[2]

[1] *Do.* Harmar's letter.

[2] State Department MSS., No. 30, p. 453. Memorial of François Carbonneaux, agent for the inhabitants of the Illinois country. Dec. 8, 1784. " Four hundred families [in the Illinois] exclusive of a like number at Post Vincent" [Vincennes]. Americans had then just begun to come in, but this enumeration did not refer to them. The population had decreased during the Revolutionary war; so that at its outbreak there were probably altogether a thousand families. They were very prolific, and four to a family is probably not too great an allowance, even when we consider that in such a community on the frontier there are always plenty of solitary adventurers. Moreover, there were a number of negro slaves. Harmar's letter of Nov. 24, 1787, states the adult males of Kaskaskia and Cahokia at four hundred and forty, not counting those at St. Philip or Prairie du Rocher. This tallies very well with the preceding. But of course the number given can only be considered approximately accurate, and a passage in a letter of Lt.-Gov. Hamilton would indicate that it was considerably smaller.

This letter is to be found in the Haldimand MSS., Series B, Vol. 123, p. 53; it is the "brief account" of his ill-starred expedition against Vincennes. He says: " On taking an account of the Inhabitants at this place [Vincennes], of all ages and sexes, we found their number to amount to 621; of this 217 fit to bear arms on the spot, several being absent hunting Buffaloe for their winter provision." But elsewhere in the same letter he alludes to the adult arms-bearing men as being three hundred in number, and of course the outlying farms and small tributary villages are not counted in. This was in December, 1778. Possibly some families had left for the

The country came into the possession of the British—not of the colonial English or Americans—at the close of Pontiac's war, the aftermath of the struggle which decided against the French the ownership of America. It was held as a new British province, not as an extension of any of the old colonies; and finally in 1774, by the famous Quebec Act, it was rendered an appanage of Canada, governed from the latter. It is a curious fact that England immediately adopted towards her own colonists the policy of the very nationality she had ousted. From the date of the triumphant peace won by Wolfe's victory, the British government became the most active foe of the spread of the English race in America. This position Britain maintained for many years after the failure of her attempt to bar her colonists out of the Ohio valley. It was the position she occupied when at Ghent in 1814 her commissioners tried to hem in the natural progress of her colonists' children by the erection of a great " neutral belt " of Indian territory, guaranteed by the British king. It was the rôle which her statesmen endeavored to make her play when at a later date they strove to keep Oregon a waste rather than see it peopled by Americans.

In the northwest she succeeded to the French policy as well as the French position. She wished the land to remain a wilderness, the home of the trapper and the fur trader, of the Indian hunter and the

Spanish possessions after the war broke out, and returned after it was ended. But as all observers seem to unite in stating that the settlements either stood still or went backwards during the Revolutionary struggle, it is somewhat difficult to reconcile the figures of Hamilton and Carbonneaux.

French voyageur. She desired it to be kept as a barrier against the growth of the seaboard colonies towards the interior. She regarded the new lands across the Atlantic as being won and settled, not for the benefit of the men who won and settled them, but for the benefit of the merchants and traders who stayed at home. It was this that rendered the Revolution inevitable ; the struggle was a revolt against the whole mental attitude of Britain in regard to America, rather than against any one special act or set of acts. The sins and shortcomings of the colonists had been many, and it would be easy to make out a formidable catalogue of grievances against them, on behalf of the mother country ; but on the great underlying question they were wholly in the right, and their success was of vital consequence to the well-being of the race on this continent.

England Adopts the French Policy.

Several of the old colonies urged vague claims to parts of the Northwestern Territory, basing them on ancient charters and Indian treaties ; but the British heeded them no more than the French had, and they were very little nearer fulfilment after the defeat of Montcalm and Pontiac than before. The French had held adverse possession in spite of them for sixty years ; the British held similar possession for fifteen more. The mere statement of the facts is enough to show the intrinsic worthlessness of the titles. The Northwest was acquired from France by Great Britain through conquest and treaty ; in a precisely similar way—Clark taking the place of Wolfe—it was

Claims of the Colonies.

afterwards won from Britain by the United States. We gained it exactly as we afterwards gained Louisiana, Florida, Oregon, California, New Mexico, and Texas : partly by arms, partly by diplomacy, partly by the sheer growth and pressure of our spreading population. The fact that the conquest took place just after we had declared ourselves a free nation, and while we were still battling to maintain our independence, does not alter its character in the least ; but it has sufficed to render the whole transaction very hazy in the minds of most subsequent historians, who generally speak as if the Northwest Territory had been part of our original possessions.

The French who dwelt in the land were at the time little affected by the change which transferred their allegiance from one European king to another. They were accustomed to obey, without question, the orders of their superiors. They accepted the results of the war submissively, and yielded a passive obedience to their new rulers.[1] Some became rather attached to the officers who came among them ; others grew rather to dislike them ; most felt merely a vague sentiment of distrust and repulsion, alike for the haughty British officer in his scarlet uniform, and for the reckless backwoodsman clad in tattered homespun or buckskin. They remained the owners of the villages, the tillers of the soil. At

---

[1] In the Haldimand MSS., Series B, Vol. 122, p. 3, the letter of M. Ste. Marie from Vincennes, May 3, 1774, gives utterance to the general feeling of the creoles, when he announces, in promising in their behalf to carry out the orders of the British commandant, that he is " remplie de respect pour tout ce qui porte l'emprinte de l'otorité." [sic.]

first few English or American immigrants, save an
occasional fur trader, came to live among them.
But their doom was assured ; their rule was at an
end forever. For a while they were still to com-
pose the bulk of the scanty population ; but nowhere
were they again to sway their own destinies. In
after years they fought for and against both whites
and Indians ; they faced each other, ranged beneath
the rival banners of Spain, England, and the insurgent
colonists ; but they never again fought for their old
flag or for their own sovereignty.

From the overthrow of Pontiac to the outbreak of
the Revolution the settlers in the Illinois and round
Vincennes lived in peace under their old laws and
customs, which were continued by the Life of the
British commandants.[1] They had been   French
originally governed, in the same way that   Creoles.
Canada was, by the laws of France, adapted, however, to the circumstances of the new country.
Moreover, they had local customs which were as
binding as the laws. After the conquest the British
commandants who came in acted as civil judges also.
All public transactions were recorded in French by
notaries public. Orders issued in English were translated into French so that they might be understood.
Criminal cases were referred to England. Before
the conquest the procureur du roi gave sentence by
his own personal decision in civil cases ; if the matters were important it was the custom for each party
to name two arbitrators, and the procureur du roi a

[1] State Department MSS., No. 48, p. 51.   Statement of M. Cerré (or
Carré), July, 1786, translated by John Pintard.

fifth ; while an appeal might be made to the council supérieur at New Orleans. The British commandant assumed the place of the procureur du roi, although there were one or two half-hearted efforts made to introduce the Common Law.

The original French commandants had exercised the power of granting to every person who petitioned as much land as the petitioner chose to ask for, subject to the condition that part of it should be cul-
Tillers of tivated within a year, under penalty of its
the Soil. reversion to "the king's demesnes."[1] The English followed the same custom. A large quantity of land was reserved in the neighborhood of each village for the common use, and a very small quantity for religious purposes. The common was generally a large patch of enclosed prairie, part of it being cultivated, and the remainder serving as a pasture for the cattle of the inhabitants.[2] The portion of the common set aside for agriculture was divided into strips of one arpent in front by forty in depth, and one or more allotted to each inhabitant according to his skill and industry as a cultivator.[3] The arpent, as used by the western French, was a rather rough measure of surface, less in size than an acre.[4] The farms held by private ownership likewise ran back in long strips from a narrow front that usually lay along some stream.[5] Several of them

[1] *Do.*

[2] State Department MSS., No. 48, p. 41. Petition of J. B. La Croix, A. Girardin, etc., dated "at Cohoe in the Illinois 15th July, 1786."

[3] Billon, 91.

[4] An arpent of land was 180 French feet square. MS. copy of Journal of Matthew Clarkson in 1766. In Durrett collection.

[5] American State Papers, Public Lands, I., 11.

generally lay parallel to one another, each including something like a hundred acres, but occasionally much exceeding this amount.

The French inhabitants were in very many cases not of pure blood. The early settlements had been made by men only, by soldiers, traders, and trappers, who took Indian wives. They were not trammelled by the queer pride which makes a man of English stock unwilling to make a red-skinned woman his wife, though anxious enough to make her his concubine. Their children were baptized in the little parish churches by the black-robed priests, and grew up holding the same position in the community as was held by their fellows both of whose parents were white. But, in addition to these free citizens, the richer inhabitants owned both red and black slaves ; negroes imported from Africa, or Indians overcome and taken in battle.[1] There were many freedmen and freedwomen of both colors, and in consequence much mixture of blood.

They were tillers of the soil, and some followed, in addition, the trades of blacksmith and carpenter. Very many of them were trappers or fur traders. Their money was composed of furs and peltries, rated at a fixed price per pound [2]; none other was used unless expressly so stated in the contract. Like the French of Europe,

Primitive Life.

[1] Fergus Historical Series, No. 12, " Illinois in the 18th Century." Edward G. Mason, Chicago, 1881. A most excellent number of an excellent series. The old parish registers of Kaskaskia, going back to 1695, contain some remarkable names of the Indian mothers—such as Maria Aramipinchicoue and Domitilla Tehuigouanakigaboucoue. Sometimes the man is only distinguished by some such title as " The Parisian," or " The Bohemian."

[2] Billon, 90.

their unit of value was the livre, nearly equivalent to the modern franc. They were not very industrious, nor very thrifty husbandmen. Their farming implements were rude, their methods of cultivation simple and primitive, and they themselves were often lazy and improvident. Near their town they had great orchards of gnarled apple-trees, planted by their forefathers when they came from France, and old pear-trees, of a kind unknown to the Americans; but their fields often lay untilled, while the owners lolled in the sunshine smoking their pipes. In consequence they were sometimes brought to sore distress for food, being obliged to pluck their corn while it was still green.[1]

The pursuits of the fur trader and fur trapper were far more congenial to them, and it was upon these that they chiefly depended. The half-savage life of toil, hardship, excitement, and long intervals of idleness attracted them strongly. This was perhaps one among the reasons why they got on so much better with the Indians than did the Americans, who, wherever they went, made clearings and settlements, cut down the trees, and drove off the game.

But even these pursuits were followed under the ancient customs and usages of the country, leave to travel and trade being first obtained from the commandant[2]; for the rule of the commandant was almost patriarchal. The inhabitants were utterly

---

[1] Letter of P. A. Laforge, Dec. 31, 1786. Billon, 268.

[2] State Department MSS., No. 150, Vol. III., p. 519. Letter of Joseph St. Marin, Aug. 23, 1788.

unacquainted with what the Americans called liberty. When they passed under our rule, it was soon found that it was impossible to make them understand such an institution as trial by jury; they throve best under the form of government to which they had been immemorially accustomed—a commandant to give them orders, with a few troops to back him up.[1] They often sought to escape from these orders, but rarely to defy them; their lawlessness was like the lawlessness of children and savages; any disobedience was always to a particular ordinance, not to the system.

The trader having obtained his permit, built his boats, — whether light, roomy bateaux made of boards, or birch-bark canoes, or pirogues, which were simply hollowed out logs. He loaded them with paint, powder, bullets, blankets, beads, and rum, manned them with hardy voyageurs, trained all their lives in the use of pole and paddle, and started off up or down the Mississippi,[2] the Ohio, or the Wabash, perhaps making a long carry or portage over into the Great Lakes. It took him weeks, often months, to get to the first trading-point, usually some large winter encampment of Indians. He might visit several of these, or stay the whole winter through at one, buying the furs.[3] Many of the French coureurs des bois, whose duty it was to traverse the wilderness, and who were expert trappers, took up their abode with the Indians, taught them how to catch the sable, fisher, otter, and

Traders and Trappers.

---

[1] *Do.*, p. 89, Harmar's letter.
[2] *Do.*, p. 519. Letter of Joseph St. Marin.   [3] *Do.*, p. 89.

beaver, and lived among them as members of the tribe, marrying copper-colored squaws, and rearing dusky children. When the trader had exchanged his goods for the peltries of these red and white skin-hunters, he returned to his home, having been absent perhaps a year or eighteen months. It was a hard life; many a trader perished in the wilderness by cold or starvation, by an upset where the icy current ran down the rapids like a mill-race, by the attack of a hostile tribe, or even in a drunken brawl with the friendly Indians, when voyageur, half-breed, and Indian alike had been frenzied by draughts of fiery liquor.[1]

Next to the commandant in power came the priest. He bore unquestioned rule over his congregation, **The** but only within certain limits; for the **Priesthood.** French of the backwoods, leavened by the presence among them of so many wild and bold spirits, could not be treated quite in the same way as the more peaceful *habitants* of Lower Canada. The duty of the priest was to look after the souls of his sovereign's subjects, to baptize, marry, and bury them, to confess and absolve them, and keep them from backsliding, to say mass, and to receive the salary due him for celebrating divine service; but, though his personal influence was of course very great, he had no temporal authority, and could not order his people either to fight or to work. Still

---

[1] Journal of Jean Baptiste Perrault, in 1783 ; in " Indian Tribes," by Henry R. Schoolcraft, Part III., Philadelphia, 1855. See also Billon, 484, for an interesting account of the adventures of Gratiot, who afterwards, under American rule, built up a great fur business, and drove a flourishing trade with Europe, as well as the towns of the American seaboard.

less could he dispose of their land, a privilege inhering only in the commandant and in the commissaries of the villages, where they were expressly authorized so to do by the sovereign.[1]

The average inhabitant, though often loose in his morals, was very religious. He was superstitious also, for he firmly believed in omens, charms, and witchcraft, and when worked upon by his dread of the unseen and the unknown he sometimes did terrible deeds, as will be related farther on.

Under ordinary circumstances he was a good-humored, kindly man, always polite—his manners offering an agreeable contrast to those of some of our own frontiersmen,—with a ready smile and laugh, and ever eager to join in any merrymaking. On Sundays and fast-days he was summoned to the little parish church by the tolling of the old bell in the small wooden belfry. The church was a rude oblong building, the walls made out of peeled logs, thrust upright in the ground, chinked with moss and coated with clay or cement. Thither every man went, clad in a capote or blanket coat, a bright silk handkerchief knotted round his head, and his feet shod with moccasins or strong rawhide sandals. If young, he walked or rode a shaggy pony ; if older, he drove his creaking, springless wooden cart, untired and unironed, in which his family sat on stools.[2]

---

[1] State Department MSS., No. 48, p. 25. A petition concerning a case in point, affecting the Priest Gibault.

[2] " History of Vincennes," by Judge John Law, Vincennes, 1858, pp. 18 and 140. They are just such carts as I have seen myself in the valley of the Red River, and in the big bend of the Missouri, carrying all the worldly

The grades of society were much more clearly marked than in similar communities of our own people. The gentry, although not numerous, possessed unquestioned social and Social Life. political headship and were the military leaders; although of course they did not have any thing like such marked preëminence of position as in Quebec or New Orleans, where the conditions were more like those obtaining in the old world. There was very little education. The common people were rarely versed in the mysteries of reading and writing, and even the wives of the gentry were often only able to make their marks instead of signing their names.[1]

The little villages in which they dwelt were pretty places,[2] with wide, shaded streets. The houses lay far apart, often a couple of hundred feet from one another. They were built of heavy hewn timbers; those of the better sort were furnished with broad verandas, and contained large, low-ceilinged rooms,

goods of their owners, the French Métis. These Métis,—ex-trappers, ex-buffalo runners, and small farmers,—are the best representatives of the old French of the west ; they are a little less civilized, they have somewhat more Indian blood in their veins, but they are substantially the same people. It may be noted that the herds of buffaloes that during the last century thronged the plains of what are now the States of Illinois and Indiana furnished to the French of Kaskaskia and Vincennes their winter meat ; exactly as during the present century the Saskatchewan Métis lived on the wild herds until they were exterminated.

[1] See the lists of signatures in the State Department MSS., also Mason's Kaskaskia Parish Records and Law's Vincennes. As an example; the wife of the Chevalier Vinsenne (who gave his name to Vincennes, and afterwards fell in the battle where the Chickasaws routed the Northern French and their Indian allies), was only able to make her mark.

Clark in his letters several times mentions the "gentry," in terms that imply their standing above the rest of the people.

[2] State Department MSS., No. 150, Vol. III., p. 89.

the high mantle-pieces and the mouldings of the doors and windows being made of curiously carved wood. Each village was defended by a palisaded fort and block-houses, and was occasionally itself surrounded by a high wooden stockade. The inhabitants were extravagantly fond of music and dancing[1] ; marriages and christenings were seasons of merriment, when the fiddles were scraped all night long, while the moccasined feet danced deftly in time to the music.

Three generations of isolated life in the wilderness had greatly changed the characters of these groups of traders, trappers, bateau-men, and adventurous warriors. It was inevitable that they should borrow many traits from their savage friends and neighbors. Hospitable, but bigoted to their old customs, ignorant, indolent, and given to drunkenness, they spoke a corrupt jargon of the French tongue ; the common people were even beginning to give up reckoning time by months and years, and dated events, as the Indians did, with reference to the phenomena of nature, such as the time of the floods, the maturing of the green corn, or the ripening of the strawberries.[2] All their attributes seemed alien to the polished army-officers of old France[3] ; they had but little more in common

Character of the Creoles.

[1] "Journal of Jean Baptiste Perrault," 1783.

[2] "Voyage en Amérique" (1796), Général Victor Collot, Paris, 1804, p. 318.

[3] *Do.* Collot calls them "un composé de traiteurs, d'aventuriers, de coureurs de bois, rameurs, et de guerriers ; ignorans, superstitieux et entêtés, qu'aucunes fatigues, aucunes privations, aucunes dangers ne peuvent arrêter dans leurs enterprises, qu'ils mettent toujours fin ; ils n'ont conservé des vertus françaises que le courage."

with the latter than with the American backwoodsmen.   But they had kept many valuable qualities,
and, in especial, they were brave and hardy, and,
after their own fashion, good soldiers.   They had
fought valiantly beside King Louis' musketeers, and
in alliance with the painted warriors of the forest;
later on they served, though perhaps with less heart,
under the gloomy ensign of Spain, shared the fate of
the red-coated grenadiers of King George, or followed
the lead of the tall Kentucky riflemen.

CHAPTER III.

WHEN we declared ourselves an independent nation there were on our borders three groups of Indian peoples. The northernmost were the Iroquois or Six Nations, who dwelt in New York, and stretched down into Pennsylvania. They had been for two centuries the terror of every other Indian tribe east of the Mississippi, as well as of the whites; but their strength had already departed. They numbered only some ten or twelve thousand all told, and though they played a bloody part in the Revolutionary struggle, it was merely as subordinate allies of the British. It did not lie in their power to strike a really decisive blow. Their chastisement did not result in our gaining new territory; nor would a failure to chastise them have affected the outcome of the war nor the terms of peace. Their fate was bound up with that of the king's cause in America and was decided wholly by events unconnected with their own success or defeat.

The very reverse was the case with the Indians, tenfold more numerous, who lived along our western frontier. There they were themselves our main opponents, the British simply acting as their supporters; and instead of their fate being settled by the treaty of peace with Britain, they continued an active warfare for twelve years after it had been signed. Had they defeated us in the early years of the contest, it is more than probable that the Alleghanies would have **Importance** been made our western boundary at the **of Indian** peace. We won from them vast stretches **Wars.** of territory because we had beaten their warriors, and we could not have won it otherwise; whereas the territory of the Iroquois was lost, not because of their defeat, but because of the defeat of the British.

There were two great groups of these Indians, the ethnic corresponding roughly with the geographic division. In the northwest, between the Ohio and the Lakes, were the Algonquin tribes, generally banded loosely together; in the southwest, between the Tennessee—then called the Cherokee—and the Gulf, the so-called Appalachians lived. Between them lay a vast and beautiful region where no tribe dared dwell, but into which all ventured now and then for war and hunting.

The southwestern Indians were called Appalachians by the olden writers, because this was the name then given to the southern Alleghanies. It is doubtful if the term has any exact racial significance; but it serves very well to indicate a number of Indian nations whose system of government, ways of life, customs, and general culture were much alike, and whose civilization was much higher than was that of most other American tribes.

The Appalachians were in the barbarous, rather than in the merely savage state. They were divided into five lax confederacies: the Cherokees, Chickasaws, Choctaws, Creeks, and Seminoles. The latter were merely a southern offshoot of the Creeks or Muscogees.   They   were   far   more   numer-   The ous than the northwestern Indians, were   Southern less nomadic, and in consequence had more   Indian. definite possession of particular localities; so that their lands were more densely peopled.

In all they amounted to perhaps seventy thousand souls.[1]   It is more difficult to tell the numbers of the different tribes; for the division lines between them were very ill defined, and were subject to wide fluctuations.   Thus the Creeks, the most formidable of all, were made up of many bands, differing from each other both in race and speech.   The languages of the Chickasaws and Choctaws did not differ more from the tongue of the Cherokees, than the two divisions of the latter did from each other.   The Cherokees of the hills, the Otari, spoke a dialect that could not be understood by the Cherokees of the lowlands, or Erati.   Towns or bands continually broke up and split off from their former associations, while ambitious and warlike chiefs kept forming new settlements, and if successful drew large numbers of young warriors from the older communities.   Thus

[1] Letter of Commissioners Hawkins, Pickens, Martin, and McIntosh, to the President of the Continental Congress, Dec. 2, 1785. (Given in Senate Documents, 33d Congress, 2d session, Boundary between Ga. and Fla.) They give 14,200 " gun-men," and say that " at a moderate calculation " there are four times as many old men, women, and children, as there are gun-men.   The estimates of the numbers are very numerous and very conflicting.   After carefully consulting all accessible authorities, I have come to the conclusion that the above is probably pretty near the truth.   It is the deliberate, official opinion of four trained experts, who had ample opportunities for investigation, and who examined the matter with care. But it is very possible that in allotting the several tribes their numbers they err now and then, as the boundaries between the tribes shifted continually, and there were always large communities of renegades, such as the Chickamaugas, who were drawn from the ranks of all.

the boundary lines between the confederacies were ever shifting.[1] Judging from a careful comparison of the different authorities, the following estimate of the numbers of the southern tribes at the outbreak of the Revolution may be considered as probably approximately correct.

The Cherokees, some twelve thousand strong,[2] were the mountaineers of their race. They dwelt **The Four Tribes.** among the blue-topped ridges and lofty peaks of the southern Alleghanies,[3] in the wild and picturesque region where the present States

---

[1] This is one of the main reasons why the estimates of their numbers vary so hopelessly. As a specimen case, among many others, compare the estimate of Professor Benj. Smith Barton (" Origin of the Tribes and Nations of America," Phila., 1798) with the report of the Commissioner of Indian Affairs for 1827. Barton estimated that in 1793 the Appalachian nations numbered in all 13,000 warriors ; considering these as one fifth of the total population, makes it 65,000. In 1837 the Commissioner reports their numbers at 65,304—almost exactly the same. Probably both statements are nearly correct, the natural rate of increase having just about offset the loss in consequence of a partial change of home, and of Jackson's slaughtering wars against the Creeks and Seminoles. But where they agree in the total, thay vary hopelessly in the details. By Barton's estimate, the Cherokees numbered but 7,500, the Chocktaws 30,000 ; by the Commissioner's census the Cherokees numbered 21,911, the Choctaws 15,000. It is of course out of the question to believe that while in 44 years the Cherokees had increased threefold, the Choctaws had diminished one half. The terms themselves must have altered their significance or else there was extensive inter-tribal migration. Similarly, according to the reports, the Creeks had increased by 4,000—the Seminoles and Choctaws had diminished by 3,000.

[2] "Am. Archives," 4th Series, III., 790. Drayton's account, Sept. 23, '75. This was a carefully taken census, made by the Indian traders. Apart from the outside communities, such as the Chickamaugas at a later date, there were :

737 gun-men in the 10 overhill towns
908   "   "   23 middle   "
356   "   "   9 lower   "

a total of 2,021 warriors. The outlying towns, who had cast off their allegiance for the time being, would increase the amount by three or four hundred more.

[3] " History of the American Indians, Particularly Those Nations Adjoin-

of Tennessee, Alabama, Georgia, and the Carolinas join one another.

To the west of the Cherokees, on the banks of the Mississippi, were the Chickasaws, the smallest of the southern nations, numbering at the outside but four thousand souls [1]; but they were also the bravest and most warlike, and of all these tribal confederacies theirs was the only one which was at all closely knit together. The whole tribe acted in unison. In consequence, though engaged in incessant warfare with the far more numerous Choctaws, Creeks, and Cherokees, they more than held their own against them all; besides having inflicted on the French two of the bloodiest defeats they ever suffered from Indians. Most of the remnants of the Natchez, the strange sun-worshippers, had taken refuge with the Chickasaws and become completely identified with them, when their own nationality was destroyed by the arms of New Orleans.

The Choctaws, the rudest and historically the least important of these Indians, lived south of the Chickasaws. They were probably rather less numerous than the Creeks. [2] Though accounted brave they

ing to the Mississippi, East and West Florida, Georgia, South and North Carolina, and Virginia." By James Adair (an Indian trader and resident in the country for forty years), London, 1775. A very valuable book, but a good deal marred by the author's irrepressible desire to twist every Indian utterance, habit, and ceremony into a proof that they are descended from the Ten Lost Tribes. He gives the number of Cherokee warriors at 2,300.

[1] Hawkins, Pickens, Martin, and McIntosh, in their letter, give them 800 warriors; most other estimates make the number smaller.

[2] Almost all the early writers make them more numerous. Adair gives them 4,500 warriors, Hawkins 6,000. But much less seems to have been known about them than about the Creeks, Cherokees, and Chickasaws; and most early estimates of Indians were largest when made of the least-known tribes. Adair's statement is probably the most trustworthy. The first accurate census showed the Creeks to be more numerous.

were treacherous and thievish, and were not as well armed as the others. They rarely made war or peace as a unit, parties frequently acting in conjunction with some of the rival European powers, or else joining in the plundering inroads made by the other Indians upon the white settlements. Beyond thus furnishing auxiliaries to our other Indian foes, they had little to do with our history.

The Muscogees or Creeks were the strongest of all. Their southern bands, living in Florida, were generally considered as a separate confederacy, under the name of Seminoles. They numbered between twenty-five and thirty thousand souls,[1] three fourths of them being the Muscogees proper, and the remainder Seminoles. They dwelt south of the Cherokees and east of the Choctaws, adjoining the Georgians.

The Creeks and Cherokees were thus by their position the barrier tribes of the South, who had to The Bar- stand the brunt of our advance, and who rier Tribes. acted as a buffer between us and the French and Spaniards of the Gulf and the lower Mississippi. Their fate once decided, that of the Chickasaws and Chocktaws inevitably followed.

The customs and the political and social systems of these two tribes were very similar; and those of their two western neighbors were merely ruder copies thereof. They were very much further ad-

[1] Hawkins, Pickens, etc., make them "at least" 27,000 in 1789; the Indian report for 1837 make them 26,844. During the half century they had suffered from devastating wars and forced removals, and had probably slightly decreased in number. In Adair's time their population was increasing.

vanced than were the Algonquin nations of the north.

Unlike most mountaineers the Cherokees were not held to be very formidable fighters, when compared with their fellows of the lowlands.[1]   In 1760 and 1761 they had waged a fierce war with the whites, had ravaged the Carolina borders, had captured British forts, and successfully withstood British armies; but though they had held their own in the field, it had been at the cost of ruinous losses.   Since that period they had been engaged in long wars with the Chickasaws and Creeks, and had been worsted by both.   Moreover, they had been much harassed by the northern Indians.   So they were steadily declining in power and numbers.[2]

Though divided linguistically into two races, speaking different dialects, the Otari and Erati, the political divisions did not follow the lines of language.   There were three groups of towns, the Upper, Lower, and Middle; and these groups often acted independently of one another.   The Upper towns lay for the most part on the Western Waters, as they were called by the Americans,—the streams running into the Tennessee.   Their inhabitants were known as Overhill Cherokees and were chiefly Otari; but the towns were none of them permanent, and sometimes shifted their positions, even changing from one group to another.   The Lower towns, inhabited by the Erati, lay in the flat lands of upper Georgia and South Carolina, and were the least im-

[1] "Am. Archives," 5th Series, I., 95.   Letter of Charles Lee.
[2] Adair, 227.   Bartram, 390.

portant. The third group, larger than either of the others and lying among the hills and mountains between them, consisted of the Middle towns. Its borders were ill-marked and were ever shifting.

Thus the towns of the Cherokees stretched from the high upland region, where rise the loftiest mountains of eastern America, to the warm, level, low country, the land of the cypress and the long-leaved pine. Each village stood by itself, in some fertile river-bottom, with around it apple orchards and fields of maize. Like the other southern Indians, the Cherokees were more industrious than their northern neighbors, lived by tillage and agriculture as much as by hunting, and kept horses, hogs, and poultry. The oblong, story-high houses were made of peeled logs, morticed into each other and plastered with clay; while the roof was of chestnut bark or of big shingles. Near to each stood a small cabin, partly dug out of the ground, and in consequence very warm; to this the inmates retired in winter, for they were sensitive to cold. In the centre of each village stood the great council-house or rotunda, capable of containing the whole population; it was often thirty feet high, and sometimes stood on a raised mound of earth.[1]

The Cherokees were a bright, intelligent race, better fitted to "follow the white man's road" than any other Indians. Like their neighbors, they were exceedingly fond of games of chance and skill, as well as of athletic sports. One of the most striking of their national amusements was the kind of ball-

The Cherokees.

---

[1] Bartram, 365.

play from which we derive the game of lacrosse.
The implements consisted of ball sticks or rackets,
two feet long, strung with raw-hide webbing, and of
a deer-skin ball, stuffed with hair, so as to be very
solid, and about the size of a base ball. Sometimes
the game was played by fixed numbers, sometimes
by all the young men of a village; and there were
often tournaments between different towns and even
different tribes. The contests excited the most intense interest, were waged with desperate resolution,
and were preceded by solemn dances and religious
ceremonies; they were tests of tremendous physical
endurance, and were often very rough, legs and arms
being occasionally broken. The Choctaws were
considered to be the best ball players.[1]

The Cherokees were likewise fond of dances.
Sometimes these were comic or lascivious, sometimes
they were religious in their nature, or were undertaken prior to starting on the war-trail. Often the
dances of the young men and maidens were very picturesque. The girls, dressed in white, with silver
bracelets and gorgets, and a profusion of gay ribbons, danced in a circle in two ranks; the young
warriors, clad in their battle finery, danced in a ring
around them; all moving in rhythmic step, as they
kept time to the antiphonal chanting [2] and singing,
the young men and girls responding alternately to
each other.

The great confederacy of the Muscogees or Creeks,
consisting of numerous tribes, speaking at least five
distinct languages, lay in a well-watered land of small

---

[1] Adair, Bartram.   [2] Bartram.

timber.[1] The rapid streams were bordered by narrow flats of rich soil, and were margined by cane-
The   brakes and reed beds. There were fine open
Creek Con- pastures, varied by sandy pine barrens, by
federacy.   groves of palmetto and magnolia, and by
great swamps and cypress ponds. The game had been
largely killed out, the elk and buffalo having been exterminated and even the deer much thinned, and in
consequence the hunting parties were obliged to travel
far into the uninhabited region to the northward in
order to kill their winter supply of meat. But panthers, wolves, and bears still lurked in the gloomy
fastnesses of the swamps and canebrakes, whence
they emerged at night to prey on the hogs and cattle.
The bears had been exceedingly abundant at one
time, so much so as to become one of the main props
of the Creek larder, furnishing flesh, fat, and especially oil for cooking and other purposes ; and so
valued were they that the Indians hit upon the novel
plan of preserving them, exactly as Europeans preserve deer and pheasants. Each town put aside a
great tract of land which was known as " the beloved
bear ground," [2] where the persimmons, haws, chestnuts, muscadines, and fox grapes abounded, and let
the bears dwell there unmolested, except at certain
seasons, when they were killed in large numbers.
However, cattle were found to be more profitable
than bears, and the " beloved bear grounds " were
by degrees changed into stock ranges.[3]

[1] " A Sketch of the Creek Country," Benjamin Hawkins. In Coll. Ga.
Hist. Soc. Written in 1798, but not published till fifty years afterwards.

[2] *Do.*, p. 33.

[3] The use of the word " beloved " by the Creeks was quite peculiar. It
is evidently correctly translated, for Milfort likewise gives it as " bien

The Creeks had developed a very curious semi-civilization of their own. They lived in many towns, of which the larger, or old towns, bore rule **Creek Civ-** over the smaller,[1] and alone sent representa- **ilization.** tives to the general councils. Many of these were as large as any in the back counties of the colonies[2]; but they were shifted from time to time, as the game was totally killed off and the land exhausted by the crops.[3] The soil then became covered by a growth of pines, and a so-called "old field" was formed. This method of cultivation was, after all, much like that of the southern whites, and the "old fields," or abandoned plantations grown up with pines, were common in the colonies.

Many of the chiefs owned droves of horses and horned cattle, sometimes as many as five hundred head,[4] besides hogs and poultry ; and some of them, in addition, had negro slaves. But the tillage of the land was accomplished by communal labor ; and, indeed, the government, as well as the system of life, was in many respects a singular compound of communism and extreme individualism. The fields of rice, corn, tobacco, beans, and potatoes were sometimes rudely fenced in with split hickory poles, and were sometimes left unfenced, with huts or

---

aimé." It was the title used for any thing held in especial regard, whether for economic or supernatural reasons ; and sometimes it was used as western tribes use the word "medicine" at the present day. The old chiefs and conjurers were called the "beloved old men" ; what in the west we would now call the "medicine squaws," were named "the beloved old women." It was often conferred upon the chief dignitaries of the whites in writing to them.   [1] Hawkins, 37.

[2] Bartram, 386. The Uchee town contained at least 1,500 people.

[3] *Do.*   [4] Hawkins, 30.

high scaffolds, where watchers kept guard. They were planted when the wild fruit was so ripe as to draw off the birds, and while ripening the swine were kept penned up and the horses were tethered with tough bark ropes. Pumpkins, melons, marsh-mallows, and sunflowers were often grown between the rows of corn. The planting was done on a given day, the whole town being summoned; no man was excepted or was allowed to go out hunting. The under-headman supervised the work.[1]

For food they used all these vegetables, as well as beef and pork, and venison stewed in bear's oil; they **Mode of** had hominy and corn-cakes, and a cool **Life.** drink made from honey and water,[2] besides another made from fermented corn, which tasted much like cider.[3] They sifted their flour in wicker-work sieves, and baked the bread in kettles or on broad, thin stones. Moreover, they gathered the wild fruits, strawberries, grapes, and plums, in their season, and out of the hickory-nuts they made a thick, oily paste, called the hickory milk.

Each town was built round a square, in which the old men lounged all day long, gossiping and wrangling. Fronting the square, and surrounding it, were the four long, low communal houses, eight feet high, sixteen feet deep, and forty to sixty in length. They were wooden frames, supported on pine posts, with roof-tree and rafters of hickory. Their fronts were open piazzas, their sides were lathed and plastered, sometimes with white marl, sometimes with reddish clay, and they had plank doors and were roofed

[1] Hawkins, 39 ; Adair, 408.　　[2] Bartram, 184.　　[3] Milfort, 212.

neatly with cypress bark or clapboards. The eave boards were of soft poplar. The barrier towns, near white or Indian enemies, had log houses, with port-holes cut in the walls.

The communal houses were each divided into three rooms. The House of the Micos, or Chiefs and Headmen, was painted red and fronted the rising sun; it was highest in rank. The Houses of the Warriors and the Beloved Men—this last being painted white—fronted south and north respectively, while the House of the Young People stood opposite that of the Micos. Each room was divided into two terraces; the one in front being covered with red mats, while that in the rear, a kind of raised dais or great couch, was strewn with skins. They contained stools hewed out of poplar logs, and chests made of clapboards sewed together with buffalo thongs.[1]

The rotunda or council-house stood near the square on the highest spot in the village. It was round, and fifty or sixty feet across, with a high peaked roof; the rafters were fastened with splints and covered with bark. A raised dais ran around the wall, strewed with mats and skins. Sometimes in the larger council-houses there were painted eagles, carved out of poplar wood, placed close to the red and white seats where the chiefs and warriors sat; or in front of the broad dais were great images of the full and the half moon, colored white or black; or rudely carved and painted figures of the panther, and of men with

The Creek Villages.

[1] Hawkins, 67.   Milfort, 203.   Bartram, 386.   Adair, 418.

buffalo horns. The tribes held in reverence both the panther and the rattlesnake..

The corn-cribs, fowl-houses, and hot-houses or dug-outs for winter use were clustered near the other cabins.

Although in tillage they used only the hoe, they had made much progress in some useful arts. They spun the coarse wool of the buffalo into blankets, which they trimmed with beads. They wove the wild hemp in frames and shuttles. They made their own saddles. They made beautiful baskets of fine cane splints, and very handsome blankets of turkey feathers; while out of glazed clay they manufactured bowls, pitchers, platters, and other pottery.

In summer they wore buckskin shirts and breech-clouts; in winter they were clad in the fur of the bear and wolf or of the shaggy buffalo. They had moccasins of elk or buffalo hide, and high thigh-boots of thin deer-skin, ornamented with fawns' trotters, or turkey spurs that tinkled as they walked. In their hair they braided eagle plumes, hawk wings, or the brilliant plumage of the tanager and redbird. Trousers or breeches of any sort they despised as marks of effeminacy.

Vermilion was their war emblem; white was only worn at the time of the Green-Corn Dance. In each town stood the war pole or painted post, a small peeled tree-trunk colored red. Some of their villages **Red and** were called white or peace towns; others **White** red or bloody towns. The white towns **Towns.** were sacred to peace; no blood could be spilt within their borders. They were towns of refuge, where not even an enemy taken in war could

be slain; and a murderer who fled thither was safe
from vengeance. The captives were tortured to
death in the red towns, and it was in these that
the chiefs and warriors gathered when they were
planning or preparing for war.

They held great marriage-feasts; the dead were
buried with the goods they had owned in their
lifetime.

Every night all the people of a town gathered in
the council-house to dance and sing and talk. Besides
this, they held there on stated occasions the cere-
monial dances: such were the dances of war and of
triumph, when the warriors, painted red and black,
returned, carrying the scalps of their slain foes on
branches of evergreen pine, while they chanted the
sonorous song of victory; and such was the Dance
of the Serpent, the dance of lawless love, where the
women and young girls were allowed to do whatso-
ever they listed.

Once a year, when the fruits ripened, they held
the Green-Corn Dance, a religious festival that lasted
eight days in the larger towns and four in *The Green-*
the smaller. Then they fasted and feasted *Corn*
alternately. They drank out of conch-shells *Dance.*
the Black Drink, a bitter beverage brewed from the
crushed leaves of a small shrub. On the third day
the high-priest or fire-maker, the man who sat in the
white seat, clad in snowy tunic and moccasins,
kindled the holy fire, fanning it into flames with the
unsullied wing of a swan, and burning therein offer-
ings of the first-fruits of the year. Dance followed
dance. The beloved men and beloved women, the

priest and priestesses, danced in three rings, singing the solemn song of which the words were never uttered at any other time; and at the end the warriors, in their wild war-gear, with white-plume head-dresses, took part, and also the women and girls, decked in their best, with ear-rings and armlets, and terrapin shells filled with pebbles fastened to the outside of their legs. They kept time with foot and voice; the men in deep tones, with short accents, the women in a shrill falsetto; while the clay drums, with heads of taut deer-hide, were beaten, the whistles blown, and the gourds and calabashes rattled, until the air resounded with the deafening noise.[1]

Though they sometimes burnt their prisoners or violated captive women, they generally were more merciful than the northern tribes.[2]

But their political and military systems could not compare with those of the Algonquins, still less with **Looseness of the Confederacy.** those of the Iroquois. Their confederacy was of the loosest kind. There was no central authority. Every town acted just as it pleased, making war or peace with the other towns, or with whites, Choctaws, or Cherokees. In each there was a nominal head for peace and war, the high chief and the head warrior; the former was supposed to be supreme, and was elected for life from some one powerful family—as, for instance, the families having for their totems the wind or the eagle. But these chiefs had little control, and could not do much more than influence or advise their subjects; they were dependent on the will of the majority. Each

---

[1] Hawkins and Adair, *passim*.   [2] *Do.*   Also *vide* Bartram.

town was a little hotbed of party spirit; the inhabitants divided on almost every question. If the head-chief was for peace, but the war-chief nevertheless went on the war-path, there was no way of restraining him. It was said that never, in the memory of the oldest inhabitant, had half the nation " taken the war talk " at the same time.[1] As a consequence, war parties of Creeks were generally merely small bands of marauders, in search of scalps and plunder. In proportion to its numbers, the nation never, until 1813, undertook such formidable military enterprises as were undertaken by the Wyandots, Shawnees, and Delawares; and, though very formidable individual fighters, even in this respect it may be questioned if the Creeks equalled the prowess of their northern kinsmen.

Yet when the Revolutionary war broke out the Creeks were under a chieftain whose consummate craft and utterly selfish but cool and masterly diplomacy enabled them for a generation to hold their own better than any other native race against the restless Americans. This was the half-breed Alexander McGillivray, perhaps the most gifted man who was ever born on the soil of Alabama.[2]

His father was a Scotch trader, Lachlan McGillivray by name, who came when a boy to Charleston, then the head-quarters of the commerce carried on by the British with the southern Indians. On visiting the traders' quarter of the town, the young Scot was strongly attracted by the

The Chief McGillivray.

---

[1] Hawkins, 29, 70. Adair, 428.
[2] " History of Alabama," by Albert James Pickett, Charleston, 1851, II., 30. A valuable work.

sight of the weather-beaten packers, with their gaudy, half-Indian finery, their hundreds of pack-horses, their curious pack-saddles, and their bales of merchandise. Taking service with them, he was soon helping to drive a pack-train along one of the narrow trails that crossed the lonely pine wilderness. To strong, coarse spirits, that were both shrewd and daring, and willing to balance the great risks incident to their mode of life against its great gains, the business was most alluring. Young Lachlan rose rapidly, and soon became one of the richest and most influential traders in the Creek country.

Like most traders, he married into the tribe, wooing and wedding, at the Hickory Ground, beside the Coosa River, a beautiful half-breed girl, Sehoy Marchand, whose father had been a French officer, and whose mother belonged to the powerful Creek family of the Wind. There were born to them two daughters and one son, Alexander. All the traders, though facing danger at every moment, from the fickle and jealous temper of the savages, wielded immense influence over them, and none more than the elder McGillivray, a far-sighted, unscrupulous Scotchman, who sided alternately with the French and English interests, as best suited his own policy and fortunes.

His son was felt by the Creeks to be one of themselves. He was born about 1746, at Little Tallasee, **His Bring-** on the banks of the clear-flowing Coosa, **ing Up.** where he lived till he was fourteen years old, playing, fishing, hunting, and bathing with the other Indian boys, and listening to the tales of the old chiefs and warriors. He was then taken to

Charleston, where he was well educated, being taught Greek and Latin, as well as English history and literature. Tall, dark, slender, with commanding figure and immovable face, of cool, crafty temper, with great ambition and a keen intellect, he felt himself called to play no common part. He disliked trade, and at the first opportunity returned to his Indian home. He had neither the moral nor the physical gifts requisite for a warrior; but he was a consummate diplomat, a born leader, and perhaps the only man who could have used aright such a rope of sand as was the Creek confederacy.

The Creeks claimed him as of their own blood, and instinctively felt that he was their only possible ruler. He was forthwith chosen to be their head chief. From that time on he **His Chief-** remained among them, at one or the other **tainship.** of his plantations, his largest and his real home being at Little Tallasee, where he lived in barbaric comfort, in a great roomy log-house with a stone chimney, surrounded by the cabins of his sixty negro slaves. He was supported by many able warriors, both of the half and the full blood. One of them is worthy of passing mention. This was a young French adventurer, Milfort, who in 1776 journeyed through the insurgent colonies and became an adopted son of the Creek nation. He first met McGillivray, then in his early manhood, at the town of Coweta, the great war-town on the Chattahoochee, where the half-breed chief, seated on a bear-skin in the council-house, surrounded by his wise men and warriors, was planning to give aid to the British.

Afterwards he married one of McGillivray's sisters, whom he met at a great dance—a pretty girl, clad in a short silk petticoat, her chemise of fine linen clasped with silver, her ear-rings and bracelets of the same metal, and with bright-colored ribbons in her hair.[1]

The task set to the son of Sehoy was one of incredible difficulty, for he was head of a loose array of towns and tribes from whom no man could get perfect, and none but himself even imperfect, obedience. The nation could not stop a town from going to war, nor, in turn, could a town stop its own young men from committing ravages. Thus the whites were always being provoked, and the frontiersmen were molested as often when they were quiet and peaceful as when they were encroaching on Indian land. The Creeks owed the land which they possessed to murder and rapine; they mercilessly destroyed all weaker communities, red or white; they had no idea of showing justice or generosity towards their fellows who lacked their strength, and now the measure they had meted so often to others was at last to be meted to them. If the whites treated them

[1] Milfort, 23, 326. Milfort's book is very interesting, but as the man himself was evidently a hopeless liar and braggart, it can only be trusted where it was not for his interest to tell a falsehood. His book was written after McGillivray's death, the object being to claim for himself the glory belonging to the half-breed chief. He insisted that he was the war-chief, the arm, and McGillivray merely the head, and boasts of his numerous successful war enterprises. But the fact is, that during this whole time the Creeks performed no important stroke in war; the successful resistance to American encroachments was due to the diplomacy of the son of Sehoy. Moreover, Milfort's accounts of his own war deeds are mainly sheer romancing. He appears simply to have been one of a score of war chiefs, and there were certainly a dozen other Creek chiefs, both half-breeds and natives, who were far more formidable to the frontier than he was; all their names were dreaded by the settlers, but his was hardly known.

well, it was set down to weakness. It was utterly
impossible to restrain the young men from murdering and plundering, either the neighboring Indians
or the white settlements. Their one ideal of glory
was to get scalps, and these the young braves were
sure to seek, no matter how much the older and
cooler men might try to prevent them. Whether
war was declared or not, made no difference. At
one time the English exerted themselves successfully to bring about a peace between the Creeks
and Cherokees. At its conclusion a Creek chief
taunted the mediators as follows : " You have sweated
yourselves poor in our smoky houses to make peace
between us and the Cherokees, and thereby enable
our young people to give you in a short time a far
worse sweat than you have yet had." [1] The result
justified his predictions; the young men, having no
other foe, at once took to ravaging the settlements.
It soon became evident that it was hopeless to
expect the Creeks to behave well to the whites
merely because they were themselves well treated,
and from that time on the English fomented, instead
of striving to put a stop to, their quarrels with the
Choctaws and Chickasaws.

The record of our dealings with them must in
many places be unpleasant reading to us, for it
shows grave wrong-doing on our part; yet the
Creeks themselves lacked only the power, but not
the will, to treat us worse than we treated them, and
the darkest pages of their history recite the wrongs
that we ourselves suffered at their hands.

[1] Adair, 279.

CHAPTER IV.

THE ALGONQUINS OF THE NORTHWEST, 1769–1774.

BETWEEN the Ohio and the Great Lakes, directly
north of the Appalachian confederacies, and separated
from them by the unpeopled wilderness
now forming the States of Tennessee and
Kentucky, dwelt another set of Indian
tribes. They were ruder in life and manners than
their southern kinsmen, less advanced towards civilization, but also far more warlike; they depended
more on the chase and fishing, and much less on
agriculture; they were savages, not merely barbarians; and they were fewer in numbers and scattered
over a wider expanse of territory. But they were farther advanced than the almost purely nomadic tribes
of horse Indians whom we afterwards encountered
west of the Mississippi. Some of their villages were
permanent, at any rate for a term of years, and
near them they cultivated small crops of corn and
melons. Their usual dwelling was the conical wigwam
covered with bark, skins, or mats of plaited reeds
but in some of the villages of the tribes nearest the
border there were regular blockhouses, copied from
their white neighbors. They went clad in skins or
blankets; the men were hunters and warriors, who
painted their bodies and shaved from their crowns

*The Algon-
quins.*

all the hair except the long scalp-lock, while the squaws were the drudges who did all the work.

Their relations with the Iroquois, who lay east of them, were rarely very close, and in fact were generally hostile. They were also usually at odds with the southern Indians, but among themselves they were frequently united in time of war into a sort of lax league, and were collectively designated by the Americans as the northwestern Indians. All the tribes belonged to the great Algonquin family, with two exceptions, the Winnebagos and the Wyandots. The former, a branch of the Dakotahs, dwelt west of Lake Michigan ; they came but little in contact with us, although many of their young men and warriors joined their neighbors in all the wars against us. The Wyandots or Hurons lived near Detroit and along the south shore of Lake Erie, and were in battle our most redoubtable foes. They were close kin to the Iroquois though bitter enemies to them, and they shared the desperate valor of these, their hostile kinsfolk, holding themselves above the surrounding Algonquins, with whom, nevertheless, they lived in peace and friendship.

The Algonquins were divided into many tribes, of ever shifting size. It would be impossible to place them all, or indeed to enumerate them, with any degree of accuracy ; for the tribes were continually splitting up, absorbing others, being absorbed in turn, or changing their abode, and, in addition, there were numerous small sub-tribes or bands of renegades, which sometimes were and sometimes were not considered as portions

Their
Tribal
Relations.

of their larger neighbors. Often, also, separate bands, which would vaguely regard themselves as all one nation in one generation, would in the next have lost even this sense of loose tribal unity.

The chief tribes, however, were well known and occupied tolerably definite locations. The Delawares or Leni-Lenappe, dwelt farthest east, lying northwest of the upper Ohio, their lands adjoining those of the Senecas, the largest and most westernmost of the Six Nations. The Iroquois had been their most relentless foes and oppressors in time gone by ; but on the eve of the Revolution all the border tribes were forgetting their past differences and were drawing together to make a stand against the common foe. Thus it came about that parties of young Seneca braves fought with the Delawares in all their wars against us.

Westward of the Delawares lay the Shawnee villages, along the Scioto and on the Pickaway plains ; but it must be remembered that the Shawnees, Delawares, and Wyandots were closely united and their villages were often mixed in together. Still farther to the west, the Miamis or Twigtees lived between the Miami and the Wabash, together with other associated tribes, the Piankeshaws and the Weas or Ouatinous. Farther still, around the French villages, dwelt those scattered survivors of the Illinois who had escaped the dire fate which befell their fellow-tribesmen because they murdered Pontiac. Northward of this scanty people lived the Sacs and Foxes, and around the upper Great Lakes the numerous and powerful Pottawattamies, Ottawas, and Chippewas ; fierce and treacherous warriors, who did not till the soil, and were hunters and fishers only, more savage even than the tribes that lay southeast of them.[1]   In the works of the early travellers we read the names of many other Indian nations; but whether these were indeed separate peoples, or branches of some of those already mentioned, or whether the different travellers spelled the Indian names in widely different ways, we cannot say. All that is certain is that there were many tribes and sub-tribes, who roamed and warred and hunted over the fair lands now forming the heart of our mighty nation, that to some of these tribes the whites gave names and to some they did not, and that the named and the nameless alike were swept down to the same inevitable doom.

Moreover, there were bands of renegades or discontented Indians, who for some cause had severed their tribal connections.   Two of the most prominent of these bands were the Cherokees and Mingos, both being noted for their predatory and murderous nature and their incessant raids on the frontier settlers.   The Cherokees were fugitives from the rest of their nation, who had fled north, beyond the Ohio, and dwelt in the land shared by the Delawares and Shawnees, drawing to themselves many of the lawless young warriors, not only of these tribes, but of the others still farther off.   The Mingos were likewise a mongrel banditti, made up of outlaws and wild spirits from among the Wyandots and Miamis, as well as from the Iroquois and the Munceys (a sub-tribe of the Delawares).

The Broken Bands.

[1] See papers by Stephen D. Peet, on the northwestern tribes, read before the State Archæological Society of Ohio, 1878.

All these northwestern nations had at one time been conquered by the Iroquois, or at least they had been defeated, their lands overrun, and they themselves forced to acknowledge a vague over-lordship on the part of their foes. But the power of the Iroquois was now passing away; when our national history began, with the assembling of the first continental congress, they had ceased to be a menace to the western tribes, and the latter no longer feared or obeyed them, regarding them merely as allies or neutrals. Yet not only the Iroquois, but their kindred folk, notably the Wyandots, still claimed, and received, for the sake of their ancient superiority, marks of formal respect from the surrounding Algonquins. Thus, among the latter, the Leni-Lenappe possessed the titular headship, and were called " grandfathers " at all the solemn councils as well as in the ceremonious communications that passed among the tribes; yet in turn they had to use similar titles of respect in addressing not only their former oppressors, but also their Huron allies, who had suffered under the same galling yoke.[1]

The northwestern nations had gradually come to equal the Iroquois as warriors; but among themselves **The** the palm was still held by the Wyandots, **Wyandots.** who, although no more formidable than the others as regards skill, hardihood, and endurance, nevertheless stood alone in being willing to suffer heavy punishment in order to win a victory.[2]

The Wyandots had been under the influence of the

[1] Barton, xxv.

[2] General W. H. Harrison, " Aborigines of the Ohio Valley." Old " Tippecanoe " was the best possible authority for their courage.

French Jesuits, and were nominally Christians [1]; and though the attempt to civilize them had not been very successful, and they remained in most respects precisely like the Indians aronnd them, there had been at least one point gained, for they were not, as a rule, nearly so cruel to their prisoners. Thus they surpassed their neighbors in mercifulness as well as valor. All the Algonquin tribes stood, in this respect, much on the same plane. The Delewares, whose fate it had been to be ever buffeted about by both the whites and the reds, had long cowered under the Iroquois terror, but they had at last shaken it off, had reasserted the superiority which tradition says they once before held, and had become a formidable and warlike race. Indeed it is curious to study how the Delawares have changed in respect to their martial prowess since the days when the whites first came in contact with them. They were then not accounted a formidable people, and were not feared by any of their neighbors. By the time the Revolution broke out they had become better warriors, and during the twenty years' Indian warfare that ensued were as formidable as most of the other redskins. But when moved west of the Mississippi, instead of their spirit being broken, they became more warlike than ever, and throughout the present century they have been the most renowned

---

[1] " Remarkable Occurrences in the Life and Travels of Col. James Smith," etc., written by himself, Lexington, Ky., 1799. Smith is our best contemporary authority on Indian warfare ; he lived with them for several years, and fought them in many campaigns. Besides several editions of the above, he also published in 1812, at Paris, Ky., a " Treatise" on Indian warfare, which holds much the same matter.

fighters of all the Indian peoples, and, moreover, they have been celebrated for their roving, adventurous nature. Their numbers have steadily dwindled, owing to their incessant wars and to the dangerous nature of their long roamings.[1]

It is impossible to make any but the roughest guess at the numbers of these northwestern Indians. It The Indian seems probable that there were considerably Numbers. over fifty thousand of them in all; but no definite assertion can be made even as to the different tribes. As with the southern Indians, old-time writers certainly greatly exaggerated their numbers, and their modern followers show a tendency to fall into the opposite fault, the truth being that any number of isolated observations to support either position can be culled from the works of the contemporary travellers and statisticians.[2] No two independent observers give the same figures. One main reason for this is doubtless the exceedingly loose way in which the word " tribe " was used. If a man speaks of the Miamis and the Delawares, for instance, before we can understand him we must know whether he includes therein the Weas and the Munceys, for he may or may not. By quoting the

[1] See Parkman's " Oregon Trail." In 1884 I myself met two Delawares hunting alone, just north of the Black Hills. They were returning from a trip to the Rocky Mountains. I could not but admire their strong, manly forms, and the disdainful resolution with which they had hunted and travelled for so many hundred miles, in defiance of the white frontiersmen and of the wild native tribes as well. I think they were in more danger from the latter than the former ; but they seemed perfectly confident of their ability to hold their own against both.

[2] See Barton, the Madison MSS., Schoolcraft, Thos. Hutchins (who accompanied Bouquet), Smythe, Pike, various reports of the U. S. Indian Commissioners, etc., etc.

numbers attributed by the old writers to the various sub-tribes, and then comparing them with the numbers given later on by writers using the same names, but speaking of entire confederacies, it is easy to work out an apparent increase, while a reversal of the process shows an appalling decrease. Moreover, as the bands broke up, wandered apart, and then rejoined each other or not as events fell out, two successive observers might make widely different estimates. Many tribes that have disappeared were undoubtedly actually destroyed; many more have simply changed their names or have been absorbed by other tribes. Similarly, those that have apparently held their own have done so at the expense of their neighbors. This was made all the easier by the fact that the Algonquins were so closely related in customs and language; indeed, there was constant intermarriage between the different tribes. On the whole, however, there is no question that, in striking contrast to the southern or Appalachian Indians, these northwestern tribes have suffered a terrible diminution in numbers.

With many of them we did not come into direct contact for long years after our birth as a nation. Perhaps those tribes with all or part of whose warriors we were brought into collision at some time during or immediately succeeding the Revolutionary war may have amounted to thirty thousand souls.[1] But though they acknowledged kinship with one another, and though they all alike

Their Lack of Cohesion.

---

[1] I base this number on a careful examination of the tribes named above, discarding such of the northern bands of the Chippewas, for instance, as were unlikely at that time to have been drawn into war with us.

hated the Americans, and though, moreover, all at times met in the great councils, to smoke the calumet of peace and brighten the chain of friendship [1] among themselves, and to take up the tomahawk [2] against the white foes, yet the tie that bound them together was so loose, and they were so fickle and so split up by jarring interests and small jealousies, that never more than half of them went to war at the same time. Very frequently even the members of a tribe would fail to act together.

Thus it came about that during the forty years intervening between Braddock's defeat and Wayne's victory, though these northwestern tribes waged incessant, unending, relentless warfare against our borders, yet they never at any one time had more than three thousand warriors in the field, and frequently not half that number [3]; and in all the battles they fought with British and American troops there was not one in which they were eleven hundred strong. [4]

[1] The expressions generally used by them in sending their war talks and peace talks to one another or the whites. Hundreds of copies of these " talks " are preserved at Washington.   [2] *Do.*

[3] Smith, " Remarkable Occurrences," etc., p. 154. Smith gives a very impartial account of the Indian discipline and of their effectiveness, and is one of the few men who warred against them who did not greatly over-estimate their numbers and losses. He was a successful Indian fighter himself. For the British regulars he had the true backwoods contempt, although having more than the average backwoods sense in acknowledging their effectiveness in the open. He had lived so long among the Indians, and estimated so highly their personal prowess, that his opinion must be accepted with caution where dealing with matters of discipline and command.

[4] The accounts of the Indian numbers in any battle given by British or Americans, soldiers or civilians, are ludicrously exaggerated as a rule ; even now it seems a common belief of historians that the whites were generally outnumbered in battles, while in reality they were generally much more numerous than their foes.

But they were superb individual fighters, beauti-
fully drilled in their own discipline[1]; and they
were favored beyond measure by the na-   Their
ture of their ground, of which their whole   Prowess
system of warfare enabled them to take the   in War.
utmost possible benefit. Much has been written and
sung of the advantages possessed by the mountaineer
when striving in his own home against invaders from
the plains ; but these advantages are as nothing when
weighed with those which make the warlike dweller
in forests unconquerable by men who have not his
training. A hardy soldier, accustomed only to war
in the open, will become a good cragsman in fewer
weeks than it will take him years to learn to be so
much as a fair woodsman ; for it is beyond all comparison more difficult to attain proficiency in woodcraft than in mountaineering.[2]

The Wyandots, and the Algonquins who surrounded them, dwelt in a region of sunless, tangled
forests ; and all the wars we waged for the   The
possession of the country between the Alle-   Endless
ghanies and the Mississippi were carried on   Forests.
in the never-ending stretches of gloomy woodland. It

[1] Harrison (*loc. cit.*) calls them "the finest light troops in the world";
and he had had full experience in serving with American and against
British infantry.

[2] Any one who is fond of the chase can test the truth of this proposition
for himself, by trying how long it will take him to learn to kill a bighorn
on the mountains, and how long it will take him to learn to kill white-tail
deer in a dense forest, by fair still-hunting, the game being equally plenty.
I have known many novices learn to equal the best old hunters, red or white,
in killing mountain game ; I have never met one who could begin to do as well
as an Indian in the dense forest, unless brought up to it—and rarely even then.
Yet, though woodcraft is harder to learn, it does not imply the possession
of such valuable qualities as mountaineering ; and when cragsman and
woodman meet on neutral ground, the former is apt to be the better man.

was not an open forest. The underbrush grew, dense and rank, between the boles of the tall trees, making a cover so thick that it was in many places impenetrable, so thick that it nowhere gave a chance for human eye to see even as far as a bow could carry. No horse could penetrate it save by following the game trails or paths chopped with the axe; and a stranger venturing a hundred yards from a beaten road would be so helplessly lost that he could not, except by the merest chance, even find his way back to the spot he had just left. Here and there it was broken by a rare hillside glade or by a meadow in a stream valley; but elsewhere a man might travel for weeks as if in a perpetual twilight, never once able to see the sun, through the interlacing twigs that formed a dark canopy above his head.

This dense forest was to the Indians a home in which they had lived from childhood, and where they were as much at ease as a farmer on his own acres. To their keen eyes, trained for generations to more than a wild beast's watchfulness, the wilderness was an open book; nothing at rest or in motion escaped them. They had begun to track game as soon as they could walk; a scrape on a tree trunk, a bruised leaf, a faint indentation of the soil, which the eye of no white man could see, all told them a tale as plainly as if it had been shouted in their ears.[1] With moccasined feet they trod among

[1] To this day the wild—not the half-tame—Indians remain unequalled as trackers. Even among the old hunters not one white in a hundred can come near them. In my experience I have known a very few whites who had spent all their lives in the wilderness who equalled the Indian average; but I never met any white who came up to the very best Indian. But, because of their better shooting and their better nerve, the whites often make the better hunters.

brittle twigs, dried leaves, and dead branches as
silently as the cougar, and they equalled the great
wood-cat in stealth and far surpassed it in cunning
and ferocity. They could no more get lost in the
trackless wilderness than a civilized man could get
lost on a highway. Moreover, no knight of the
middle ages was so surely protected by his armor as
they were by their skill in hiding; the whole forest
was to the whites one vast ambush, and to them
a sure and ever-present shield. Every tree trunk
was a breastwork ready prepared for battle; every
bush, every moss-covered boulder, was a defence
against assault, from behind which, themselves
unseen, they watched with fierce derision the
movements of their clumsy white enemy. Lurking,
skulking, travelling with noiseless rapidity, they left
a trail that only a master in woodcraft could follow,
while, on the other hand, they could dog a white
man's footsteps as a hound runs a fox. Their silence,
their cunning and stealth, their terrible prowess and
merciless cruelty, makes it no figure of speech to call
them the tigers of the human race.

Unlike the southern Indians, the villages of
the northwestern tribes were usually far from the
frontier. Tireless, and careless of all hard- Their Mode
ship, they came silently out of unknown   of War.
forests, robbed and murdered, and then disappeared again into the fathomless depths of the
woods. Half of the terror they caused was due
to the extreme difficulty of following them, and
the absolute impossibility of forecasting their attacks. Without warning, and unseen until the moment they dealt the death stroke, they emerged

from their forest fastnesses, the horror they caused
being heightened no less by the mystery that
shrouded them than by the dreadful nature of
their ravages. Wrapped in the mantle of the unknown, appalling by their craft, their ferocity, their
fiendish cruelty, they seemed to the white settlers
devils and not men; no one could say with cer-
tainty whence they came nor of what tribe they
were; and when they had finished their dreadful
work they retired into a wilderness that closed over
their trail as the waves of the ocean close in the
wake of a ship.

They were trained to the use of arms from their
youth up, and war and hunting were their two chief
occupations, the business as well as the pleasure of
their lives. They were not as skilful as the white
hunters with the rifle [1]—though more so than the
average regular soldier,—nor could they equal the
frontiersman in feats of physical prowess, such as
boxing and wrestling; but their superior endurance
and the ease with which they stood fatigue and exposure made amends for this. A white might out-
run them for eight or ten miles; but on a long journey they could tire out any man, and any beast except
a wolf. Like most barbarians they were fickle and
inconstant, not to be relied on for pushing through
a long campaign, and after a great victory apt to go
off to their homes, because each man desired to

[1] It is curious how to this day the wild Indians retain the same traits. I
have seen and taken part in many matches between frontiersmen and the
Sioux, Cheyennes, Grosventres, and Mandans, and the Indians were beaten
in almost every one. On the other hand the Indians will stand fatigue,
hunger, and privation better, but they seem more susceptible to cold.

secure his own plunder and tell his own tale of glory. They are often spoken of as undisciplined; but in reality their discipline in the battle itself was very high. They attacked, retreated, rallied or repelled a charge at the signal of command; and they were able to fight in open order in thick covers without losing touch of each other—a feat that no European regiment was then able to perform.

On their own ground they were far more formidable than the best European troops. The British grenadiers throughout the eighteenth century showed themselves superior, in the actual shock of battle, to any infantry of continental Europe; if they ever met an over-match, it was when pitted against the Scotch highlanders. Yet both grenadier and highlander, the heroes of Minden, the heirs to the glory of Marlborough's campaigns, as well as the sinewy soldiers who shared in the charges of Prestonpans and Culloden, proved helpless when led against the dark tribesmen of the forest. On the march they could not be trusted thirty yards from the column without getting lost in the woods [1] —the mountain training of the highlanders apparently standing them in no stead whatever,—and were only able to get around at all when convoyed by backwoodsmen. In fight they fared even worse. The British regulars at Braddock's battle, and the highlanders at Grant's defeat a few years Their Superiority to later, suffered the same fate. Both battles European were fair fights; neither was a surprise; yet Troops. the stubborn valor of the red-coated grenadier and the

[1] See Parkman's "Conspiracy of Pontiac"; also "Montcalm and Wolfe."

headlong courage of the kilted Scot proved of less
than no avail. Not only were they utterly routed
and destroyed in each case by an inferior force of
Indians (the French taking little part in the conflict), but they were able to make no effective resistance whatever; it is to this day doubtful whether
these superb regulars were able, in the battles where
they were destroyed, to so much as kill one Indian
for every hundred of their own men who fell. The
provincials who were with the regulars were the
only troops who caused any loss to the foe; and
this was true in but a less degree of Bouquet's fight
at Bushy Run. Here Bouquet, by a clever stratagem, gained the victory over an enemy inferior in
numbers to himself; but only after a two days'
struggle in which he suffered a fourfold greater
loss than he inflicted.[1]

When hemmed in so that they had no hope of
escape, the Indians fought to the death; but when a
way of retreat was open they would not stand cutting like British, French, or American regulars, and
so, though with a nearly equal force, would retire if
they were suffering heavily, even if they were causing their foes to suffer still more. This was not
due to lack of courage; it was their system, for they
were few in numbers, and they did not believe in
losing their men.[2] The Wyandots were exceptions

---

[1] Bouquet, like so many of his predecessors and successors, greatly exaggerated the numbers and loss of the Indians in this fight. Smith, who derived his information both from the Indians and from the American rangers,
states that but eighteen Indians were killed at Bushy Run.

[2] Most of the plains Indians feel in the same way at present. I was once
hunting with a Sioux half-breed who illustrated the Indian view of the matter in a rather striking way, saying : " If there were a dozen of you white

to this rule, for with them it was a point of honor
not to yield, and so they were of all the tribes the
most dangerous in an actual pitched battle.[1]

But making the attack, as they usually did,
with the expectation of success, all were equally
dangerous. If their foes were clustered **The**
together in a huddle they attacked them **Attack.**
without hesitation, no matter what the difference
in numbers, and shot them down as if they had been
elk or buffalo, they themselves being almost absolutely safe from harm, as they flitted from cover to
cover. It was this capacity for hiding, or taking
advantage of cover, that gave them their great superiority; and it is because of this that the wood tribes
were so much more formidable foes in actual battle
than the horse Indians of the plains afterwards proved
themselves. In dense woodland a body of regular
soldiers are almost as useless against Indians as they
would be if at night they had to fight foes who could
see in the dark; it needs special and long-continued
training to fit them in any degree for wood-fighting
against such foes. Out on the plains the white hunter's skill with the rifle and his cool resolution give
him an immense advantage; a few determined men
can withstand a host of Indians in the open, although helpless if they meet them in thick cover:

hunters and you found six or eight bears in the brush, and you knew you
could go in and kill them all, but that in the fight you would certainly lose
three or four men yourselves, you would n't go in, would you ? You 'd wait
until you got a better chance, and could kill them without so much risk.
Well, Indians feel the same way about attacking whites that you would feel
about attaking those bears."

[1] All the authorities from Smith to Harrison are unanimous on this
point.

and our defeats by the Sioux and other plains tribes
have generally taken the form of a small force being
overwhelmed by a large one.

Not only were the Indians very terrible in battle,
but they were cruel beyond all belief in victory;
Their and the gloomy annals of border war-
Cruelty. fare are stained with their darkest hues
because it was a war in which helpless women and
children suffered the same hideous fate that so often
befell their husbands and fathers. It was a war
waged by savages against armed settlers, whose families followed them into the wilderness. Such a war
is inevitably bloody and cruel; but the inhuman
love of cruelty for cruelty's sake,[1] which marks the
red Indian above all other savages, rendered these
wars more terrible than any others. For the hideous,
unnamable, unthinkable tortures practised by the
red men on their captured foes, and on their foes'
tender women and helpless children, were such
as we read of in no other struggle, hardly even
in the revolting pages that tell the deeds of the
Holy Inquisition. It was inevitable—indeed it was
in many instances proper—that such deeds should
awake in the breasts of the whites the grimmest,
wildest spirit of revenge and hatred.

The history of the border wars, both in the ways

---

[1] Any one who has ever been in an encampment of wild Indians, and
has had the misfortune to witness the delight the children take in torturing
little animals, will admit that the Indian's love of cruelty for cruelty's sake
cannot possibly be exaggerated. The young are so trained that when old
they shall find their keenest pleasure in inflicting pain in its most appalling
form. Among the most brutal white borderers a man would be instantly
lynched if he practised on any creature the fiendish torture which in an Indian camp either attracts no notice at all, or else excites merely laughter.

they were begun and in the ways they were waged,
makes a long tale of injuries inflicted, suffered, and
mercilessly revenged. It could not be otherwise
when brutal, reckless, lawless borderers, despising
all men not of their own color, were thrown in contact with savages who esteemed cruelty and treachery as the highest of virtues, and rapine and murder
as the worthiest of pursuits. Moreover, it was sadly
inevitable that the law-abiding borderer as well as
the white ruffian, the peaceful Indian as well as the
painted marauder, should be plunged into the struggle to suffer the punishment that should only have
fallen on their evil-minded fellows.

Looking back, it is easy to say that much of the
wrong-doing could have been prevented; but if we
examine the facts to find out the truth,   **Border**
not to establish a theory, we are bound   **Wars**
to admit that the struggle was really one **Inevitable.**
that could not possibly have been avoided.
The sentimental historians speak as if the blame
had been all ours, and the wrong all done to
our foes, and as if it would have been possible by
any exercise of wisdom to reconcile claims that were
in their very essence conflicting; but their utterances are as shallow as they are untruthful.[1] Unless we were willing that the whole continent west
of the Alleghanies should remain an unpeopled
waste, the hunting-ground of savages, war was
inevitable; and even had we been willing, and had
we refrained from encroaching on the Indians' lands,
the war would have come nevertheless, for then the

[1] See Appendix A.

Indians themselves would have encroached on ours.
Undoubtedly we have wronged many tribes; but
equally undoubtedly our first definite knowledge of
many others has been derived from their unprovoked
outrages upon our people.   The Chippewas, Ottawas, and Pottawatamies furnished hundreds of
young warriors to the parties that devastated our
frontiers generations before we in any way encroached upon or wronged them.

Mere outrages could be atoned for or settled;
the question which lay at the root of our difficulties
Struggle was that of the occupation of the land
for the itself, and to this there could be no so-
Land. lution save war. The Indians had no
ownership of the land in the way in which we
understand the term.   The tribes lived far apart;
each had for its hunting-grounds all the territory
from which it was not barred by rivals.   Each
looked with jealousy upon all interlopers, but each
was prompt to act as an interloper when occasion
offered.   Every good hunting-ground was claimed
by many nations. It was rare, indeed, that any tribe
had an uncontested title to a large tract of land;
where such title existed, it rested, not on actual occu-
pancy and cultivation, but on the recent butchery of
weaker rivals.   For instance, there were a dozen
tribes, all of whom hunted in Kentucky, and fought
each other there, all of whom had equally good
titles to the soil, and not one of whom acknowledged
the right of any other; as a matter of fact they had
therein no right, save the right of the strongest.
The land no more belonged to them than it be-

longed to Boon and the white hunters who first
visited it.

On the borders there are perpetual complaints of
the encroachments of whites upon Indian lands; and
naturally the central government at Washington, and
before it was at Washington, has usually been inclined to sympathize with the feeling that considers
the whites the aggressors, for the government does
not wish a war, does not itself feel any land hunger,
hears of not a tenth of the Indian outrages, and
knows by experience that the white borderers are
not easy to rule. As a consequence, the official
reports of the people who are not on the ground are
apt to paint the Indian side in its most favorable
light, and are often completely untrustworthy, this
being particularly the case if the author of the
report is an eastern man, utterly unacquainted with
the actual condition of affairs on the frontier.

Such a man, though both honest and intelligent,
when he hears that the whites have settled on
Indian lands, cannot realize that the act has Encroach-
no resemblance whatever to the forcible ment on In-
occupation of land already cultivated. The dian Lands.
white settler has merely moved into an uninhabited
waste; he does not feel that he is committing a
wrong, for he knows perfectly well that the land is
really owned by no one. It is never even visited,
except perhaps for a week or two every year, and
then the visitors are likely at any moment to be
driven off by a rival hunting-party of greater
strength. The settler ousts no one from the land; if
he did not chop down the trees, hew out the logs for

a building, and clear the ground for tillage, no one else would do so. He drives out the game, however, and of course the Indians who live thereon sink their mutual animosities and turn against the intruder. The truth is, the Indians never had any real title to the soil; they had not half as good a claim to it, for instance, as the cattlemen now have to all eastern Montana, yet no one would assert that the cattlemen have a right to keep immigrants off their vast unfenced ranges. The settler and pioneer have at bottom had justice on their side; this great continent could not have been kept as nothing but a game preserve for squalid savages. Moreover, to the most oppressed Indian nations the whites often acted as a protection, or, at least, they deferred instead of hastening their fate. But for the interposition of the whites it is probable that the Iroquois would have exterminated every Algonquin tribe before the end of the eighteenth century; exactly as in recent time the Crows and Pawnees would have been destroyed by the Sioux, had it not been for the wars we have waged against the latter.

Again, the loose governmental system of the Indians made it as difficult to secure a perma-**Difficulties** nent peace with them as it was to negotiate **in Way of** the purchase of the lands. The sachem, **Peace.** or hereditary peace chief, and the elective war chief, who wielded only the influence that he could secure by his personal prowess and his tact, were equally unable to control all of their tribes-men, and were powerless with their confederated nations. If peace was made with the Shawnees, the war was continued by the Miamis; if peace was made with the latter, nevertheless perhaps one small band was dissatisfied, and continued the contest on its own account; and even if all the recognized bands were dealt with, the parties of renegades or outlaws had to be considered; and in the last resort the full recognition accorded by the Indians to the right of private warfare, made it possible for any individual warrior who possessed any influence to go on raiding and murdering unchecked. Every tribe, every sub-tribe, every band of a dozen souls ruled over by a petty chief, almost every individual warrior of the least importance, had to be met and pacified. Even if peace were declared, the Indians could not exist long without breaking it. There was to them no temptation to trespass on the white man's ground for the purpose of settling; but every young brave was brought up to regard scalps taken and horses stolen, in war or peace, as the highest proofs and tokens of skill and courage, the sure means of attaining glory and honor, the admiration of men and the love of women. Where the young men thought thus, and the chiefs had so little real control, it was inevitable that there should be many unprovoked forays for scalps, slaves, and horses made upon the white borderers.[1]

As for the whites themselves, they too have many and grievous sins against their red neighbors for which to answer. They cannot be severely blamed for trespassing upon what was called the Indian's

[1] Similarly the Crows, who have always been treated well by us, have murdered and robbed any number of peaceful, unprotected travellers during the past three decades, as I know personally.

land; for let sentimentalists say what they will, the
man who puts the soil to use must of right dispossess the man who does not, or the world will come
to a standstill; but for many of their other deeds there
can be no pardon. On the border each man was a law
unto himself, and good and bad alike were left in per-
Misdeeds fect freedom to follow out to the uttermost
of the limits their own desires; for the spirit of
Borderers. individualism so characteristic of American
life reached its extreme of development in the backwoods. The whites who wished peace, the magistrates and leaders, had little more power over their
evil and unruly fellows than the Indian sachems had
over the turbulent young braves. Each man did
what seemed best in his own eyes, almost without
let or hindrance; unless, indeed, he trespassed upon
the rights of his neighbors, who were ready enough
to band together in their own defence, though slow
to interfere in the affairs of others.

Thus the men of lawless, brutal spirit who are
found in every community and who flock to places
where the reign of order is lax, were able to follow
the bent of their inclinations unchecked. They utterly
despised the red man; they held it no crime whatever to cheat him in trading, to rob him of his
peltries or horses, to murder him if the fit seized
them. Criminals who generally preyed on their own
neighbors, found it easier, and perhaps hardly as
dangerous, to pursue their calling at the expense of
the redskins, for the latter, when they discovered
that they had been wronged, were quite as apt
to vent their wrath on some outsider as on the

original offender. If they injured a white, all the whites might make common cause against them; but if they injured a red man, though there were sure to be plenty of whites who disapproved of it, there were apt to be very few indeed whose disapproval took any active shape.

Each race stood by its own members, and each held all of the other race responsible for the misdeeds of a few uncontrollable spirits; and this **Each Race** clannishness among those of one color, and **Held Accountable** the refusal or the inability to discriminate **for Individ-** between the good and the bad of the other **ual Deeds.** color were the two most fruitful causes of border strife.[1] When, even if he sought to prevent them, the innocent man was sure to suffer for the misdeeds of the guilty, unless both joined together for defence, the former had no alternative save to make common cause with the latter. Moreover, in a sparse backwoods settlement, where the presence of a strong, vigorous fighter was a source of safety to the whole community, it was impossible to expect that he would be punished with severity for offences which, in their hearts, his fellow townsmen could not help regarding as in some sort a revenge for the in-

[1] It is precisely the same at the present day. I have known a party of Sioux to steal the horses of a buffalo-hunting outfit, whereupon the latter retaliated by stealing the horses of a party of harmless Grosventres: and I knew a party of Cheyennes, whose horses had been taken by white thieves, to, in revenge, assail a camp of perfectly orderly cowboys. Most of the ranchmen along the Little Missouri in 1884, were pretty good fellows, who would not wrong Indians, yet they tolerated for a long time the presence of men who did not scruple to boast that they stole horses from the latter; while our peaceful neighbors, the Grosventres, likewise permitted two notorious red-skinned horse thieves to use their reservation as a harbor of refuge, and a starting-point from which to make forays against the cattlemen.

juries they had themselves suffered. Every quiet, peaceable settler had either himself been grievously wronged, or had been an eye-witness to wrongs done to his friends; and while these were vivid in his mind, the corresponding wrongs done the Indians were never brought home to him at all. If his son was scalped or his cattle driven off, he could not be expected to remember that perhaps the Indians who did the deed had themselves been cheated by a white trader, or had lost a relative at the hands of some border ruffian, or felt aggrieved because a hundred miles off some settler had built a cabin on lands they considered their own. When he joined with other exasperated and injured men to make a retaliatory inroad, his vengeance might or might not fall on the heads of the real offenders; and, in any case, he was often not in the frame of mind to put a stop to the outrages sure to be committed by the brutal spirits among his allies—though these brutal spirits were probably in a small minority.

The excesses so often committed by the whites, when, after many checks and failures, they at last **Provoca-** grasped victory, are causes for shame and **tions Suf-** regret; yet it is only fair to keep in mind **fered by the** **Whites.** the terrible provocations they had endured. Mercy, pity, magnanimity to the fallen, could not be expected from the frontiersmen gathered together to war against an Indian tribe. Almost every man of such a band had bitter personal wrongs to avenge. He was not taking part in a war against a civilized foe; he was fighting in a contest where women and children suffered the fate of the strong men, and instead of enthusiasm for his country's flag and a general national animosity towards its enemies, he was actuated by a furious flame of hot anger, and was goaded on by memories of which merely to think was madness. His friends had been treacherously slain while on messages of peace; his house had been burned, his cattle driven off, and all he had in the world destroyed before he knew that war existed and when he felt quite guiltless of all offence; his sweetheart or wife had been carried off, ravished, and was at the moment the slave and concubine of some dirty and brutal Indian warrior; his son, the stay of his house, had been burned at the stake with torments too horrible to mention[1]; his sister, when ransomed and returned to him, had told of the weary journey through the woods, when she carried around her neck as a horrible necklace the bloody scalps of her husband and children[2]; seared into his eyeballs, into his very brain, he bore ever with him, waking or sleeping, the sight of the skinned, mutilated, hideous body of the baby who had just grown old enough to recognize him and to crow and laugh when taken in his arms. Such incidents as

[1] The expression "too horrible to mention" is to be taken literally, not figuratively. It applies equally to the fate that has befallen every white man or woman who has fallen into the power of hostile plains Indians during the last ten or fifteen years. The nature of the wild Indian has not changed. Not one man in a hundred, and not a single woman, escapes torments which a civilized man cannot look another in the face and so much as speak of. Impalement on charred stakes, finger-nails split off backwards, finger-joints chewed off, eyes burned out—these tortures can be mentioned, but there are others equally normal and customary which cannot even be hinted at, especially when women are the victims.

[2] For the particular incident see M'Ferrin's "History of Methodism in Tennessee," p. 145.

these were not exceptional ; one or more, and often all of them, were the invariable attendants of every one of the countless Indian inroads that took place during the long generations of forest warfare. It was small wonder that men who had thus lost every thing should sometimes be fairly crazed by their wrongs. Again and again on the frontier we hear of some such unfortunate who has devoted all the remainder of his wretched life to the one object of taking vengeance on the whole race of the men who had darkened his days forever. Too often the squaws and pappooses fell victims of the vengeance that should have come only on the warriors ; for the whites regarded their foes as beasts rather than men, and knew that the squaws were more cruel than others in torturing the prisoner, and that the very children took their full part therein, being held up by their fathers to tomahawk the dying victims at the stake.[1]

Thus it is that there are so many dark and bloody pages in the book of border warfare, that grim and iron-bound volume, wherein we read how our fore-fathers won the wide lands that we inherit. It con-tains many a tale of fierce heroism and adventurous ambition, of the daring and resolute courage of men and the patient endurance of women ; it shows us a

---

[1] As was done to the father of Simon Girty.   Any history of any Indian inroad will give examples such as I have mentioned above.   See McAfee MSS., John P. Hale's " Trans-Alleghany Pioneers," De Haas' " Indian Wars," Wither's " Border War," etc.   In one respect, however, the In-dians east of the Mississippi were better than the tribes of the plains from whom our borders have suffered during the present century ; their female captives were not invariably ravished by every member of the band captur-ing them, as has ever been the custom among the horse Indians. Still, they were often made the concubines of their captors.

stern race of freemen who toiled hard, endured greatly, and fronted adversity bravely, who prized strength and courage and good faith, whose wives were chaste, who were generous and loyal to their friends. But it shows us also how they spurned at restraint and fretted under it, how they would brook no wrong to themselves, and yet too often inflicted wrong on others; their feats of terrible prowess are interspersed with deeds of the foulest and most wanton aggression, the darkest treachery, the most revolting cruelty; and though we meet with plenty of the rough, strong, coarse virtues, we see but little of such qualities as mercy for the fallen, the weak, and the helpless, or pity for a gallant and vanquished foe.

Among the Indians of the northwest, generally so much alike that we need pay little heed to tribal distinctions, there was one body deserving especial and separate mention. Among the turbulent and jarring elements tossed The Moravian Indians. into wild confusion by the shock of the contact between savages and the rude vanguard of civilization, surrounded and threatened by the painted warriors of the woods no less than by the lawless white riflemen who lived on the stump-dotted clearings, there dwelt a group of peaceful beings who were destined to suffer a dire fate in the most lamentable and pitiable of all the tragedies which were played out in the heart of this great wilderness. These were the Moravian Indians.[1] They were mostly Delawares,

[1] The missionaries called themselves United Brethren; to outsiders they were known as Moravians. Loskiel, "History of the Mission of the United Brethren," London, 1794. Heckewelder, "Narrative of the Mission of the United Brethren," Phil., 1820.

and had been converted by the indefatigable German missionaries, who taught the tranquil, Quaker-like creed of Count Zinzendorf. The zeal and success of the missionaries were attested by the marvellous change they had wrought in these converts; for they had transformed them in one generation from a restless, idle, blood-thirsty people of hunters and fishers, into an orderly, thrifty, industrious folk, believing with all their hearts the Christian religion in the form in which their teachers both preached and practised it. At first the missionaries, surrounded by their Indian converts, dwelt in Pennsylvania; but, harried and oppressed by their white neighbors, the submissive and patient Moravians left their homes and their cherished belongings, and in 1771 moved out into the wilderness northwest of the Ohio. It is a bitter and unanswerable commentary on the workings of a non-resistant creed when reduced to practice, that such outrages and massacres as those committed on these helpless Indians were more numerous and flagrant in the colony the Quakers governed than in any other; their vaunted policy of peace, which forbade them to play a true man's part and put down wrong-doing, caused the utmost possible evil to fall both on the white man and the red. An avowed policy of force and fraud carried out in the most cynical manner could hardly have worked more terrible injustice; their system was a direct incentive to crime and wrong-doing between the races, for they punished the aggressions of neither, and hence allowed any blow to always fall heaviest on those least deserving to suffer. No other colony made such futile, contemptible efforts to deal with the Indian problem; no other colony showed such supine, selfish helplessness in allowing her own border citizens to be mercilessly harried; none other betrayed such inability to master the hostile Indians, while, nevertheless, utterly failing to protect those who were peaceful and friendly.

When the Moravians removed beyond the Ohio, they settled on the banks of the Muskingum, made clearings in the forest, and built them- **Moravian** selves little towns, which they christened **Settle-** by such quaint names as Salem and **the West.** Gnadenhütten; names that were pathetic symbols of the peace which the harmless and sadly submissive wanderers so vainly sought. Here, in the forest, they worked and toiled, surrounded their clean, neatly kept villages with orchards and grain-fields, bred horses and cattle, and tried to do wrong to no man; all of each community meeting every day to worship and praise their Creator. But the mission-aries who had done so much for them had also done one thing which more than offset it all: for they had taught them not to defend themselves, and had thus exposed the poor beings who trusted their teaching to certain destruction. No greater wrong can ever be done than to put a good man at the mercy of a bad, while telling him not to defend himself or his fellows; in no way can the success of evil be made surer and quicker; but the wrong was peculiarly great when at such a time and in such a place the defenceless Indians were thrust between the anvil of their savage red brethren and the ham-

mer of the lawless and brutal white borderers. The
awful harvest which the poor converts reaped had
in reality been sown for them by their own friends
and would-be benefactors.

So the Moravians, seeking to deal honestly with
Indians and whites alike, but in return suspected
and despised by both, worked patiently year in and
year out, as they dwelt in their lonely homes, meekly
awaiting the stroke of the terrible doom which hung
over them.

CHAPTER V.

THE BACKWOODSMEN OF THE ALLEGHANIES.
1769–1774.

ALONG the western frontier of the colonies that
were so soon to be the United States, among the
foothills of the Alleghanies, on the slopes of the
wooded mountains, and in the long trough-like
valleys that lay between the ranges, dwelt a peculiar
and characteristically American people.

These frontier folk, the people of the up-country,
or back-country, who lived near and among the
forest-clad mountains, far away from the The People
long-settled districts of flat coast plain and   of the
sluggish tidal river, were known to them-   Frontier.
selves and to others as backwoodsmen. They all
bore a strong likeness to one another in their habits
of thought and ways of living, and differed markedly
from the people of the older and more civilized communities to the eastward. The western border of
our country was then formed by the great barrier-
chains of the Alleghanies, which ran north and south
from Pennsylvania through Maryland, Virginia, and
the Carolinas,[1] the trend of the valleys being parallel
to the sea-coast, and the mountains rising highest to
the southward.   It was difficult to cross the ranges

[1] Georgia was then too weak and small to contribute much to the backwoods stock ; her frontier was still in the low country.

from east to west, but it was both easy and natural to follow the valleys between. From Fort Pitt to the high hill-homes of the Cherokees this great tract of wooded and mountainous country possessed nearly the same features and characteristics, differing utterly in physical aspect from the alluvial plains bordering the ocean.

So, likewise, the backwoods mountaineers who dwelt near the great water-shed that separates the Atlantic streams from the springs of the Watauga, the Kanawha, and the Monongahela, were all cast in the same mould, and resembled each other much more than any of them did their immediate neighbors of the plains. The backwoodsmen of Pennsylvania had little in common with the peaceful population of Quakers and Germans who lived between the Delaware and the Susquehanna; and their near kinsmen of the Blue Ridge and the Great Smoky Mountains were separated by an equally wide gulf from the aristocratic planter communities that flourished in the tide-water regions of Virginia and the Carolinas. Near the coast the lines of division between the colonies corresponded fairly well with the differences between the populations; but after striking the foot-hills, though the political boundaries continued to go east and west, those both of ethnic and of physical significance began to run north and south.

The backwoodsmen were Americans by birth and parentage, and of mixed race; but the dominant strain in their blood was that of the Presbyterian Irish— the Scotch-Irish as they were often called. Full credit has been awarded the Roundhead and the

Cavalier for their leadership in our history; nor have we been altogether blind to the deeds of the Hollander and the Huguenot; but it is doubtful if we have wholly realized the importance of the part played by that stern and virile peo- **The Backwoods** ple, the Irish whose preachers taught the **Stock.** creed of Knox and Calvin. These Irish representatives of the Covenanters were in the west almost what the Puritans were in the northeast, and more than the Cavaliers were in the south. Mingled with the descendants of many other races, they nevertheless formed the kernel of the distinctively and intensely American stock who were the pioneers of our people in their march westward, the vanguard of the army of fighting settlers, who with axe and rifle won their way from the Alleghanies to the Rio Grande and the Pacific.[1]

The Presbyterian Irish were themselves already a mixed people. Though mainly descended from Scotch ancestors—who came originally from both lowlands and highlands, from among both the Scotch Saxons and the Scotch Celts,[2]—many of them were of Eng-

---

[1] Among the dozen or so most prominent backwoods pioneers of the west and southwest, the men who were the leaders in exploring and settling the lands, and in fighting the Indians, British, and Mexicans, the Presbyterian Irish stock furnished Andrew Jackson, Samuel Houston, David Crockett, James Robertson; Lewis, the leader of the backwoods hosts in their first great victory over the northwestern Indians; and Campbell, their commander in their first great victory over the British. The other pioneers who stand beside the above were such men as Sevier, a Shenandoah Huguenot; Shelby, of Welsh blood; and Boon and Clark, both of English stock, the former from Pennsylvania, the latter from Virginia.

[2] Of course, generations before they ever came to America, the McAfees, McClungs, Campbells, McCoshes, etc., had become indistinguishable from the Todds, Armstrongs, Elliotts, and the like.

lish, a few of French Huguenot,[1] and quite a number
of true old Milesian Irish[2] extraction. They were
the Protestants of the Protestants; they detested and
The Pres-   despised the Catholics, whom their ances-
byterian   tors had conquered, and regarded the Epis-
Irish.   copalians by whom they themselves had
been oppressed, with a more sullen, but scarcely less
intense, hatred.[3] They were a truculent and obsti-
nate people, and gloried in the warlike renown of
their forefathers, the men who had followed Cromwell, and who had shared in the defence of Derry
and in the victories of the Boyne and Aughrim.[4]

They did not begin to come to America in any
numbers till after the opening of the eighteenth
century; by 1730 they were fairly swarming across
the ocean, for the most part in two streams, the
larger going to the port of Philadelphia, the smaller

[1] A notable instance being that of the Lewis family, of Great Kanawha
fame.

[2] The Blount MSS. contain many muster-rolls and pay-rolls of the
frontier forces of North Carolina during the year 1788. In these, and in
the lists of names of settlers preserved in the Am. State Papers, Public
Lands, II., etc., we find numerous names such as Shea, Drennan, O'Neil,
O'Brien, Mahoney, Sullivan, O'Connell, Maguire, O'Donohue,—in fact
hardly a single Irish name is unrepresented. Of course, many of these
were the descendants of imported Irish bondservants ; but many also were
free immigrants, belonging to the Presbyterian congregations, and sometimes appearing as pastors thereof. For the numerous Irish names of
prominent pioneers (such as Donelly, Hogan, etc.) see McClung's "Western Adventures" (Louisville, 1879), 52, 167, 207, 308, etc.; also DeHaas,
236, 289, etc.; Doddridge, 16, 288, 301, etc., etc.

[3] "Sketches of North Carolina," William Henry Foote, New York,
1846. An excellent book, written after much research.

[4] For a few among many instances : Houston (see Lane's " Life of Houston") had ancestors at Derry and Aughrim ; the McAfees (see McAfee
MSS.) and Irvine, one of the commanders on Crawford's expedition, were
descendants of men who fought at the Boyne ("Crawford's Campaign," G.
W. Butterfield, Cincinnati, 1873, p. 26) ; so with Lewis, Campbell, etc.

to the port of Charleston.[1] Pushing through the
long settled lowlands of the seacoast, they at once
made their abode at the foot of the mountains, and
became the outposts of civilization. From Pennsylvania, whither the great majority had come, they
drifted south along the foothills, and down the long
valleys, till they met their brethren from Charleston
who had pushed up into the Carolina back-country.
In this land of hills, covered by unbroken forest,
they took root and flourished, stretching in a broad
belt from north to south, a shield of sinewy men
thrust in between the people of the seaboard and the
red warriors of the wilderness. All through this
region they were alike ; they had as little kinship
with the Cavalier as with the Quaker ; the west was
won by those who have been rightly called the Round-
heads of the south, the same men who, before any
others, declared for American independence.[2]

The two facts of most importance to remember in
dealing with our pioneer history are, first, that the
western portions of Virginia and the Caro- The Back-
linas were peopled by an entirely different woodsmen
stock from that which had long existed in Form One
.   People.
the tide-water regions of those colonies ; and, second-
ly, that, except for those in the Carolinas who came
from Charleston, the immigrants of this stock were
mostly from the north, from their great breeding-
ground and nursery in western Pennsylvania.[3]

[1] Foote, 78.
[2] Witness the Mecklenburg Declaration.
[3] McAfee MSS. "Trans-Alleghany Pioneers" (John P. Hale), 17.
Foote, 188. See also *Columbian Magazine*, I., 122, and Schöpf, 406.
Boon, Crockett, Houston, Campbell, Lewis, were among the southwestern

That these Irish Presbyterians were a bold and hardy race is proved by their at once pushing past the settled regions, and plunging into the wilderness as the leaders of the white advance. They were the first and last set of immigrants to do this; all others have merely followed in the wake of their predecessors. But, indeed, they were fitted to be Americans from the very start; they were kinsfolk of the Covenanters; they deemed it a religious duty to interpret their own Bible, and held for a divine right the election of their own clergy. For generations their whole ecclesiastic and scholastic systems had been fundamentally democratic. In the hard life of the frontier they lost much of their religion, and they had but scant opportunity to give their children the schooling in which they believed; but what few meeting-houses and school-houses there were on the border were theirs.[1] The numerous families of colonial English who came among them adopted their religion if they adopted any. The creed of the backwoodsman who had a creed at all was Presbyterianism; for the Episcopacy of the tide-water lands obtained no foothold in the mountains, and the Methodists and Baptists had but just begun to appear in the west when the Revolution broke out.[2]

pioneers whose families originally came from Pennsylvania. See " Annals of Augusta County, Va.," by Joseph A. Waddell, Richmond, 1888 (an excellent book), pp. 4, 276, 278, for a clear showing of the Presbyterian Irish origin of the West Virginians, and of the large German admixture.

[1] The Irish schoolmaster was everywhere a feature of early western society.

[2] McAfee MSS. MS. Autobiography of Rev. Wm. Hickman, born in Virginia in 1747 (in Col. R. T. Durrett's library). " Trans-Alleghany Pioneers," 147. " History of Kentucky Baptists," J. H. Spencer (Cincinnati, 1885).

These Presbyterian Irish were, however, far from being the only settlers on the border, although more than any others they impressed the stamp of their peculiar character on the pioneer civilization of the west and southwest. Great numbers of immigrants of English descent came among them from the settled districts on the east; and though these later arrivals soon became indistinguishable from the people among whom they settled, yet they certainly sometimes added a tone of their own to backwoods society, giving it here and there a slight dash of what we are accustomed to consider the distinctively southern or cavalier spirit.[1] There was likewise a large German admixture, not only from the Germans of Pennsylvania, but also from those of the Carolinas.[2] A good many Huguenots

Of Mixed Race.

---

[1] Boon, though of English descent, had no Virginia blood in his veins ; he was an exact type of the regular backwoodsman ; but in Clark, and still more in Blount, we see strong traces of the "cavalier spirit." Of course, the Cavaliers no more formed the bulk of the Virginia people than they did of Rupert's armies ; but the squires and yeomen who went to make up the mass took their tone from their leaders.

[2] Many of the most noted hunters and Indian fighters were of German origin. (See "Early Times in Middle Tennessee," John Carr, Nashville, 1859, pp. 54 and 56, for Steiner and Mansker—or Stoner and Mansco.) Such were the Wetzels, famous in border annals, who lived near Wheeling ; Michael Steiner, the Steiners being the forefathers of many of the numerous Kentucky Stoners of to-day ; and Kasper Mansker, the " Mr. Mansco " of Tennessee writers. Every old western narrative contains many allusions to " Dutchmen," as Americans very properly call the Germans. Their names abound on the muster-rolls, pay-rolls, lists of settlers, etc., of the day (Blount MSS., State Department MSS., McAfee MSS., Am. State Papers, etc.) ; but it must be remembered that they are often Anglicized, when nothing remains to show the origin of the owners. We could not recognize in Custer and Herkomer, Küster and Herckheimer, were not the ancestral history of the two generals already known ; and in the backwoods, a man often loses sight of his ancestors in a couple of generations. In the Carolinas the Germans seem to have been almost as plentiful on the

likewise came,[1] and a few Hollanders [2] and even Swedes,[3] from the banks of the Delaware, or perhaps from farther off still.

A single generation, passed under the hard conditions of life in the wilderness, was enough to weld together into one people the representatives of these numerous and widely different races; and the children of the next generation became indistinguishable from one another. Long before the first Continental Congress assembled, the backwoodsmen, whatever their blood, had become Americans, one in speech, thought, and character, clutching firmly the land in which their fathers and grandfathers had lived before them. They had lost all remembrance of Europe and all sympathy with things European; they had become as emphatically products native to the soil as were the tough and sup-

Intense American-ism of the Frontiers-men.

frontiers as the Irish (see Adair, 245, and Smyth's "Tour," I., 236). In Pennsylvania they lived nearer civilization (Schoolcraft, 3, 335 ; "Journey in the West in 1785," by Lewis Brantz), although also mixed with the borderers ; the more adventurous among them naturally seeking the frontier.

[1] Giving to the backwoods society such families as the Seviers and Lenoirs. The Huguenots, like the Germans, frequently had their names Anglicized. The best known and most often quoted example is that of the Blancpied family, part of whom have become Whitefoots, while the others, living on the coast, have suffered a marvellous sea-change, the name reappearing as "Blumpy."

[2] To the western American, who was not given to nice ethnic distinctions, both German and Hollander were simply Dutchmen ; but occasionally we find names like Van Meter, Van Buskirk, Van Swearingen, which carry their origin on their faces (De Haas, 317, 319 ; Doddridge, 307).

[3] The Scandinavian names, in an unlettered community, soon become indistinguishable from those of the surrounding American's—Jansen, Petersen, etc., being readily Americanized. It is therefore rarely that they show their parentage. Still, we now and then come across one that is unmistakable, as Erickson, for instance (see p. 51 of Col. Reuben T. Durrett's admirable "Life and Writings of John Filson," Louisville and Cincinnati, 1884).

ple hickories out of which they fashioned the handles of their long, light axes.   Their grim, harsh, narrow lives were yet strangely fascinating and full of adventurous toil and danger; none but natures as strong, as freedom-loving, and as full of bold defiance as theirs could have endured existence on the terms which these men found pleasurable.   Their iron surroundings made a mould which turned out all alike in the same shape.   They resembled one another, and they differed from the rest of the world—even the world of America, and infinitely more the world of Europe—in dress, in customs, and in mode of life.

Where their lands abutted on the more settled districts to the eastward, the population was of course thickest, and their peculiarities least.   Here and there at such points they built small backwoods burgs or towns, rude, straggling, unkempt villages, with a store or two, a tavern,—sometimes good, often a "scandalous hog-sty," where travellers were devoured by fleas, and every one slept and ate in one room,[1]—a small log school-house, and a little church, presided over by a hard-featured Presbyterian preacher, gloomy, earnest, and zealous, probably bigoted and narrow-minded, but nevertheless a great power for good in the community.[2]

However, the backwoodsmen as a class neither built towns nor loved to dwell therein.   They were to be seen at their best in the vast, interminable for-

[1] MS. Journal of Matthew Clarkson, 1766.   See also "Voyage dans les États-Unis," La Rochefoucauld–Liancourt, Paris, L'an, VII., I., 104.
[2] The borderers had the true Calvinistic taste in preaching.   Clarkson, in his journal of his western trip, mentions with approval a sermon he heard as being "a very judicious and alarming discourse."

ests that formed their chosen home. They won and kept their lands by force, and ever lived either at war **Not a** or in dread of war. Hence they settled **Town-Building** always in groups of several families each, all **Race.** banded together for mutual protection. Their red foes were strong and terrible, cunning in council, dreadful in battle, merciless beyond belief in victory. The men of the border did not overcome and dispossess cowards and weaklings; they marched forth to spoil the stout-hearted and to take for a prey the possessions of the men of might. Every acre, every rood of ground which they claimed had to be cleared by the axe and held with the rifle. Not only was the chopping down of the forest the first preliminary to cultivation, but it was also the surest means of subduing the Indians, to whom the unending stretches of choked woodland were an impenetrable cover behind which to move unseen, a shield in making assaults, and a strong tower of defence in repelling counter-attacks. In the conquest of the west the backwoods axe, shapely, well-poised, with long haft and light head, was a servant hardly standing second even to the rifle; the two were the national weapons of the American backwoodsman, and in their use he has never been excelled.

When a group of families moved out into the wilderness they built themselves a station or stock- **The Back-** ade fort; a square palisade of upright logs, **woods** loop-holed, with strong blockhouses as bas- **Forts.** tions at the corners. One side at least was generally formed by the backs of the cabins themselves, all standing in a row; and there was a great

door or gate, that could be strongly barred in case of
need.   Often no iron whatever was employed in any
of the buildings.   The square inside contained the
provision sheds and frequently a strong central block-
house as well.   These forts, of course, could not stand
against cannon, and they were always in danger when
attacked with fire ; but save for this risk of burning
they were very effectual defences against men without
artillery, and were rarely taken, whether by whites or
Indians, except by surprise.   Few other buildings have
played so important a part in our history as the rough
stockade fort of the backwoods.

The families only lived in the fort when there
was war with the Indians, and even then not in the
winter.   At other times they all separated out to
their own farms, universally called clearings, as they
were always made by first cutting off the timber.
The stumps were left to dot the fields of grain and
Indian corn.   The corn in especial was the stand-by
and invariable resource of the western settler ; it was
the crop on which he relied to feed his family, and
when hunting or on a war trail the parched grains
were carried in his leather wallet to serve often as
his only food.   But he planted orchards and raised
melons, potatoes, and many other fruits and vegetables as well ; and he had usually a horse or two,
cows, and perhaps hogs and sheep, if the wolves and
bears did not interfere.   If he was poor his cabin
was made of unhewn logs, and held but a Life on the
single room ; if well-to-do, the logs were Clearings.
neatly hewed, and besides the large living- and eating-
room with its huge stone fireplace, there was also a

small bedroom and a kitchen, while a ladder led to the loft above, in which the boys slept. The floor was made of puncheons, great slabs of wood hewed carefully out, and the roof of clapboards. Pegs of wood were thrust into the sides of the house, to serve instead of a wardrobe; and buck antlers, thrust into joists, held the ever-ready rifles. The table was a great clapboard set on four wooden legs; there were three-legged stools, and in the better sort of houses old-fashioned rocking-chairs.[1] The couch or bed was warmly covered with blankets, bear-skins, and deer-hides.[2]

These clearings lay far apart from one another in the wilderness. Up to the door-sills of the log-huts stretched the solemn and mysterious forest. There were no openings to break its continuity; nothing but endless leagues on leagues of shadowy, wolf-haunted woodland. The great trees towered aloft till their separate heads were lost in the mass of foliage above, and the rank underbrush choked the spaces between the trunks. On the higher peaks and ridge-crests of the mountains there were straggling birches and pines, hemlocks and balsam firs;[3] elsewhere, oaks, chestnuts, hickories, maples, beeches,

[1] McAfee MSS.

[2] In the McAfee MSS. there is an amusing mention of the skin of a huge bull elk, killed by the father, which the youngsters christened "old ellick"; they used to quarrel for the possession of it on cold nights, as it was very warm, though if the hairside was turned in it became slippery and apt to slide off the bed.

[3] On the mountains the climate, flora, and fauna were all those of the north, not of the adjacent southern lowlands. The ruffed grouse, red squirrel, snow bird, various Canadian warblers, and a peculiar species of boreal field-mouse, the *evotomys*, are all found as far south as the Great Smokies.

walnuts, and great tulip trees grew side by side with many other kinds. The sunlight could not penetrate the roofed archway of murmuring leaves; through the gray aisles of the forest men walked always in a kind of mid-day gloaming. Those who had lived in the open plains felt when they came to the back-woods as if their heads were hooded. Save on the border of a lake, from a cliff top, or on a bald knob —that is, a bare hill-shoulder,—they could not any-where look out for any distance.

All the land was shrouded in one vast forest. It covered the mountains from crest to river-bed, filled the plains, and stretched in sombre and melancholy wastes towards the Mississippi. All that it contained, all that lay hid within it and beyond it, none could tell; men only knew that their boldest hunters, how-ever deeply they had penetrated, had not yet gone through it, that it was the home of the game they followed and the wild beasts that preyed on their flocks, and that deep in its tangled depths lurked their red foes, hawk-eyed and wolf-hearted.

Backwoods society was simple, and the duties and rights of each member of the family were plain and clear. The man was the armed protector and pro-vider, the bread-winner; the woman was the house-wife and child-bearer. They married young and their families were large, for they were strong and healthy, and their success in life depended on their own stout arms and willing hearts. There was every-where great equality of conditions. Land was plenty and all else scarce; so courage, thrift, and industry were sure of their reward. All had small farms, with the few stock necessary to cultivate them ; the farms being generally placed in the hollows, the division lines between them, if they were close together, being the tops of the ridges and the water-courses, especially the former. The buildings of each farm were usually at its lowest point, as if in the centre of an amphitheatre.[1] Each was on an average of about 400 acres,[2] but sometimes more.[3] Tracts of low, swampy grounds, possibly some miles from the cabin, were cleared for meadows, the fodder being stacked, and hauled home in winter.

Each backwoodsman was not only a small farmer but also a hunter ; for his wife and children depended **Backwoods** for their meat upon the venison and bear's **Society.** flesh procured by his rifle. The people were restless and always on the move. After being a little while in a place, some of the men would settle down permanently, while others would again drift off, farming and hunting alternately to support their families.[4] The backwoodsman's dress was in great part borrowed

[1] Doddridge's "Settlements and Indian Wars," (133) written by an eye-witness ; it is the most valuable book we have on old-time frontier ways and customs.

[2] The land laws differed at different times in different colonies ; but this was the usual size at the outbreak of the Revolution, of the farms along the western frontier, as under the laws of Virginia, then obtaining from the Holston to the Alleghany, this amount was allotted every settler who built a cabin or raised a crop of corn.

[3] Beside the right to 400 acres, there was also a preëmption right to 1,000 acres more adjoining to be secured by a land-office warrant. As between themselves the settlers had what they called "tomahawk rights," made by simply deadening a certain number of trees with a hatchet. They were similar to the rights conferred in the west now by what is called a "claim shack" or hut, built to hold some good piece of land ; that is, they con-ferred no title whatever, except that sometimes men would pay for them rather than have trouble with the claimant.

[4] McAfee MSS. (particularly Autobiography of Robert McAfee).

from his Indian foes. He wore a fur cap or felt hat, moccasins, and either loose, thin trousers, or else simply leggings of buckskin or elk-hide, and the Indian breech-clout. He was always clad in the fringed hunting-shirt, of homespun or buckskin, the most picturesque and distinctively national dress ever worn in America. It was a loose smock or tunic, reaching nearly to the knees, and held in at the waist by a broad belt, from which hung the tomahawk and scalping-knife.[1] His weapon was the long, small-bore, flint-lock rifle, clumsy, and ill-balanced, but exceedingly accurate. It was very heavy, and when upright, reached to the chin of a tall man ; for the barrel of thick, soft iron, was four feet in length, while the stock was short, and the butt scooped out. Sometimes it was plain, sometimes ornamented. It was generally bored out—or, as the expression then was, "sawed out"—to carry a ball of seventy, more rarely of thirty or forty, to the pound ; and was usually of backwoods manufacture.[2] The marksman almost always fired from a rest, and rarely at a very long range ; and the shooting was marvellously accurate.[3]

The Backwoods Rifles.

In the backwoods there was very little money;

[1] To this day it is worn in parts of the Rocky Mountains, and even occasionally, here and there, in the Alleghanies.

[2] The above is the description of one of Boon's rifles, now in the possession of Col. Durrett. According to the inscription on the barrel it was made at Louisville (Ky.), in 1782, by M. Humble. It is perfectly plain ; whereas one of Floyd's rifles, which I have also seen, is much more highly finished, and with some ornamentation.

[3] For the opinion of a foreign military observer on the phenomenal accuracy of backwoods markmanship, see General Victor Collot's " Voyage en Amérique," p. 242.

barter was the common form of exchange, and peltries were often used as a circulating medium, a beaver, otter, fisher, dressed buckskin or large bear-skin being reckoned as equal to two foxes or wildcats, four coons, or eight minks.[1] A young man inherited nothing from his father but his strong frame and eager heart; but before him lay a whole continent wherein to pitch his farm, and he felt ready to marry as soon as he became of age, even though he had nothing but his clothes, his horses, his axe, and his rifle.[2] If a girl was well off, and had been careful and industrious, she might herself bring a dowry, of a cow and a calf, a brood mare, a bed well stocked with blankets, and a chest containing her clothes[3]— the latter not very elaborate, for a woman's dress consisted of a hat or poke bonnet, a " bed gown," perhaps a jacket, and a linsey petticoat, while her feet were thrust into coarse shoepacks or moccasins. Fine clothes were rare; a suit of such cost more than 200 acres of good land.[4]

The first lesson the backwoodsmen learnt was the necessity of self-help; the next, that such a community could only thrive if all joined in helping one another. Log-rollings, house-raisings, house-warm-ings, corn-shuckings, quiltings, and the like were occasions when all the neighbors came together to do what the family itself could hardly accomplish alone. Every such meeting was the occasion of a

---

[1] MS. copy of Matthew Clarkson's Journal in 1766.

[2] McAfee MSS. (Autobiography of Robert R. McAfee).

[3] *Do.*

[4] Memoirs of the Hist. Soc. of Penn., 1826. Account of first settlements, etc., by John Watson (1804).

frolic and dance for the young people, whisky and rum being plentiful, and the host exerting his utmost power to spread the table with backwoods delicacies —bear-meat and venison, vegetables from the "truck patch," where squashes, melons, beans, and the like were grown, wild fruits, bowls of milk, and apple pies, which were the acknowledged standard of luxury. At the better houses there was metheglin or small beer, cider, cheese, and biscuits.[1] Tea was so little known that many of the backwoods people were not aware it was a beverage and at first attempted to eat the leaves with salt or butter.[2]

The young men prided themselves on their bodily strength, and were always eager to contend against one another in athletic games, such as wrestling, racing, jumping, and lifting flour-barrels; and they also sought distinction in vieing with one another at their work. Sometimes **Sports and Quarrels.** they strove against one another singly, sometimes they divided into parties, each bending all its energies to be first in shucking a given heap of corn or cutting (with sickles) an allotted patch of wheat. Among the men the bravos or bullies often were dandies also in the backwoods fashions, wearing their hair long and delighting in the rude finery of hunting-shirts embroidered with porcupine quills; they were loud, boastful, and profane, given to coarsely bantering one another. Brutally savage fights were frequent; the combatants, who were surrounded by rings of interested

---

[1] *Do.* An admirable account of what such a frolic was some thirty-five years later is to be found in Edward Eggleston's "Circuit Rider."

[2] Such incidents are mentioned again and again by Watson, Milfort, Doddridge, Carr, and other writers.

spectators, striking, kicking, biting, and gouging. The fall of one of them did not stop the fight, for the man who was down was maltreated without mercy until he called "enough." The victor always bragged savagely of his prowess, often leaping on a stump, crowing and flapping his arms. This last was a thoroughly American touch; but otherwise one of these contests was less a boxing match than a kind of backwoods *pankrátion,* no less revolting than its ancient prototype of Olympic fame. Yet, if the uncouth borderers were as brutal as the highly polished Greeks, they were more manly; defeat was not necessarily considered disgrace, a man often fighting when he was certain to be beaten, while the onlookers neither hooted nor pelted the conquered. We first hear of the noted scout and Indian fighter, Simon Kenton, as leaving a rival for dead after one of these ferocious duels, and fleeing from his home in terror of the punishment that might follow the deed.[1] Such fights were specially fre-

---

[1] McClung's "Western Adventures." All eastern and European observers comment with horror on the border brawls, especially the eye-gouging. Englishmen, of course, in true provincial spirit, complacently contrasted them with their own boxing fights; Frenchmen, equally of course, were more struck by the resemblances than the differences between the two forms of combat. Milfort gives a very amusing account of the "Anglo-Américains d'une espèce particulière," whom he calls "crakeurs ou gaugeurs," (crackers or gougers). He remarks that he found them "tous borgnes," (as a result of their pleasant fashion of eye-gouging—a backwoods bully in speaking of another would often threaten to "measure the length of his eye-strings,") and that he doubts if there can exist in the world "des hommes plus méchants que ces habitants."

These fights were among the numerous backwoods habits that showed Scotch rather than English ancestry. "I attempted to keep him down, in order to improve my success, after the manner of my own country" ("Roderick Random").

quent when the backwoodsmen went into the little frontier towns to see horse races or fairs.

A wedding was always a time of festival. If there was a church anywhere near, the bride rode thither on horseback behind her father, and after the service her pillion was shifted to the **Wedding.** bridegroom's steed.[1] If, as generally happened, there was no church, the groom and his friends, all armed, rode to the house of the bride's father, plenty of whisky being drunk, and the men racing recklessly along the narrow bridle-paths, for there were few roads or wheeled vehicles in the backwoods. At the bride's house the ceremony was performed, and then a huge dinner was eaten , after which the fiddling and dancing began, and were continued all the afternoon, and most of the night as well. A party of girls stole off the bride and put her to bed in the loft above ; and a party of young men then performed the like service for the groom. The fun was hearty and coarse, and the toasts always included one to the young couple, with the wish that they might have many big children ; for as long as they could remember the backwoodsmen had lived at war, while looking ahead they saw no chance of its ever stopping, and so each son was regarded as a future warrior, a help to the whole community.[2] The neighbors all joined again in chopping and rolling the logs for the young couple's future house, then in raising the house itself, and finally in feasting and dancing at the house-warming.

Funerals were simple, the dead body being carried

[1] Watson.   [2] Doddridge.

to the grave in a coffin slung on poles and borne by four men.

There was not much schooling, and few boys or girls learnt much more than reading, writing, and **Schooling.** ciphering up to the rule of three.[1] Where the school-houses existed they were only dark, mean log-huts, and if in the southern colonies, were generally placed in the so-called " old fields," or abandoned farms grown up with pines. The schoolmaster boarded about with the families ; his learning was rarely great, nor was his discipline good, in spite of the frequency and severity of the canings. The price for such tuition was at the rate of twenty shillings a year, in Pennsylvania currency.[2]

Each family did every thing that could be done for itself. The father and sons worked with axe, hoe, **Home Em-** and sickle. Almost every house contained a **ployments.** loom, and almost every woman was a weaver. Linsey-woolsey, made from flax grown near the cabin, and of wool from the backs of the few sheep, was the warmest and most substantial cloth ; and when the flax crop failed and the flocks were destroyed by wolves, the children had but scanty covering to hide their nakedness. The man tanned the buckskin, the woman was tailor and shoemaker, and made the deer-skin sifters to be used instead of bolting-cloths. There were a few pewter spoons in use ; but the table furniture consisted mainly of hand-made trenchers, platters, noggins, and bowls. The cradle was of peeled hickory bark.[3] Ploughshares had to be imported,

---

[1] McAfee MSS.   [2] Watson.
[3] McAfee MSS.   See also Doddridge and Watson.

but harrows and sleds were made without difficulty; and the cooper work was well done. Chaff beds were thrown on the floor of the loft, if the house-owner was well off. Each cabin had a hand-mill and a hominy block; the last was borrowed from the Indians, and was only a large block of wood, with a hole burned in the top, as a mortar, where the pestle was worked. If there were any sugar maples accessible, they were tapped every year.

But some articles, especially salt and iron, could not be produced in the backwoods. In order to get them each family collected during the year all the furs possible, these being valuable and yet easily carried on pack-horses, the sole means of transport. Then, after seeding time, in the fall, the people of a neighborhood ordinarily joined in sending down a train of peltry-laden pack-horses to some large sea-coast or tidal-river trading town, where their burdens were bartered for the needed iron and salt. The unshod horses all had bells hung round their neck; the clappers were stopped during the day, but when the train was halted for the night, and the horses were hobbled and turned loose, the bells were once more unstopped.[1] Several men accompanied each little caravan, and sometimes they drove with them steers and hogs to sell on the sea-coast. A

Pack-trains.

---

[1] Doddridge, 156. He gives an interesting anecdote of one man engaged in helping such a pack-train, the bell of whose horse was stolen. The thief was recovered, and whipped as a punishment, the owner exclaiming as he laid the strokes lustily on: "Think what a rascally figure I should make in the streets of Baltimore without a bell on my horse." He had never been out of the woods before; he naturally wished to look well on his first appearance in civilized life, and it never occurred to him that a good horse was left without a bell anywhere.

bushel of alum salt was worth a good cow and calf, and as each of the poorly fed, undersized pack animals could carry but two bushels, the mountaineers prized it greatly, and instead of salting or pickling their venison, they jerked it, by drying it in the sun or smoking it over a fire.

The life of the backwoodsmen was one long struggle. The forest had to be felled, droughts, deep **Dangers of** snows, freshets, cloudbursts, forest fires, **the Life.** and all the other dangers of a wilderness life faced. Swarms of deer-flies, mosquitoes, and midges rendered life a torment in the weeks of hot weather. Rattlesnakes and copperheads were very plentiful, and, the former especially, constant sources of danger and death. Wolves and bears were incessant and inveterate foes of the live stock, and the cougar or panther occasionally attacked man as well.[1] More terrible still, the wolves sometimes went mad, and the men who then encountered them were almost certain to be bitten and to die of hydrophobia.[2]

Every true backwoodsman was a hunter. Wild turkeys were plentiful. The pigeons at times filled the woods with clouds that hid the sun and broke down the branches on their roosting grounds as

[1] An instance of this, which happened in my mother's family, has been mentioned elsewhere (" Hunting Trips of a Ranchman "). Even the wolves occasionally attacked man ; Audubon gives an example.

[2] Doddridge, 194. Dodge, in his " Hunting Grounds of the Great West," gives some recent instances. Bears were sometimes dangerous to human life. Doddridge, 64. A slave on the plantation of my great-grand-father in Georgia was once regularly scalped by a she-bear whom he had tried to rob of her cubs, and ever after he was called, both by the other negroes and by the children on the plantation, " Bear Bob."

if a whirlwind had passed. The black and gray
squirrels swarmed, devastating the corn-fields, and
at times gathering in immense companies
and migrating across mountain and river.

The hunter's ordinary game was the deer, and
after that the bear; the elk was already growing
uncommon. No form of labor is harder than the
chase, and none is so fascinating nor so excellent
as a training-school for war. The successful still-
hunter of necessity possessed skill in hiding and
in creeping noiselessly upon the wary quarry, as
well as in imitating the notes and calls of the
different beasts and birds; skill in the use of the
rifle and in throwing the tomahawk he already had;
and he perforce acquired keenness of eye, thorough
acquaintance with woodcraft, and the power of
standing the severest strains of fatigue, hardship
and exposure. He lived out in the woods for
many months with no food but meat, and no shelter
whatever, unless he made a lean-to of brush or
crawled into a hollow sycamore.

Such training stood the frontier folk in good
stead when they were pitted against the Indians;
without it they could not even have held
their own, and the white advance would
have been absolutely checked. Our frontiers were pushed westward by the war-

like skill and adventurous personal prowess of the
individual settlers; regular armies by themselves
could have done little. For one square mile the
regular armies added to our domain, the settlers
added ten,—a hundred would probably be nearer the

truth. A race of peaceful, unwarlike farmers would have been helpless before such foes as the red Indians, and no auxiliary military force could have protected them or enabled them to move westward. Colonists fresh from the old world, no matter how thrifty, steady-going, and industrious, could not hold their own on the frontier; they had to settle where they were protected from the Indians by a living barrier of bold and self-reliant American borderers.[1] The west would never have been settled save for the fierce courage and the eager desire to brave danger so characteristic of the stalwart backwoodsmen.

These armed hunters, woodchoppers, and farmers were their own soldiers. They built and manned their own forts; they did their own fighting under their own commanders. There were no regiments of regular troops along the frontier.[2] In the event of an Indian inroad each borderer had to defend himself until there was time for them all to gather together to repel or avenge it. Every man was accustomed to the use of arms from his childhood; when a boy was twelve years old he was given a rifle and made a fort-soldier, with a loophole where he was to stand if the station was attacked. The war was never-ending, for even the times of so-called peace were broken by forays and murders; a man might grow from babyhood to middle age on the border, and yet never remember a year in which some one of his neighbors did not fall a victim to the Indians.

[1] Schöpf, I., 404.
[2] The insignificant garrisons at one or two places need not be taken into account, as they were of absolutely no effect.

There was everywhere a rude military organization, which included all the able-bodied men of the community. Every settlement had its colonels and captains; but these officers, both in their training and in the authority they exercised, corresponded much more nearly to Indian chiefs than to the regular army men whose titles they bore. They had no means whatever of enforcing their orders, and their tumultuous and disorderly levies of sinewy riflemen were hardly as well disciplined as the Indians themselves.[1] The superior officer could advise, entreat, lead, and influence his men, but he could not command them, or, if he did, the men obeyed him only just so far as it suited them. If an officer planned a scout or campaign, those who thought proper accompanied him, and the others stayed at home, and even those who went out came back if the fit seized them, or perchance followed the lead of an insubordinate junior officer whom they liked better than they did his superior.[2] There was

Their Military Organization.

---

[1] Brantz Mayer, in "Tah-Gah-Jute, or Logan and Cresap" (Albany, 1867), ix., speaks of the pioneers as "comparative few in numbers," and of the Indian as "numerous, and fearing not only the superior weapons of his foe, but the organization and discipline which together made the comparatively few equal to the greater number." This sentence embodies a variety of popular misconceptions. The pioneers were more numerous than the Indians ; the Indians were generally, at least in the northwest, as well armed as the whites, and in military matters the Indians were actually (see Smith's narrative, and almost all competent authorities) superior in organization and discipline to their pioneer foes. Most of our battles against the Indians of the western woods, whether won or lost, were fought by superior numbers on our side. Individually, or in small parties, the frontiersmen gradually grew to be a match for the Indians, man for man, at least in many cases, but this was only true of large bodies of them if they were commanded by some one naturally able to control their unruly spirits.

[2] As examples take Clark's last Indian campaign and the battle of Blue Licks.

no compulsion to perform military duties beyond dread of being disgraced in the eyes of the neighbors, and there was no pecuniary reward for performing them; nevertheless the moral sentiment of a backwoods community was too robust to tolerate habitual remissness in military affairs, and the coward and laggard were treated with utter scorn, and were generally in the end either laughed out, or "hated out," of the neighborhood, or else got rid of in a still more summary manner. Among a people naturally brave and reckless, this public opinion acted fairly effectively, and there was generally but little shrinking from military service.[1]

A backwoods levy was formidable because of the high average courage and prowess of the individuals composing it; it was on its own ground **Character of the Backwoods Levies.** much more effective than a like force of regular soldiers, but of course it could not be trusted on a long campaign. The backwoodsmen used their rifles better than the Indians, and also stood punishment better, but they never matched them in surprises nor in skill in taking advantage of cover, and very rarely equalled their discipline in the battle itself. After all, the pioneer was primarily a husbandman; the time spent in chopping trees and tilling the soil his foe spent in preparing for or practising forest warfare, and so the former, thanks to the exercise of the very qualities which in the end gave him the possession of the soil, could not, as a rule, hope to rival his antagonist in the actual conflict itself. When large bodies of the red men and

[1] Doddridge, 161, 185.

white borderers were pitted against each other, the former were if any thing the more likely to have the advantage.[1] But the whites soon copied from the Indians their system of individual and private war-fare, and they probably caused their foes far more damage and loss in this way than in the large expeditions. Many noted border scouts and Indian fighters—such men as Boon, Kenton, Wetzel, Brady, McCulloch, Mansker [2]—grew to overmatch their Indian foes at their own game, and held themselves above the most renowned warriors. But these men carried the spirit of defiant self-reliance to such an extreme that their best work was always done when they were alone or in small parties of but four or five. They made long forays after scalps and horses, going a wonderful distance, enduring extreme hard-ship, risking the most terrible of deaths, and harry-ing the hostile tribes into a madness of terror and revengeful hatred.

As it was in military matters, so it was with the administration of justice by the frontiersmen; they had few courts, and knew but little law, and yet they

---

[1] At the best such a frontier levy was composed of men of the type of Leatherstocking, Ishmael Bush, Tom Hutter, Harry March, Bill Kirby, and Aaron Thousandacres. When animated by a common and overmaster-ing passion, such a body would be almost irresistible ; but it could not hold together long, and there was generally a plentiful mixture of men less trained in woodcraft, and therefore useless in forest fighting, while if, as must generally be the case in any body, there were a number of cowards in the ranks, the total lack of discipline not only permitted them to flinch from their work with impunity, but also allowed them, by their example, to infect and demoralize their braver companions.

[2] Haywood, DeHaas, Withers, McClung, and other border annalists, give innumerable anecdotes about these and many other men, illustrating their feats of fierce prowess and, too often, of brutal ferocity.

contrived to preserve order and morality with rough effectiveness, by combining to frown down on the Adminis- grosser misdeeds, and to punish the more tration of flagrant misdoers. Perhaps the spirit in Justice.   which they acted can be best shown by the recital of an incident in the career of the three McAfee brothers, who were among the pioneer hunters of Kentucky.[1] Previous to trying to move their families out to the new country, they made a cache of clothing, implements, and provisions, which in their absence was broken into and plundered. They caught the thief, " a little diminutive, red-headed white man," a runaway convict servant from one of the tide-water counties of Virginia. In the first impulse of anger at finding that he was the criminal, one of the McAfees rushed at him to kill him with his tomahawk; but the weapon turned, the man was only knocked down, and his assailant's gusty anger subsided as quickly as it had risen, giving way to a desire to do stern but fair justice. So the three captors formed themselves into a court, examined into the case, heard the man in his own defence, and after due consultation decided that " according to their opinion of the laws he had forfeited his life, and ought to be hung "; but none of them were willing to execute the sentence in cold blood, and they ended by taking their prisoner back to his master.

The incident was characteristic in more than one way. The prompt desire of the backwoodsman to avenge his own wrong; his momentary furious an-

[1] McAfee MSS. The story is told both in the "Autobiography of Robert McAfee," and in the " History of the First Settlement on Salt River."

ger, speedily quelled and replaced by a dogged determination to be fair but to exact full retribution;
the acting entirely without regard to legal forms or
legal officials, but yet in a spirit which spoke well
for the doer's determination to uphold the essentials
that make honest men law-abiding; together with the
good faith of the whole proceeding, and the amusing
ignorance that it would have been in the least un-
lawful to execute their own rather harsh sentence—
all these were typical frontier traits. Some of the
same traits appear in the treatment commonly
adopted in the backwoods to meet the case—of painfully frequent occurrence in the times of Indian wars
—where a man taken prisoner by the savages, and
supposed to be murdered, returned after two or three
years' captivity, only to find his wife married again.
In the wilderness a husband was almost a necessity
to a woman; her surroundings made the loss of the
protector and provider an appalling calamity; and
the widow, no matter how sincere her sorrow, soon
remarried—for there were many suitors where women were not over-plenty. If in such a case the one
thought dead returned, the neighbors and the parties
interested seem frequently to have held a sort of
informal court, and to have decided that the woman
should choose either of the two men she wished to
be her husband, the other being pledged to submit
to the decision and leave the settlement. Evidently
no one had the least idea that there was any legal
irregularity in such proceedings.[1]

[1] Incidents of this sort are frequently mentioned. Generally the woman
went back to her first husband. " Early Times in Middle Tennessee,"
John Carr, Nashville, 1859, p. 231.

The McAfees themselves and the escaped convict servant whom they captured typify the two prominent classes of the backwoods people. The frontier, in spite of the outward uniformity of means and manners, is preëminently the place of sharp contrasts. The two extremes of society, the strongest, best, and most adventurous, and the weakest, most shiftless, and vicious, are those which seem naturally to drift to the border. Most of the men who came to the backwoods to hew out homes and rear families were stern, manly, and honest; but there was also a large influx of people drawn from the worst immigrants that perhaps ever were brought to America—the mass of convict servants, redemptioners, and the like, who formed such an excessively undesirable substratum to the otherwise excellent population of the tidewater regions in Virginia and the Carolinas.[1] Many of the southern crackers or poor whites spring from this class, which also in the backwoods gave birth to generations of violent and hardened criminals, and to an even greater number of shiftless, lazy, cowardly cumberers of the earth's surface. They had in many places a permanently bad effect upon the tone of the whole community.

Sharp Contrasts of Backwoods Society.

Moreover, the influence of heredity was no more plainly perceptible than was the extent of individual variation. If a member of a bad family wished to reform, he had every opportunity to do so; if a member of a good family had vicious propensities,

---

[1] See "A Short History of the English Colonies in America," by Henry Cabot Lodge (New York, 1886), for an account of these people.

there was nothing to check them. All qualities, good and bad, are intensified and accentuated in the life of the wilderness. The man who in civilization is merely sullen and bad-tempered becomes a murderous, treacherous ruffian when transplanted to the wilds; while, on the other hand, his cheery, quiet neighbor develops into a hero, ready uncomplainingly to lay down his life for his friend. One who in an eastern city is merely a backbiter and slanderer, in the western woods lies in wait for his foe with a rifle; sharp practice in the east becomes highway robbery in the west; but at the same time negative good-nature becomes active self-sacrifice, and a general belief in virtue is translated into a prompt and determined war upon vice. The ne'er-do-well of a family who in one place has his debts paid a couple of times and is then forced to resign from his clubs and lead a cloudy but innocuous existence on a small pension, in the other abruptly finishes his career by being hung for horse-stealing.

In the backwoods the lawless led lives of abandoned wickedness; they hated good for good's sake, and did their utmost to destroy it. Where the bad element was large, gangs of horse thieves, highwaymen, and other criminals often united with the uncontrollable young men of vicious tastes who were given to gambling, fighting, and the like. They then formed half-secret organizations, often of great extent and with wide ramifications; and if they could control a community they established a reign of terror, driving out both ministers and magistrates, and killing with-

Wicked-ness of the Lawless.

out scruple those who interfered with them. The good men in such a case banded themselves together as regulators and put down the wicked with ruthless severity, by the exercise of lynch law, shooting and hanging the worst off-hand.[1]

Jails were scarce in the wilderness, and often were entirely wanting in a district, which, indeed, was **Summary** quite likely to lack legal officers also. If **Punish-** punishment was inflicted at all it was apt **ments.** to be severe, and took the form of death or whipping. An impromptu jury of neighbors decided with a rough and ready sense of fair play and justice what punishment the crime demanded, and then saw to the execution of their own decree. Whipping was the usual reward of theft. Occasionally torture was resorted to, but not often; and to their honor be it said, the backwoodsmen were horrified at the treatment accorded both to black slaves and to white convict servants in the lowlands.[2]

They were superstitious, of course, believing in witchcraft, and signs and omens; and it may be noted that their superstition showed a singular mixture of old-world survivals and of practices borrowed from the savages or evolved by the very force of their strange surroundings. At the bottom they were deeply religious in their tendencies; and although ministers and meeting-houses were rare, yet

[1] The regulators of backwoods society corresponded exactly to the vigilantes of the western border to-day. In many of the cases of lynch law which have come to my knowledge the effect has been healthy for the community; but sometimes great injustice is done. Generally the vigilantes, by a series of summary executions, do really good work; but I have rarely known them fail, among the men whom they killed for good reason, to also kill one or two either by mistake or to gratify private malice.

[2] See Doddridge.

the backwoods cabins often contained Bibles, and the mothers used to instil into the minds of their children reverence for Sunday,[1] while many even of the hunters refused to hunt on that day.[2] Those of them who knew the right honestly tried to live up to it, in spite of the manifold temptations to backsliding offered by their lives of hard and fierce contention.[3] But Calvinism, though more congenial to them than Episcopacy, and infinitely more so than Catholicism, was too cold for the fiery hearts of the borderers; they were not stirred to the depths of their natures till other creeds, and, above all, Methodism, worked their way to the wilderness.

Religion.

Thus the backwoodsmen lived on the clearings they had hewed out of the everlasting forest; a grim, stern people, strong and simple, powerful for good and evil, swayed by gusts of stormy passion, the love of freedom rooted in their very hearts' core. Their lives were harsh and narrow; they gained their bread by their blood and sweat, in the unending struggle with the wild ruggedness of nature. They suffered terrible injuries at the hands of the red men, and on their foes they waged a terrible warfare in return. They were relentless, revengeful, suspicious, knowing neither ruth nor pity; they were also upright, resolute, and fearless, loyal to their friends, and devoted to their country. In spite of their many failings, they were of all men the best fitted to conquer the wilderness and hold it against all comers.

[1] McAfee MSS.   [2] Doddridge.
[3] Said one old Indian fighter, a Col. Joseph Brown, of Tennessee, with quaint truthfulness, " I have tried also to be a religious man, but have not always, in a life of so much adventure and strife, been able to act consistently."—*Southwestern Monthly*, Nashville, 1851, I., 80.

CHAPTER VI.

BOON AND THE LONG HUNTERS; AND THEIR HUNTING IN NO-MAN'S-LAND, 1769–1774.

THE American backwoodsmen had surged up, wave upon wave, till their mass trembled in the troughs of the Alleghanies, ready to flood the continent beyond. The peoples threatened by them were dimly conscious of the danger which as yet only loomed in the distance. Far off, among their quiet adobe villages, in the sun-scorched lands by the Rio Grande, the slow Indo-Iberian peons and their monkish masters still walked in the tranquil steps of their fathers, ignorant of the growth of the power that was to overwhelm their children and successors; but nearer by, Spaniard and Creole Frenchman, Algonquin and Appalachian, were all uneasy as they began to feel the first faint pressure of the American advance.

As yet they had been shielded by the forest which lay over the land like an unrent mantle. All **The De-** through the mountains, and far beyond, it **batable** stretched without a break; but towards **Land.** the mouth of the Kentucky and Cumberland rivers the landscape became varied with open groves of woodland, with flower-strewn glades and great barrens or prairies of long grass. This region, one of the fairest in the world, was the debatable ground between the northern and the southern Indians. Neither dared dwell therein,[1] but both used it as their hunting-grounds; and it was traversed from end to end by the well marked war traces[2] which they followed when they invaded each other's territory. The whites, on trying to break through the barrier which hemmed them in from the western lands, naturally succeeded best when pressing along the line of least resistance; and so their first great advance was made in this debatable land, where the uncertainly defined hunting-grounds of the Cherokee, Creek, and Chickasaw marched upon those of northern Algonquin and Wyandot.

Unknown and unnamed hunters and Indian traders had from time to time pushed some little way into the wilderness; and they had been followed by others of whom we do indeed know the names, but little more. One explorer had found and named the Cumberland river and mountains, and the great pass called Cumberland Gap.[3] Others had gone far beyond the utmost

First Explorers.

---

[1] This is true as a whole; but along the Mississippi, in the extreme west of the present Kentucky and Tennessee, the Chickasaws held possession. There was a Shawnee town south of the Ohio, and Cherokee villages in southeastern Tennessee.

[2] The backwoodsmen generally used "trace," where western frontiersmen would now say "trail."

[3] Dr. Thomas Walker, of Virginia. He named them after the Duke of Cumberland. Walker was a genuine explorer and surveyor, a man of mark as a pioneer. The journal of his trip across the Cumberland to the headwaters of the Kentucky in 1750 has been preserved, and has just been published by William Cabell Rives (Boston: Little, Brown & Co.). It is very interesting, and Mr. Rives has done a real service in publishing it. Walker and five companions were absent six months. He found traces of earlier

limits this man had reached, and had hunted in the great bend of the Cumberland and in the woodland region of Kentucky, famed amongst the Indians for the abundance of the game.[1] But their accounts excited no more than a passing interest; they came and went without comment, as lonely stragglers had come and gone for nearly a century. The backwoods civilization crept slowly westward without being influenced in its movements by their explorations.[2]

wanderers—probably hunters. One of his companions was bitten by a bear; three of the dogs were wounded by bears, and one killed by an elk; the horses were frequently bitten by rattlesnakes; once a bull-buffalo threatened the whole party. They killed 13 buffaloes, 8 elks, 53 bears, 20 deer, 150 turkeys, and some other game.

[1] Hunters and Indian traders visited portions of Kentucky and Tennessee years before the country became generally known even on the border. (Not to speak of the French, who had long known something of the country, where they had even made trading posts and built furnaces, as see Haywood, etc.) We know the names of a few. Those who went down the Ohio, merely landing on the Kentucky shore, do not deserve mention; the French had done as much for a century. Whites who had been captured by the Indians, were sometimes taken through Tennessee or Kentucky, as John Salling in 1730, and Mrs. Mary Inglis in 1756 (see " Trans-Alleghany Pioneers," Collins, etc.). In 1654 a certain Colonel Wood was in Kentucky. The next real explorer was nearly a century later, though Doherty in 1690, and Adair in 1730, traded with the Cherokees in what is now Tennessee. Walker struck the head-water of the Kentucky in 1750; he had been to the Cumberland in 1748. He made other exploring trips. Christopher Gist went up the Kentucky in 1751. In 1756 and 1758 Forts Loudon and Chissel were built on the Tennessee head-waters, but were soon afterwards destroyed by the Cherokees. In 1761, '62, '63, and for a year or two afterwards, a party of hunters under the lead of one Wallen, hunted on the western waters, going continually farther west. In 1765 Croghan made a sketch of the Ohio River. In 1766 James Smith and others explored Tennessee. Stoner, Harrod, and Lindsay, and a party from South Carolina were near the present site of Nashville in 1767; in the same year John Finley and others were in Kentucky; and it was Finley who first told Boon about it and led him thither.

[2] The attempt to find out the names of the men who first saw the different portions of the western country is not very profitable. The first

Finally, however, among these hunters one arose whose wanderings were to bear fruit; who was destined to lead through the wilderness the first body of settlers that ever established a community in the far west, completely cut off from the seaboard colonies. This was Daniel Boon. He was born in Pennsylvania in 1734,[1] but when only a boy had been brought with the rest of his family to the banks of the Yadkin in North Carolina. Here he grew up, and as soon as he came of age he married, built a log hut, and made a clearing, whereon to farm like the rest of his backwoods neighbors. They all tilled their own clearings, guiding the plow among the charred stumps left when the trees were chopped down and the land burned over, and they were all, as a matter of course, hunters. With Boon hunting and exploration were passions, and the lonely life of the wilderness, with its bold, wild freedom, the only existence for which he really cared. He was a tall, spare, sinewy man, with eyes like an eagle's, and muscles that never tired; the toil and hardship of his life made no impress on his iron frame, unhurt by intemperance of any kind, and

Daniel Boon.

visitors were hunters, simply wandering in search of game, not with any settled purpose of exploration. Who the individual first-comers were, has generally been forgotten. At the most it is only possible to find out the name of some one of several who went to a given locality. The hunters were wandering everywhere. By chance some went to places we now consider important. By chance the names of a few of these have been preserved. But the credit belongs to the whole backwoods race, not to the individual backwoodsman.

[1] August 22, 1734 (according to James Parton, in his sketch of Boon). His grandfather was an English immigrant; his father had married a Quakeress. When he lived on the banks of the Delaware, the country was still a wilderness. He was born in Berks Co.

he lived for eighty-six years, a backwoods hunter to the end of his days. His thoughtful, quiet, pleasant face, so often portrayed, is familiar to every one; it was the face of a man who never blustered or bullied, who would neither inflict nor suffer any wrong, and who had a limitless fund of fortitude, endurance, and indomitable resolution upon which to draw when fortune proved adverse. His self-command and patience, his daring, restless love of adventure, and, in time of danger, his absolute trust in his own powers and resources, all combined to render him peculiarly fitted to follow the career of which he was so fond.

Boon hunted on the western waters at an early date. In the valley of Boon's Creek, a tributary of the Watauga, there is a beech tree still standing, on which can be faintly traced an inscription setting forth that " D. Boon cilled a bar on (this) tree in the year 1760." [1] On the expeditions of which this is the earliest record he was partly hunting on **Henderson,** his own account, and partly exploring on **the Land** behalf of another, Richard Henderson. **Speculator.** Henderson was a prominent citizen of North Carolina,[2] a speculative man of great ambition and energy. He stood high in the colony, was

[1] The inscription is first mentioned by Ramsey, p. 67. See Appendix C, for a letter from the Hon. John Allison, at present (1888) Secretary of State for Tennessee, which goes to prove that the inscription has been on the tree as long as the district has been settled. Of course it cannot be proved that the inscription is by Boon; but there is much reason for supposing that such is the case, and little for doubting it.

[2] He was by birth a Virginian, of mixed Scotch and Welsh descent. See Collins, II., 336; also Ramsey. For Boon's early connection with Henderson, in 1764, see Haywood, 35.

extravagant and fond of display, and his fortune being jeopardized he hoped to more than retrieve it by going into speculations in western lands on an unheard of scale; for he intended to try to establish on his own account a great proprietary colony beyond the mountains. He had great confidence in Boon; and it was his backing which enabled the latter to turn his discoveries to such good account.

Boon's claim to distinction rests not so much on his wide wanderings in unknown lands, for in this respect he did little more than was done by a hundred other backwoods hunters of his generation, but on the fact that he was able to turn his daring woodcraft to the advantage of his fellows. As he himself said, he was an instrument "ordained of God to settle the wilderness." He inspired confidence in all who met him,[1] so that the men of means and influence were willing to trust adventurous enterprises to his care; and his success as an explorer, his skill as a hunter, and his prowess as an Indian fighter, enabled him to bring these enterprises to a successful conclusion, and in some degree to control the wild spirits associated with him.

Boon's expeditions into the edges of the wilderness whetted his appetite for the unknown. He had heard of great hunting-grounds in the far interior from a stray hunter and Indian trader,[2] who had himself seen them, and on May 1, 1769, he left his

---

[1] Even among his foes; he is almost the only American praised by Lt.-Gov. Henry Hamilton of Detroit, for instance (see *Royal Gazette*, July 15, 1780).   [2] John Finley.

home on the Yadkin "to wander through the wilderness of America in quest of the country of **Boon** Kentucky."[1] He was accompanied by five **Goes to** other men, including his informant, and **Kentucky.** struck out towards the northwest, through the tangled mass of rugged mountains and gloomy forests. During five weeks of severe toil the little band journeyed through vast solitudes, whose utter loneliness can with difficulty be understood by those who have not themselves dwelt and hunted in primæval mountain forests. Then, early in June, the adventurers broke through the interminable wastes of dim woodland, and stood on the threshold of the beautiful blue-grass region of Kentucky; a land of running waters, of groves and glades, of prairies, cane-brakes, and stretches of lofty forest. It was teeming with game. The shaggy-maned herds of unwieldy buffalo —the bison as they should be called—had beaten out broad roads through the forest, and had furrowed the prairies with trails along which they had travelled for countless generations. The round-horned elk, with spreading, massive antlers, the lordliest of the deer tribe throughout the world, abounded, and like the buffalo travelled in bands not only through the woods but also across the reaches of waving grass land. The deer were extraordinarily numerous, and so were bears, while wolves and panthers were plentiful.

---

[1] " The Adventures of Colonel Daniel Boon, formerly a hunter "; nominally written by Boon himself, in 1784, but in reality by John Filson, the first Kentucky historian,—a man who did history good service, albeit a true sample of the small hedge-school pedant. The old pioneer's own language would have been far better than that which Filson used ; for the latter's composition is a travesty of Johnsonese in its most aggravated form. For Filson see Durrett's admirable " Life " in the Filson Club Publications.

Wherever there was a salt spring the country was fairly thronged with wild beasts of many kinds. For six months Boon and his companions enjoyed such hunting as had hardly fallen to men of their race since the Germans came out of the Hercynian forest.[1]

In December, however, they were attacked by Indians. Boon and a companion were captured; and when they escaped they found their camp broken up, and the rest of the party scattered and gone home. About this time they were joined by Squire Boon, the brother of the great hunter, and himself a woodsman of but little less skill, together with another adventurer; the two had travelled through the immense wilderness, partly to explore it and partly with the hope of finding the original adventurers, which they finally succeeded in doing more by good luck than design. Soon afterwards Boon's companion in his first short captivity was again surprised by the Indians, and this time was slain [2]—the first of the thousands of human beings

Wanderings in Kentucky.

---

[1] The Nieblung Lied tells of Siegfried's feats with bear, buffalo, elk, wolf, and deer :

> " Danach schlug er wieder einen Büffel und einen Elk
> Vier starkes Auer nieder und einen grimmen Schelk,
> So schnell trug ihn die Mähre, dasz ihm nichts entsprang ;
> Hinden und Hirsche wurden viele sein Fang.
> . . . . ein Waldthier fürchterlich,
> Einen wilden Bären."

Siegfried's elk was our moose ; and like the American frontiersmen of to-day, the old German singer calls the Wisent or Bison a buffalo—European sportsmen now committing an equally bad blunder by giving it the name of the extinct aurochs. Be it observed also that the hard fighting, hard drinking, boastful hero of Nieblung fame used a " spür hund," just as his representative of Kentucky or Tennessee used a track hound a thousand years later.

[2] His name was John Stewart.

with whose life-blood Kentucky was bought. The attack was entirely unprovoked. The Indians had wantonly shed the first blood. The land belonged to no one tribe, but was hunted over by all, each feeling jealous of every other intruder; they attacked the whites, not because the whites had wronged them, but because their invariable policy was to kill any strangers on any grounds over which they themselves ever hunted, no matter what man had the best right thereto. The Kentucky hunters were promptly taught that in this no-man's-land, teeming with game and lacking even a solitary human habitation, every Indian must be regarded as a foe.

The man who had accompanied Squire Boon was terrified by the presence of the Indians, and now re-

Boon's Lonely Sojourn.

turned to the settlements. The two brothers remained alone on their hunting-grounds throughout the winter, living in a little cabin. About the first of May Squire set off alone to the settlements to procure horses and ammunition. For three months Daniel Boon remained absolutely alone in the wilderness, without salt, sugar, or flour, and without the companionship of so much as a horse or a dog.[1] But the solitude-loving hunter,

[1] His remaining absolutely alone in the wilderness for such a length of time is often spoken of with wonder; but here again Boon stands merely as the backwoods type, not as an exception. To this day many hunters in the Rockies do the same. In 1880, two men whom I knew wintered to the west of the Bighorns, 150 miles from any human beings. They had salt and flour, however; but they were nine months without seeing a white face. They killed elk, buffalo, and a moose; and had a narrow escape from a small Indian war party. Last winter (1887–88) an old trapper, a friend of mine in the days when he hunted buffalo, spent five months entirely alone in the mountains north of the Flathead country.

dauntless and self-reliant, enjoyed to the full his
wild, lonely life ; he passed his days hunting and
exploring, wandering hither and thither over the
country, while at night he lay off in the canebrakes
or thickets, without a fire, so as not to attract the
Indians.   Of the latter he saw many signs, and they
sometimes came to his camp, but his sleepless wari-
ness enabled him to avoid capture.

Late in July his brother returned, and met him
according to appointment at the old camp.   Other
hunters also now came into the Kentucky   Other
wilderness, and Boon joined a small party   Hunters
of them for a short time.   Such a party of   Join Him.
hunters is always glad to have any thing wherewith
to break the irksome monotony of the long evenings
passed round the camp fire ; and a book or a greasy
pack of cards was as welcome in a camp of Kentucky
riflemen in 1770 as it is to a party of Rocky Mountain hunters in 1888.   Boon has recorded in his own
quaint phraseology an incident of his life during this
summer, which shows how eagerly such a little band
of frontiersmen read a book, and how real its characters became to their minds.   He was encamped with
five other men on Red River, and they had with
them for their " amusement the history of Samuel
Gulliver's travels, wherein he gave an account of
his young master, Glumdelick, careing [sic] him on a
market day for a show to a town called Lulbegrud."
In the party who, amid such strange surroundings,
read and listened to Dean Swift's writings was a
young man named Alexander Neely.   One night he
came into camp with two Indian scalps, taken from

a Shawnese village he had found on a creek running
into the river; and he announced to the circle of
grim wilderness veterans that "he had been that day
to Lulbegrud, and had killed two Brobdignags in
their capital." To this day the creek by which the
two luckless Shawnees lost their lives is known as
Lulbegrud Creek.[1]

Soon after this encounter the increasing danger
from the Indians drove Boon back to the valley of
the Cumberland River, and in the spring of 1771 he
returned to his home on the Yadkin.

A couple of years before Boon went to Kentucky,
Steiner, or Stoner, and Harrod, two hunters from
Pittsburg, who had passed through the Illinois, came
down to hunt in the bend of the Cumberland, where
Nashville now stands; they found vast numbers of
buffalo, and killed a great many, especially around
the licks, where the huge clumsy beasts had fairly
destroyed most of the forest, treading down the
young trees and bushes till the ground was left bare
or covered with a rich growth of clover. The

[1] Deposition of Daniel Boon, September 15, 1796. Certified copy from
Deposition Book No. 1, page 156, Clarke County Court, Ky. First published by Col. John Mason Brown, in " Battle of the Blue Licks," p. 40
(Frankfort, 1882). The book which these old hunters read around their
camp-fire in the Indian-haunted primæval forest a century and a quarter
ago has by great good-luck been preserved, and is in Col. Durrett's library
at Louisville. It is entitled the " Works of Dr. Jonathan Swift, London,
MDCCLXV," and is in two small volumes. On the title-page is written
" A. Neely, 1770."

Frontiersmen are often content with the merest printed trash ; but the
better men among them appreciate really good literature quite as much as
any other class of people. In the long winter evenings they study to good
purpose books as varied as Dante, Josephus, Macaulay, Longfellow, Parton's " Life of Jackson," and the Rollo stories—to mention only volumes
that have been especial favorites with my own cowboys and hunters.

bottoms and the hollows between the hills were
thickset with cane. Sycamore grew in the low
ground, and towards the Mississippi were to be
found the persimmon and cottonwood. Sometimes
the forest was open and composed of huge trees;
elsewhere it was of thicker, smaller growth.[1] Everywhere game abounded, and it was nowhere very wary.

Other hunters of whom we know even the names
of only a few, had been through many parts of the
wilderness before Boon, and earlier still Frenchmen
had built forts and smelting furnaces on the Cumberland, the Tennessee, and the head tributaries of the
Kentucky.[2] Boon is interesting as a leader and explorer; but he is still more interesting as a type.
The west was neither discovered, won, nor settled
by any single man. No keen-eyed statesman planned
the movement, nor was it carried out by any great
military leader; it was the work of a whole people,
of whom each man was impelled mainly by sheer
love of adventure; it was the outcome of the ceaseless strivings of all the dauntless, restless backwoods
folk to win homes for their descendants and to
each penetrate deeper than his neighbors into the
remote forest hunting-grounds where the perilous
pleasures of the chase and of war could be best en-

[1] MS. diary of Benj. Hawkins, 1796. Preserved in Nash. Historical
Soc. In 1796 buffalo were scarce ; but some fresh signs of them were still
seen at licks.

[2] Haywood, p. 75, etc. It is a waste of time to quarrel over who first discovered a particular tract of this wilderness. A great many hunters
traversed different parts at different times, from 1760 on, each practically
exploring on his own account. We do not know the names of most of
them ; those we do know are only worth preserving in county histories and
the like ; the credit belongs to the race, not the indvidual.

joyed. We owe the conquest of the west to all the backwoodsmen, not to any solitary individual among them ; where all alike were strong and daring there was no chance for any single man to rise to unquestioned preëminence.

In the summer of 1769 a large band of hunters[1] crossed the mountains to make a long hunt in the **The Long** western wilderness, the men clad in hunt- **Hunters.** ing-shirts, moccasins, and leggings, with traps, rifles, and dogs, and each bringing with him two or three horses. They made their way over the mountains, forded or swam the rapid, timber-choked streams, and went down the Cumberland, till at last they broke out of the forest and came upon great barrens of tall grass. One of their number was killed by a small party of Indians ; but they saw no signs of human habitations. Yet they came across mounds and graves and other remains of an ancient people who had once lived in the land, but had died out of it long ages before the incoming of the white men.[2]

The hunters made a permanent camp in one place, and returned to it at intervals to deposit their skins and peltries. Between times they scattered out singly or in small bands. They hunted all through the year, killing vast quantities of every kind of game. Most of it they got by fair still-hunting,

[1] From twenty to forty. Compare Haywood and Marshall, both of whom are speaking of the same bodies of men ; Ramsey makes the mistake of supposing they are speaking of different parties ; Haywood dwells on the feats of those who descended the Cumberland ; Marshall of those who went to Kentucky.

[2] The so-called mound builders ; now generally considered to have been simply the ancestors of the present Indian races.

but some by methods we do not now consider legitimate, such as calling up a doe by imitating the bleat of a fawn, and shooting deer from a scaffold when they came to the salt licks at night. Nevertheless, most of the hunters did not approve of "crusting" the game—that is, of running it down on snowshoes in the deep mid-winter snows.

At the end of the year some of the adventurers returned home; others [1] went north into the Kentucky country, where they hunted for several months before recrossing the mountains; while the remainder, led by an old hunter named Kasper Mansker, [2] built two boats and hollowed out of logs two pirogues or dugouts—clumsier but tougher craft than the light birch-bark canoes—and started down the Cumberland. At the French Lick, where Nashville now stands, they saw enormous quantities of buffalo, elk, and other game, more than they had ever seen before in any one place. Some of their goods were taken by a party of Indians they met, but some French traders whom they likewise encountered, treated them well and gave them salt, flour, tobacco, and taffia, the last being especially prized, as they had had no spirits for a year. They went down to Natchez, sold their furs, hides, oil, and tallow, and some returned by sea, while others, including Mansker, came overland with a drove of horses that was being taken through the Indian nations to Georgia. From the length of time all these men, as well as Boon and his companions,

[1] Led by one James Knox.

[2] His real name was Kasper Mansker, as his signature shows, but he was always spoken of as Mansco.

were absent, they were known as the Long Hunters, and the fame of their hunting and exploring spread all along the border and greatly excited the young men.[1]

In 1771 many hunters crossed over the mountains and penetrated far into the wilderness, to work huge havoc among the herds of game. Some of them came in bands, and others singly, and many of the mountains, lakes, rivers, and creeks of Tennessee are either called after the leaders among these old hunters and wanderers, or else by their names perpetuate the memory of some incident of their hunting trips.[2]

Mansker himself came back, a leader among his comrades, and hunted many years in the woods **The** alone or with others of his kind, and saw **Hunter** and did many strange things. One winter **Mansker.** he and those who were with him built a skin house from the hides of game, and when their ammunition gave out they left three of their number and all of their dogs at the skin house and went to the settlements for powder and lead. When they returned they found that two of the men had been killed and the other chased away by the Indians, who, however, had not found the camp. The dogs, having seen no human face for three months, were very wild, yet in a few days became as tame and well trained as ever. They killed such

[1] McAfee MSS. ("Autobiography of Robt. McAfee"). Sometimes the term Long Hunters was used as including Boon, Finley, and their companions, sometimes not ; in the McAfee MSS. it is explicitly used in the former sense.

[2] See Haywood for Clinch River, Drake's Pond, Mansco's Lick, **Greasy** Rock, etc., etc.

enormous quantities of buffalo, elk, and especially deer, that they could not pack the hides into camp, and one of the party, during an idle moment and in a spirit of protest against fate,[1] carved on the peeled trunk of a fallen poplar, where it long remained, the sentence: " 2300 deer skins lost; ruination by God!" The soul of this thrifty hunter must have been further grieved when a party of Cherokees visited their camp and took away all the camp utensils and five hundred hides. The whites found the broad track they made in coming in, but could not find where they had gone out, each wily redskin then covering his own trail, and the whole number apparently breaking up into several parties.

Sometimes the Indians not only plundered the hunting camps but killed the hunters as well, and the hunters retaliated in kind. Often the white men and red fought one another whenever they met, and displayed in their conflicts all the cunning and merciless ferocity that made forest warfare so dreadful. Terrible deeds of prowess were done by the mighty men on either side. It was a war of stealth and cruelty, and ceaseless, sleepless watchfulness. The contestants had sinewy frames and iron wills, keen eyes and steady hands, hearts as bold as they were ruthless. Their moccasined feet made no sound as they stole softly on the camp of a sleeping enemy or crept to ambush him while he himself still-hunted or waylaid the deer, A favorite stratagem was to imitate the call of game. especially the gobble of the wild turkey, and thus to

Life in the Wilderness.

[1] A hunter named Bledsoe ; Collins, II., 418.

lure the would-be hunter to his fate. If the deceit was guessed at, the caller was himself stalked. The men grew wonderfully expert in detecting imitation. One old hunter, Castleman by name, was in after years fond of describing how an Indian nearly lured him to his death. It was in the dusk of the evening, when he heard the cries of two great wood owls near him. Listening attentively, he became convinced that all was not right. " The woo-woo call and the woo-woo answer were not well timed and toned, and the babel-chatter was a failure. More than this, they seemed to be on the ground." Creeping cautiously up, and peering through the brush, he saw something the height of a stump between two forked trees. It did not look natural; he aimed, pulled trigger, and killed an Indian.

Each party of Indians or whites was ever on the watch to guard against danger or to get the chance of taking vengeance for former wrongs. The dark woods saw a myriad lonely fights where red warrior or white hunter fell and no friend of the fallen ever knew his fate, where his sole memorial was the scalp that hung in the smoky cabin or squalid wigwam of the victor.

The rude and fragmentary annals of the frontier are filled with the deeds of men, of whom Mansker **Mansker's** can be taken as a type. He was a won-**Adven-** derful marksman and woodsman, and was **tures.** afterwards made a colonel of the frontier militia, though, being of German descent, he spoke only broken English.[1] Like most of the hunters

---

[1] Carr's " Early Times in Middle Tennessee," pp. 52, 54, 56, etc.

he became specially proud of his rifle, calling it
" Nancy "; for they were very apt to know each
his favorite weapon by some homely or endearing
nickname.   Every forest sight or sound was familiar to him.   He knew the cries of the birds and
beasts so well that no imitation could deceive him.
Once he was nearly taken in by an unusually perfect imitation of a wild gobbler; but he finally
became suspicious, and " placed " his adversary behind a large tree.   Having perfect confidence in his
rifle, and knowing that the Indians rarely fired except at close range—partly because they were poor
shots, partly because they loaded their guns too lightly
—he made no attempt to hide.   Feigning to pass to
the Indian's right, the latter, as he expected, tried
to follow him; reaching an opening in a glade,
Mansker suddenly wheeled and killed his foe.   When
hunting he made his home sometimes in a hollow
tree, sometimes in a hut of buffalo hides; for the
buffalo were so plenty that once when a lick was
discovered by himself and a companion,[1] the latter,
though on horseback, was nearly trampled to death
by the mad rush of a herd they surprised and
stampeded.

He was a famous Indian fighter; one of the earliest of his recorded deeds has to do with an Indian
adventure.   He and three other men were trapping
on Sulphur Fork and Red River, in the great bend
of the Cumberland.   Moving their camp, they came
on recent traces of Indians : deer-carcases and wicker
frames for stretching hides.   They feared to tarry

[1] The hunter Bledsoe mentioned in a previous note.

longer unless they knew something of their foes, and Mansker set forth to explore, and turned towards Red River, where, from the sign, he thought to find the camp. Travelling some twenty miles, he perceived by the sycamore trees in view that he was near the river. Advancing a few steps farther he suddenly found himself within eighty or ninety yards of the camp. He instantly slipped behind a tree to watch. There were only two Indians in camp; the rest he supposed were hunting at a distance. Just as he was about to retire, one of the Indians took up a tomahawk and strolled off in the opposite direction; while the other picked up his gun, put it on his shoulder, and walked directly towards Mansker's hiding-place. Mansker lay close, hoping that he would not be noticed; but the Indian advanced directly towards him until not fifteen paces off. There being no alternative, Mansker cocked his piece, and shot the Indian through the body. The Indian screamed, threw down his gun, and ran towards camp; passing it he pitched headlong down the bluff, dead, into the river. The other likewise ran to camp at the sound of the shot; but Mansker outran him, reached the camp first, and picked up an old gun that was on the ground; but the gun would not go off, and the Indian turned and escaped. Mansker broke the old gun, and returned speedily to his comrades. The next day they all went to the spot, where they found the dead Indian and took away his tomahawk, knife, and bullet-bag; but they never found his gun. The other Indian had come back, had loaded his horses with furs, and was gone. They followed him all that day and all night with a torch of dry cane, and could never overtake him. Finding that there were other bands of Indians about, they then left their hunting grounds. Towards the close of his life old Mansker, like many another fearless and ignorant backwoods fighter, became so much impressed by the fiery earnestness and zeal of the Methodists that he joined himself to them, and became a strong and helpful prop of the community whose first foundations he had helped to lay.

Sometimes the hunters met creole trappers, who sent their tallow, hides, and furs in pirogues and bateaux down the Mississippi to Natchez or Orleans, instead of having to transport them on pack-horses through the perilous forest-tracks across the mountains. They had to encounter dangers from beasts as well as men. More than once we hear of one who, in a canebrake or tangled thicket, was mangled to death by the horns and hoofs of a wounded buffalo.[1] All of the wild beasts were then comparatively unused to contact with rifle-bearing hunters; they were, in consequence, much more ferocious and ready to attack man than at present. The bear were the most numerous of all, after the deer; their chase was a favorite sport. There was just enough danger in it to make it exciting, for though hunters were frequently bitten or clawed, they were hardly ever killed. The wolves were generally very wary; yet in rare instances they, too, were dangerous. The panther was a much more dreaded foe,

Perils of the Hunters.

[1] As Haywood, 81.

and lives were sometimes lost in hunting him ; but even with the panther, the cases where the hunter was killed were very exceptional.

The hunters were in their lives sometimes clean and straight, and sometimes immoral, with a gross and uncouth viciousness. We read of one party of six men and a woman, who were encountered on the Cumberland River ; the woman acted as the wife of a man named Big John, but deserted him for one of his companions, and when he fell sick persuaded the whole party to leave him in the wilderness to die of disease and starvation. Yet those who left him did not in the end fare better, for they were ambushed and cut off, when they had gone down to Natchez, apparently by Indians.

At first the hunters, with their small-bore rifles, were unsuccessful in killing buffalo. Once, when George Rogers Clark had long resided in Kentucky, he and two companions discovered a camp of some forty new-comers actually starving, though buffalo were plenty. Clark and his friends speedily relieved their necessities by killing fourteen of the great beasts; for when once the hunters had found out the knack, the buffalo were easier slaughtered than any other game.[1]

The hunters were the pioneers ; but close behind them came another set of explorers quite as hardy

[1] This continued to be the case until the buffalo were all destroyed. When my cattle came to the Little Missouri, in 1882, buffalo were plenty ; my men killed nearly a hundred that winter, though tending the cattle ; yet an inexperienced hunter not far from us, though a hardy plainsman, killed only three in the whole time. See also Parkman's " Oregon Trail " for an instance of a party of Missouri backwoodsmen who made a characteristic failure in an attempt on a buffalo band.

and resolute. These were the surveyors. The men of chain and compass played a part in the explora-tion of the west scarcely inferior to that of the heroes of axe and rifle. Often, indeed, the parts were combined; Boon himself was a sur-veyor.[1] Vast tracts of western land were continually being allotted either to actual settlers or as bounties to soldiers who had served against the French and Indians. These had to be explored and mapped and as there was much risk as well as reward in the task, it naturally proved attractive to all adventurous young men who had some education, a good deal of ambition, and not too much fortune. A great number of young men of good families, like Washington and Clark, went into the business. Soon after the return of Boon and the Long Hunters, parties of surveyors came down the Ohio,[2] mapping out its course and exploring the Kentucky lands that lay beside it.[3]

The Surveyors.

Among the hunters, surveyors, and explorers who came into the wilderness in 1773 was a band led by three young men named McAfee,—typical backwoodsmen, hardy, adventurous, their frontier recklessness and license tempered by the Calvinism they had learned in their rough log home. They were fond of hunting, but they came to spy out the land and see if it could be made into homes for their children; and in their party were several surveyors. They descended the

The Mc-Afees Visit Kentucky.

---

[1] See Appendix.

[2] An English engineer made a rude survey or table of distances of the Ohio in 1766.

[3] Collins states that in 1770 and 1772 Washington surveyed small tracts in what is now northeastern Kentucky; but this is more than doubtful.

Ohio in dugout canoes, with their rifles, blankets, tomahawks, and fishing-tackle. They met some Shawnees and got on well with them; but while their leader was visiting the chief, Cornstalk, and listening to his fair speeches at his town of Old Chilicothe, the rest of the party were startled to see a band of young Shawnee braves returning from a successful foray on the settlements, driving before them the laden pack-horses they had stolen.[1]

They explored part of Kentucky, and visited the different licks. One, long named Big Bone Lick, was famous because there were scattered about it in incredible quantity the gigantic remains of the extinct mastodon; the McAfees made a tent by stretching their blankets over the huge fossil ribs, and used the disjointed vertebræ as stools on which to sit. Game of many kinds thronged the spaces round the licks; herds of buffalo, elk, and deer, as well as bears and wolves, were all in sight at once. The ground round about some of them was trodden down so that there was not as much grass left as would feed a sheep; and the game trails were like streets, or the beaten roads round a city. A little village to this day recalls by its name the fact that it stands on a former "stamping ground" of the buffalo. At one lick the explorers met with what might have proved a serious adventure. One of the McAfees and a companion were passing round its outskirts, when some others of the party fired at a gang of buffaloes, which stampeded directly towards

[1] All of this is taken from the McAfee MSS., in Colonel Durrett's library.

the two. While his companion scampered up a
leaning mulberry bush, McAfee, less agile, leaped
behind a tree trunk, where he stood sideways till the
buffalo passed, their horns scraping off the bark on
either side ; then he looked round to see his friend
" hanging in the mulberry bush like a coon." [1]

When the party left this lick they followed a
buffalo trail, beaten out in the forest, " the size of
the wagon road leading out of Williamsburg," then
the capital of Virginia It crossed the Kentucky
River at a riffle below where Frankfort now stands.
Thence they started homewards across the Cumberland Mountains, and suffered terribly while making
their way through the " desolate and voiceless solitudes " ; mere wastes of cliffs, crags, caverns, and
steep hillsides covered with pine, laurel, and underbrush.   Twice they were literally starving and were
saved in the nick of time by the killing, on the first
occasion, of a big bull elk, on the next, of a small
spike buck.   At last, sun-scorched and rain-beaten,
foot-sore and leg-weary, their thighs torn to pieces
by the stout briars,[2] and their feet and hands blis-
tered and scalded, they came out in Powell's Valley,
and followed the well-worn hunter's trail across it.
Thence it was easy to reach home, where the tale of
their adventures excited still more the young frontiersmen.

Their troubles were ended for the time being ; but
in Powell's Valley they met other wanderers whose

[1] McAfee MSS. A similar adventure befell my brother Elliott and my
cousin John Roosevelt while they were hunting buffalo on the staked plains
of Texas in 1877.

[2] They evidently wore breech-clouts and leggings, not trowsers.

toil and peril had just begun. There they encountered the company[1] which Daniel Boon was just
Boon Tries leading across the mountains, with the hope
to Settle of making a permanent settlement in far dis-
Kentucky. tant Kentucky.[2] Boon had sold his farm on
the Yadkin and all the goods he could not carry with
him, and in September, 1773, he started for Kentucky
with his wife and his children; five families, and forty
men besides, went with him, driving their horses and
cattle.   It was the first attempt that was made to
settle a region separated by long stretches of wilderness from the already inhabited districts; and it was
doomed to failure.   On approaching the gloomy and
forbidding defiles of the Cumberland Mountains the
party was attacked by Indians.[3]   Six of the men, including Boon's eldest son, were slain, and the cattle
scattered ; and though the backwoodsmen rallied
and repulsed their assailants, yet they had suffered
such loss and damage that they retreated and took
up their abode temporarily on the Clinch River.

In the same year Simon Kenton, afterwards famous
as a scout and Indian fighter, in company with other
hunters, wandered through Kentucky.   Kenton, like
every one else, was astounded at the beauty and
fertility of the land and the innumerable herds of
buffalo, elk, and other game that thronged the trampled ground around the licks. One of his companions
was taken by the Indians, who burned him alive.

McAfee MSS.

[2] Filson's " Boon."

[3] October 10, 1773, Filson's " Boon." The McAfee MSS. speak of
meeting Boon in Powell's Valley and getting home in September ; if so, it
must have been the very end of the month.

In the following year numerous parties of surveyors visited the land. One of these was headed by
Floyd's John Floyd, who was among the ablest
Party Visits of the Kentucky pioneers, and after-
Kentucky. wards played a prominent part in the
young commonwealth, until his death at the hands
of the savages. Floyd was at the time assistant surveyor of Fincastle County; and his party went out
for the purpose of making surveys "by virtue of the
Governor's warrant for officers and soldiers on the
Ohio and its waters." [1]

They started on April 9, 1774,—eight men in all,
—from their homes in Fincastle County.[2] They
went down the Kanawha in a canoe, shooting bear
and deer, and catching great pike and catfish. The
first survey they made was one of two thousand
acres for " Colo. Washington "; and they made another for Patrick Henry. On the way they encountered other parties of surveyors, and learned that an
Indian war was threatened; for a party of thirteen
would-be settlers on the upper Ohio had been attacked, but had repelled their assailants, and in
consequence the Shawnees had declared for war, and

[1] The account of this journey of Floyd and his companions is taken from a
very interesting MS. journal, kept by one of the party—Thomas Hanson.
It was furnished me, together with other valuable papers, through the courtesy of Mr. and Mrs. Daniel Trigg, of Abingdon, Va., and of Dr. George
Ben. Johnston, of Richmond, to whom I take this opportunity of returning
my warm thanks.

[2] From the house of Col. William Preston, " at one o'clock, in high spirits." They took the canoe at the mouth of Elk River, on the 16th. Most
of the diary is, of course, taken up with notes on the character and fertility
of the lands, and memoranda of the surveys made. Especial comment is
made on a burning spring by the Kanawha, which is dubbed " one of the
wonders of the world."

threatened thereafter to kill the Virginians and rob
the Pennsylvanians wherever they found them.[1] The
reason for this discrimination in favor of the citizens
of the Quaker State was that the Virginians with
whom the Indians came chiefly in contact were settlers, whereas the Pennsylvanians were traders. The
marked difference in the way the savages looked at
the two classes received additional emphasis in Lord
Dunmore's war.

At the mouth of the Kanawha [2] the adventurers
found twenty or thirty men gathered together; some
had come to settle, but most wished to explore or
survey the lands. All were in high spirits, and resolute to go to Kentucky, in spite of Indian hostilities.
Some of them joined Floyd, and raised his party to
eighteen men, who started down the Ohio in four
canoes.[3] They found " a battoe loaded with corn,"
apparently abandoned, and took about three bushels
with them. Other parties joined them from time to
time, as they paddled and drifted down stream; and
one or two of their own number, alarmed by further
news of Indian hostilities, went back. Once they
met a party of Delawares, by whom they were not
molested ; and again, two or three of their number
encountered a couple of hostile savages ; and though
no one was hurt, the party were kept on the watch
all the time. They marvelled much at the great
trees—one sycamore was thirty-seven feet in circum-

[1] They received this news on April 17th, and confirmation thereof on the
19th. The dates should be kept in mind, as they show that the Shawnees
had begun hostilities from a fortnight to a month before Cresap's attack and
the murder of Logan's family, which will be described hereafter.

[2] Which they reached on the 20th.   [3] On the 22d.

ference,—and on a Sunday, which they kept as a day of rest, they examined with interest the forest-covered embankments of a fort at the mouth of the Scioto, a memorial of the mound-builders who had vanished centuries before.

When they reached the mouth of the Kentucky[1] they found two Delawares and a squaw, to whom they gave corn and salt. Here they split up, and Floyd and his original party spent a week in the neighborhood, surveying land, going some distance up the Kentucky to a salt lick, where they saw a herd of three hundred buffalo.[2] They then again embarked, and drifted down the Ohio. On May 26th they met two Delawares in a canoe flying a red flag; they had been sent down the river with a pass from the commandant at Fort Pitt to gather their hunters and get them home, in view of the threatened hostilities between the Shawnees and Virginians.[3] The actions of the two Indians were so suspicious, and the news they brought was so alarming, that some of Floyd's companions became greatly alarmed, and wished to go straight on down the Mississippi; but Floyd swore that he would finish his work unless

[1] On May 13th.

[2] There were quarrels among the surveyors. The entry for May 13th runs : " Our company divided, eleven men went up to Harrad's company one hundred miles up the Cantucky or Louisa river (n. b. one Capt. Harrad has been there many months building a kind of Town &c) in order to make improvements. This day a quarrel arose between Mr. Lee and Mr. Hyte ; Lee cut a Stick and gave Hyte a Whiping with it, upon which Mr. Floyd demanded the King's Peace which stopt it sooner that it would have ended if he had not been there."

[3] They said that in a skirmish the whites had killed thirteen Shawnees, two Mingos, and one Delaware (this may or may not mean the massacres by Cresap and Greathouse ; see, *post*, chapter on Lord Dunmore's War).

actually forced off. Three days afterwards they reached the Falls.

Here Floyd spent a fortnight, making surveys in every direction, and then started off to explore the land between the Salt River and the Kentucky. Like the others, he carried his own pack, which consisted of little but his blanket and his instruments. He sometimes had difficulties with his men ; one of them refused to carry the chain one day, and went off to hunt, got lost, and was not found for thirty-six hours. Another time it was noticed that two of the hunters had become sullen, and seemed anxious to leave camp. The following morning, while on the march, the party killed an elk and halted for breakfast ; but the two hunters walked on, and, says the journal, " we never saw them more " ; but whether they got back to the settlements or perished in the wilderness, none could tell.

The party suffered much hardship. Floyd fell sick, and for three days could not travel. They gave him an " Indian sweat," probably building just such a little sweat-house as the Indians use to this day. Others of their number at different times fell ill ; and they were ever on the watch for Indians. In the vast forests, every sign of a human being was the sign of a probable enemy. Once they heard a gun, and another time a sound as of a man calling to another ; and on each occasion they redoubled their caution, keeping guard as they rested, and at night extinguishing their camp-fire and sleeping a mile or two from it.

They built a bark canoe in which to cross the

Kentucky, and on the 1st of July they met another party of surveyors on the banks of that stream.[1] Two or three days afterwards, Floyd and three companions left the others, agreeing to meet them on August 1st, at a cabin built by a man named Harwood, on the south side of the Kentucky, a few miles from the mouth of the Elkhorn. For three weeks they surveyed and hunted, enchanted with the beauty of the country.[2] They then went to the cabin, several days before the appointed time; but to their surprise found every thing scattered over the ground, and two fires burning, while on a tree near the landing was written, "Alarmed by finding some people killed and we are gone down." This left the four adventurers in a bad plight, as they had but fifteen rounds of powder left, and none of them knew the way home. However there was no help for it, and they started off.[3] When they came to the mountains they found it such hard going that they were obliged to throw away their blankets and every thing else except their rifles, hunting-shirts, leggings, and moccasins. Like the other parties of returning explorers, they found this portion of their journey extremely distressing; and they suffered much from sore feet, and also from want of food, until they came on a gang of buffaloes, and killed two. At

---

[1] Where the journal says the land "is like a paradise, it is so good and beautiful.

[2] The journal for July 8th says: "The Land is so good that I cannot give it its due Praise. The undergrowth is Clover, Pea-vine, Cane & Nettles; intermingled with Rich Weed. It's timber is Honey Locust, Black Walnut, Sugar Tree, Hickory, Iron-Wood, Hoop Wood, Mulberry, Ash and Elm and some Oak." And later it dwells on the high limestone cliffs facing the river on both sides.   [3] On July 25th.

last they struck Cumberland Gap, followed a blazed trail across it to Powell's Valley, and on August 9th came to the outlying settlements on Clinch River, where they found the settlers all in their wooden forts, because of the war with the Shawnees.[1]

In this same year many different bodies of hunters and surveyors came into the country, drifting down the Ohio in pirogues. Some forty men led by Harrod and Sowdowsky[2] founded Harrodsburg, where they built cabins and sowed corn; but the Indians killed one of their number, and the rest dispersed. Some returned across the mountains; but Sowdowsky and another went through the woods to the Cumberland River, where they built a canoe, paddled down the muddy Mississippi between unending reaches of lonely marsh and forest, and from New Orleans took ship to Virginia.

Other Attempts at Settlement.

At that time, among other parties of surveyors there was one which had been sent by Lord Dunmore

[1] I have given the account of Floyd's journey at some length as illustrating the experience of a typical party of surveyors. The journal has never hitherto been alluded to, and my getting hold of it was almost accidental.

There were three different kinds of explorers: Boon represents the hunters; the McAfees represent the would-be settlers; and Floyd's party the surveyors who mapped out the land for owners of land grants. In 1774, there were parties of each kind in Kentucky. Floyd's experience shows that these parties were continually meeting others and splitting up; he started out with eight men, at one time was in a body with thirty-seven, and returned home with four.

The journal is written in a singularly clear and legible hand, evidently by a man of good education.

[2] The latter, from his name presumably of Sclavonic ancestry, came originally from New York, always a centre of mixed nationalities. He founded a most respectable family, some of whom have changed their name to Sandusky; but there seems to be no justification for their claim that they gave Sandusky its name, for this is almost certainly a corruption of its old Algonquin title. "American Pioneer" (Cincinnati, 1843), II., p. 325.

to the Falls of the Ohio.   When the war broke out
between the Shawnees and the Virginians, Lord Dunmore, being very anxious for the fate of these surveyors, sent Boon and Stoner to pilot them in; which
the two bush veterans accordingly did, making the
round trip of 800 miles in 64 days.   The outbreak of
the Indian war caused all the hunters and surveyors
to leave Kentucky; and at the end of 1774 there were
no whites left, either there or in what is now middle
Tennessee.   But on the frontier all men's eyes were
turned towards these new and fertile regions.   The
pioneer work of the hunter was over, and that of the
axe-bearing settler was about to begin.

CHAPTER VII.

SEVIER, ROBERTSON, AND THE WATAUGA COMMONWEALTH, 1769-1774.

Soon after the successful ending of the last colonial struggle with France, and the conquest of Canada, the British king issued a proclamation forbidding the English colonists from trespassing on Indian grounds, or moving west of the mountains. But in 1768, at the treaty of Fort Stanwix, the Six Nations agreed to surrender to the English all the lands lying between the Ohio and the Tennessee[1]; and this treaty was at once seized upon by the backwoodsmen as offering an excuse for settling beyond the mountains. However, the Iroquois had ceded lands to which they had no more right than a score or more other Indian tribes; and these latter, not having been consulted, felt at perfect liberty to make war on the intruders. In point of fact, no one tribe or set of tribes could cede Kentucky or Tennessee, because no one tribe or set of tribes owned either. The great hunting-grounds between the Ohio and the Tennessee formed a debatable land, claimed by every tribe that could hold its own against its rivals.[2]

---

[1] Then called the Cherokee.

[2] Volumes could be filled—and indeed it is hardly too much to say, have been filled—with worthless " proofs " of the ownership of Iroquois,

The eastern part of what is now Tennessee consists of a great hill-strewn, forest-clad valley, running from northeast to southwest, bounded on one side by the Cumberland, and on the other by the Great Smoky and Unaka Mountains ; the latter separating it from North Carolina. In this valley arise and end the Clinch, the Holston, the Watauga, the Nolichucky, the French Broad, and the other streams, whose combined volume makes the Tennessee River. The upper end of the valley lies in southwestern Virginia, the head-waters of some of the rivers being well within that State ; and though the province was really part of North Carolina, it was separated therefrom by high mountain chains, while from Virginia it was easy to follow the watercourses down the valley. Thus, as elsewhere among the mountains forming the western frontier, the first movements of population went parallel with, rather than across, the ranges. As in western Virginia the first settlers came, for the most part, from Pennsylvania, so, in turn, in what was then western North Carolina, and is now eastern Tennessee, the first settlers came mainly from Virginia, and, indeed, in great part, from this same Pennsylvanian stock.[1] Of course, in each case

First Settlements in Tennessee. (side note)

Shawnees, or Cherokees, as the case might be. In truth, it would probably have been difficult to get any two members of the same tribe to have pointed out with precision the tribal limits. Each tribe's country was elastic, for it included all lands from which it was deemed possible to drive out the possessors. In 1773 the various parties of Long Hunters had just the same right to the whole of the territory in question that the Indians themselves had.

[1] Campbell MSS.

" The first settlers on Holston River were a remarkable race of people for their intelligence, enterprise, and hardy adventure. The greater por-

there was also a very considerable movement directly westward.[1]   They were a sturdy race, enterprising

tion of them had emigrated from the counties of Botetourt, Augusta, and Frederick, and others along the same valley, and from the upper counties of Maryland and Pennsylvania; were mostly descendants of Irish stock, and generally where they had any religious opinions, were Presbyterians. A very large proportion were religious, and many were members of the church. There were some families, however, and amongst the most wealthy, that were extremely wild and dissipated in their habits.

"The first clergyman that came among them was the Rev. Charles Cummings, an Irishman by birth, but educated in Pennsylvania. This gentleman was one of the first settlers, defended his domicile for years with his rifle in hand, and built his first meeting-house on the very spot where he and two or three neighbors and one of his servants had had a severe skirmish with the Indians, in which one of his party was killed and another wounded. Here he preached to a very large and most respectable congregation for twenty or thirty years. He was a zealous whig, and contributed much to kindle the patriotic fire which blazed forth among these people in the revolutionary struggle."

This is from a MS. sketch of the Holston Pioneers, by the Hon. David Campbell, a son of one of the first settlers. The Campbell family, of Presbyterian Irish stock, first came to Pennsylvania, and drifted south. In the revolutionary war it produced good soldiers and commanders, such as William and Arthur Campbell. The Campbells intermarried with the Prestons, Breckenridges, and other historic families; and their blood now runs in the veins of many of the noted men of the States south of the Potomac and Ohio.

[1] The first settlers on the Watauga included both Virginians (as "Captain" William Bean, whose child was the first born in what is now Tennessee; Ramsey, 94) and Carolinians (Haywood, 37). But many of these Carolina hill people were, like Boon and Henderson, members of families who had drifted down from the north. The position of the Presbyterian churches in all this western hill country shows the origin of that portion of the people which gave the tone to the rest; and, as we have already seen, while some of the Presbyterians penetrated to the hills from Charleston, most came down from the north. The Presbyterian blood was, of course, Irish or Scotch; and the numerous English from the coast regions also mingled with the two former kindred stocks, and adopted their faith. The Huguenots, Hollanders, and many of the Germans, being of Calvinistic creed, readily assimilated themselves to the Presbyterians. The absence of Episcopacy on the western border, while in part indicating merely the lack of religion in the backwoods, and the natural growth of dissent in such a society, also indicates that the people were not of pure English descent, and were of different stock from those east of them.

and intelligent, fond of the strong excitement inherent in the adventurous frontier life. Their untamed and turbulent passions, and the lawless freedom **The First** of their lives, made them a population very **Settlers.** productive of wild, headstrong characters; yet, as a whole, they were a God-fearing race, as was but natural in those who sprang from the loins of the Irish Calvinists. Their preachers, all Presbyterians, followed close behind the first settlers, and shared their toil and dangers; they tilled their fields rifle in hand, and fought the Indians valorously. They felt that they were dispossessing the Canaanites, and were thus working the Lord's will in preparing the land for a race which they believed was more truly His chosen people than was that nation which Joshua led across the Jordan. They exhorted no less earnestly in the bare meeting-houses on Sunday, because their hands were roughened with guiding the plow and wielding the axe on week-days; for they did not believe that being called to preach the word of God absolved them from earning their living by the sweat of their brows. The women, the wives of the settlers, were of the same iron temper. They fearlessly fronted every danger the men did, and they worked quite as hard. They prized the knowledge and learning they themselves had been forced to do without; and many a backwoods woman by thrift and industry, by the sale of her butter and cheese, and the calves from her cows, enabled her husband to give his sons good schooling, and perhaps to provide for some favored member of the family the opportunity to secure a really first-class education.[1]

[1] Campbell MSS.

The valley in which these splendid pioneers of our people settled, lay directly in the track of the Indian marauding parties, for the great war trail used by the Cherokees and by their northern foes ran along its whole length. This war trail, or war trace as it was then called, was in places very distinct, although apparently never as well marked as were some of the buffalo trails. It sent off a branch to Cumberland Gap, whence it ran directly north through Kentucky to the Ohio, being there known as the warriors' path. Along these trails the northern and southern Indians passed and repassed when they went to war against each other; and of course they were ready and eager to attack any white man who might settle down along their course.

In 1769, the year that Boon first went to Kentucky, the first permanent settlers came to the banks of the **Growth of the Settlement.** Watauga,[1] the settlement being merely an enlargement of the Virginia settlement, which had for a short time existed on the head-waters of the Holston, especially near Wolf Hills.[2] At first the settlers thought they were still in the domain of Virginia, for at that time the line marking her southern boundary had not been run so far west.[3] Indeed, had they not considered the land

---

[1] For this settlement see especially " Civil and Political History of the State of Tennessee," John Haywood (Knoxville, 1823), p. 37 ; also " Annals of Tennessee," J. G. M. Ramsey (Charleston, 1853), p. 92 ; " History of Middle Tennessee," A. W. Putnam (Nashville, 1859), p. 21; the " Address " of the Hon. John Allison to the Tennessee Press Association (Nashville, 1887) ; and the " History of Tennessee," by James Phelan (Boston, 1888).

[2] Now Abingdon.

[3] It only went to Steep Rock.

as belonging to Virginia, they would probably not at the moment have dared to intrude farther on territory claimed by the Indians. But while the treaty between the crown and the Iroquois at Fort Stanwix[1] had resulted in the cession of whatever right the Six Nations had to the southwestern territory, another treaty was concluded about the same time[2] with the Cherokees, by which the latter agreed to surrender their claims to a small portion of this country, though as a matter of fact before the treaty was signed white settlers had crowded beyond the limits allowed them. These two treaties, in the first of which one set of tribes surrendered a small portion of land, while in the second an entirely different confederacy surrendered a larger tract, which, however, included part of the first cession, are sufficient to show the absolute confusion of the Indian land titles.

But in 1771, one of the new-comers,[3] who was a practical surveyor, ran out the Virginia boundary line some distance to the westward, and discovered that the Watauga settlement came within the limits of North Carolina. Hitherto the settlers had supposed that they themselves were governed by the Virginian law, and that their rights as against the Indians were guaranteed by the Virginian government ; but this discovery threw them back upon their own resources. They suddenly found themselves

---

[1] November 5, 1768.

[2] October 14, 1768, at Hard Labor, S. C., confirmed by the treaty of October 18, 1770, at Lockabar, S. C. Both of these treaties acknowledged the rights of the Cherokees to the major part of these northwestern hunting-grounds.

[3] Anthony Bledsoe.

obliged to organize a civil government, under which they themselves should live, and at the same time to enter into a treaty on their own account with the neighboring Indians, to whom the land they were on apparently belonged.

The first need was even more pressing than the second. North Carolina was always a turbulent and disorderly colony, unable to enforce law and justice even in the long-settled districts; so that it was wholly out of the question to appeal to her for aid in governing a remote and outlying community. Moreover, about the time that the Watauga commonwealth was founded, the troubles in North Carolina came to a head. Open war ensued between the adherents of the royal governor, Tryon, on the one hand, and the Regulators, as the insurgents styled themselves, on the other, the struggle ending with the overthrow of the Regulators at the battle of the Alamance.[1]

As a consequence of these troubles, many people from the back counties of North Carolina crossed the mountains, and took up their abode among the pioneers on the Watauga[2] and upper Holston; the beautiful valley of the Nolichucky soon receiving its share of this stream of immigration. Among the first comers were many members of the class of desperate

[1] May 16, 1771.

[2] It is said that the greatest proportion of the early settlers came from Wake County, N. C., as did Robertson; but many of them, like Robertson, were of Virginian birth; and the great majority were of the same stock as the Virginian and Pennsylvanian mountaineers. Of the five members of the " court " or governing committee of Watauga, three were of Virginian birth, one came from South Carolina, and the origin of the other is not specified. Ramsey, 107.

adventurers always to be found hanging round the outskirts of frontier civilization. Horse-thieves, murderers, escaped bond-servants, runaway debtors—all, in fleeing from the law, sought to find a secure asylum in the wilderness. The brutal and lawless wickedness of these men, whose uncouth and raw savagery was almost more repulsive than that of city criminals, made it imperative upon the decent members of the community to unite for self-protection. The desperadoes were often mere human beasts of prey; they plundered whites and Indians impartially. They not only by their thefts and murders exasperated the Indians into retaliating on innocent whites, but, on the other hand, they also often deserted their own color and went to live among the redskins, becoming their leaders in the worst outrages.[1]

But the bulk of the settlers were men of sterling worth ; fit to be the pioneer fathers of a mighty and beautiful state. They possessed the courage *Character* that enabled them to defy outside foes, to- *of the* gether with the rough, practical common- *Settlers.* sense that allowed them to establish a simple but effective form of government, so as to preserve order among themselves. To succeed in the wilderness, it

[1] In Collins, II., 345, is an account of what may be termed a type family of these frontier barbarians. They were named Harpe ; and there is something revoltingly bestial in the record of their crimes ; of how they travelled through the country, the elder brother, Micajah Harpe, with two wives, the younger with only one ; of the appalling number of murders they committed, for even small sums of money ; of their unnatural proposal to kill all their children, so that they should not be hampered in their flight ; of their life in the woods, like wild beasts, and the ignoble ferocity of their ends. Scarcely less sombre reading is the account of how they were hunted down, and of the wolfish eagerness the borderers showed to massacre the women and children as well as the men.

was necessary to possess not only daring, but also
patience and the capacity to endure grinding toil.
The pioneers were hunters and husbandmen.   Each,
by the aid of axe and brand, cleared his patch of corn
land in the forest, close to some clear, swift-flowing
stream, and by his skill with the rifle won from
canebrake and woodland the game on which his
family lived until the first crop was grown.

A few of the more reckless and foolhardy, and
more especially of those who were either merely hunters and not farmers, or else who were of doubtful
character, lived entirely by themselves; but, as a rule,
each knot of settlers was gathered together into a
little stockaded hamlet, called a fort or station.   This
system of defensive villages was very distinctive of
pioneer backwoods life, and was unique of its kind ;
without it the settlement of the west and southwest
would have been indefinitely postponed.   In no other
way could the settlers have combined for defence,
while yet retaining their individual ownership of the
land.   The Watauga forts or palisaded villages were
of the usual kind, the cabins and blockhouses connected by a heavy loop-holed picket.   They were
admirably adapted for defence with the rifle.   As
there was no moat, there was a certain danger from an
attack with fire unless water was stored within ; and
it was of course necessary to guard carefully against
surprise.   But to open assault they were practically
impregnable, and they therefore offered a sure haven
of refuge to the settlers in case of an Indian inroad.
In time of peace, the inhabitants moved out, to live
in their isolated log-cabins and till the stump-dotted

clearings. Trails led through the dark forests from
one station to another, as well as to the settled districts beyond the mountains ; and at long intervals
men drove along them bands of pack-horses, laden
with the few indispensable necessaries the settlers
could not procure by their own labor. The pack-
horse was the first, and for a long time the only,
method of carrying on trade in the backwoods ; and
the business of the packer was one of the leading
frontier industries.

The settlers worked hard and hunted hard, and lived
both plainly and roughly. Their cabins were roofed
with clapboards, or huge shingles, split from Their Mode
the log with maul and wedge, and held in   of Life.
place by heavy stones, or by poles ; the floors were
made of rived puncheons, hewn smooth on one surface ; the chimney was outside the hut, made of rock
when possible, otherwise of logs thickly plastered
with clay that was strengthened with hogs' bristles
or deer hair ; in the great fire-place was a tongue on
which to hang pot-hooks and kettle ; the unglazed
window had a wooden shutter, and the door was
made of great clapboards.[1] The men made their own
harness, farming implements, and domestic utensils ;
and, as in every other community still living in the
heroic age, the smith was a person of the utmost importance. There was but one thing that all could
have in any quantity, and that was land ; each had
all of this he wanted for the taking,—or if it
was known to belong to the Indians, he got its use

[1] In "American Pioneers," II., 445, is a full description of the better
sort of backwoods log-cabin.

for a few trinkets or a flask of whisky. A few of the settlers still kept some of the Presbyterian austerity of character, as regards amusements; but, as a rule, they were fond of horse-racing, drinking, dancing, and fiddling. The corn-shuckings, flax-pullings, log-rollings (when the felled timber was rolled off the clearings), house-raisings, maple-sugar-boilings, and the like were scenes of boisterous and light-hearted merriment, to which the whole neighborhood came, for it was accounted an insult if a man was not asked in to help on such occasions, and none but a base churl would refuse his assistance. The backwoods people had to front peril and hardship without stint, and they loved for the moment to leap out of the bounds of their narrow lives and taste the coarse pleasures that are always dear to a strong, simple, and primitive race. Yet underneath their moodiness and their fitful light-heartedness lay a spirit that when roused was terrible in its ruthless and stern intensity of purpose.

Such were the settlers of the Watauga, the founders of the commonwealth that grew into the State of Tennessee, who early in 1772 decided that they must form some kind of government that would put down wrong-doing and work equity between man and man. Two of their number already towered head and shoulders above the rest in importance and merit especial mention; for they were destined for the next thirty years to play the chief parts in the history of that portion of the Southwest which largely through their own efforts became the State of Tennessee. These two men, neither of them yet thirty years of age, were John Sevier and James Robertson.[1]

Robertson first came to the Watauga early in 1770.[2] He had then been married for two years, and had been "learning his letters and to spell" from his well-educated wife; for he belonged to a backwoods family, even poorer than the average, and he had not so much as received the rudimentary education that could be acquired at an "old-field" school. But he was a man of remarkable natural powers, above the medium height,[3] with wiry, robust form, light-blue eyes, fair complexion, and dark hair; his somewhat sombre face had in it a look of self-contained strength that made it impressive; and his taciturn, quiet, masterful way of dealing with men and affairs, together with his singular mixture of cool caution and most adventurous daring, gave him an immediate hold even upon such lawless spirits as those of the border. He was a mighty hunter; but, unlike Boon, hunting and exploration were to him secondary affairs, and he came to examine the lands with the eye of a pioneer settler. He intended to

James Robertson.

---

[1] Both were born in Virginia; Sevier in Rockingham County, September 23, 1745, and Robertson in Brunswick County, June 28, 1742.

[2] Putnam, p. 21; who, however, is evidently in error in thinking he was accompanied by Boon, as the latter was then in Kentucky. A recent writer revives this error in another form, stating that Robertson accompanied Boon to the Watauga in 1769. Boon, however, left on his travels on May 1, 1769, and in June was in Kentucky; whereas Putnam not only informs us definitely that Robertson went to the Watauga for the first time in 1770, but also mentions that when he went his eldest son was already born, and this event took place in June, 1769, so that it is certain Boon and Robertson were not together.

[3] The description of his looks is taken from the statements of his descendants, and of the grandchildren of his contemporaries.

have a home where he could bring up his family, and, if possible, he wished to find rich lands, with good springs, whereto he might lead those of his neighbors who, like himself, eagerly desired to rise in the world, and to provide for the well-being of their children.

To find such a country Robertson, then dwelling in North Carolina, decided to go across the mountains. **He Goes** He started off alone on his exploring expe- **to the** dition, rifle in hand, and a good horse under **Watauga.** him. He crossed the ranges that continue northward the Great Smokies, and spent the summer in the beautiful hill country where the springs of the western waters flowed from the ground. He had never seen so lovely a land. The high valleys, through which the currents ran, were hemmed in by towering mountain walls, with cloud-capped peaks. The fertile loam forming the bottoms was densely covered with the growth of the primæval forest, broken here and there by glade-like openings, where herds of game grazed on the tall, thick grass.

Robertson was well treated by the few settlers, and stayed long enough to raise a crop of corn, the stand-by of the backwoods pioneer ; like every other hunter, explorer, Indian fighter, and wilderness wanderer, he lived on the game he shot, and the small quantity of maize he was able to carry with him.[1] In the late fall, however, when recrossing the mountain on his way home through the trackless forests, both game and corn failed him. He lost his way, was forced to abandon his horse among impassable preci-

[1] The importance of maize to the western settler is shown by the fact that in our tongue it has now monopolized the title of corn.

pices, and finally found his rifle useless owing to the powder having become soaked. For fourteen days he lived almost wholly on nuts and wild berries, and was on the point of death from starvation, when he met two hunters on horseback, who fed him and let him ride their horses by turns, and brought him safely to his home.

Such hardships were little more than matter-of-course incidents in a life like his; and he at once prepared to set out with his family for the new land. His accounts greatly excited his neighbors, and sixteen families made ready to accompany him. The little caravan started, under Robertson's guidance, as soon as the ground had dried after the winter rains in the spring of 1771.[1] They travelled in the usual style of backwoods emigrants: the men on foot, rifle on shoulder, the elder children driving the lean cows, while the women, the young children, and the few household goods, and implements of husbandry, were carried on the backs of the pack-horses; for in settling the backwoods during the last century, the pack-horse played the same part that in the present century was taken by the canvas-covered emigrant wagon, the white-topped "prairie schooner."

He Leads a Band of Settlers Thither.

Once arrived at the Watauga, the Carolina new-comers mixed readily with the few Virginians already on the ground; and Robertson speedily became one of the leading men in the little settlement. On an island in the river he built a house of logs with the

[1] Putnam, p. 24, says it was after the battle of the Great Alamance, which took place May 16, 1771. An untrustworthy tradition says March.

bark still on them on the outside, though hewed smooth within; tradition says that it was the largest in the settlement. Certainly it belonged to the better class of backwoods cabins, with a loft and several rooms, a roof of split saplings, held down by weighty poles, a log veranda in front, and a huge fire-place, of sticks or stones laid in clay, wherein the pile of blazing logs roared loudly in cool weather. The furniture was probably precisely like that in other houses of the class; a rude bed, table, settee, and chest of drawers, a spinning-jenny, and either three-legged stools or else chairs with backs and seats of undressed deer hides. Robertson's energy and his remarkable natural ability brought him to the front at once, in every way; although, as already said, he had much less than even the average backwoods education, for he could not read when he was married, while most of the frontiersmen could not only read but also write, or at least sign their names.[1]

Sevier, who came to the Watauga early in 1772, nearly a year after Robertson and his little colony John had arrived, differed widely from his friend Sevier. in almost every respect save highmindedness and dauntless, invincible courage. He was a gentleman by birth and breeding, the son of a Huguenot who had settled in the Shenandoah Valley. He had received a fair education, and though never fond of books, he was to the end of his days an interested and intelligent observer of men and things, both in

[1] In examining numerous original drafts of petitions and the like, signed by hundreds of the original settlers of Tennessee and Kentucky, I have been struck by the small proportion—not much over three or four per cent. at the outside—of men who made their mark instead of signing.

America and Europe. He corresponded on intimate
and equal terms with Madison, Franklin, and others
of our most polished statesmen; while Robertson's
letters, when he had finally learned to write them
himself, were almost as remarkable for their phenom-
enally bad spelling as for their shrewd common-sense
and homely, straightforward honesty. Sevier was a
very handsome man; during his lifetime he was
reputed the handsomest in Tennessee. He was tall,
fair-skinned, blue-eyed, brown-haired, of slender
build, with erect, military carriage and commanding
bearing, his lithe, finely proportioned figure being
well set off by the hunting-shirt which he almost
invariably wore. From his French forefathers he
inherited a gay, pleasure-loving temperament, that
made him the most charming of companions. His
manners were polished and easy, and he had great
natural dignity. Over the backwoodsmen he exercised an almost unbounded influence, due as much to
his ready tact, invariable courtesy, and lavish, generous hospitality, as to the skill and dashing prowess
which made him the most renowned Indian fighter
of the Southwest. He had an eager, impetuous nature, and was very ambitious, being almost as fond
of popularity as of Indian-fighting.[1] He was already
married, and the father of two children, when he

[1] See, in the collection of the Tenn. Hist. Soc., at Nashville, the MS.
notes containing an account of Sevier, given by one of the old settlers
named Hillsman. Hillsman especially dwells on the skill with which Sevier
could persuade the backwoodsmen to come round to his own way of thinking, while at the same time making them believe that they were acting on
their own ideas, and adds—" whatever he had was at the service of his
friends and for the promotion of the Sevier party, which sometimes embraced
nearly all the population."

came to the Watauga, and, like Robertson, was seeking a new and better home for his family in the west. So far, his life had been as uneventful as that of any other spirited young borderer; his business had been that of a frontier Indian trader; he had taken part in one or two unimportant Indian skirmishes.[1] Later he was commissioned by Lord Dunmore as a captain in the Virginia line.

Such were Sevier and Robertson, the leaders in the little frontier outpost of civilization that was struggling to maintain itself on the Watauga; and these two men afterwards proved themselves to be,

[1] Mr. James Gilmore (Edmund Kirke), in his "John Sevier," makes some assertions, totally unbacked by proof, about his hero's alleged feats, when only a boy, in the wars between the Virginians and the Indians. He gives no dates, but can only refer to Pontiac's war. Sevier was then eighteen years old, but nevertheless is portrayed, among other things, as leading "a hundred hardy borderers" into the Indian country, burning their villages and "often defeating bodies of five times his own numbers." These statements are supported by no better authority than traditions gathered a century and a quarter after the event, and must be dismissed as mere fable. They show a total and rather amusing ignorance not only of the conditions of Indian warfare, but also of the history of the particular contest referred to. Mr. Gilmore forgets that we have numerous histories of the war in which Sevier is supposed to have distinguished himself, and that in not one of them is there a syllable hinting at what he says. Neither Sevier nor any one else ever with a hundred men defeated "five times his number" of northwestern Indians in the woods; and during Sevier's life in Virginia, the only defeat ever suffered by such a body of Indians was at Bushy Run, when Bouquet gained a hard-fought victory. After the end of Pontiac's war there was no expedition of importance undertaken by Virginians against the Indians until 1774, and of Pontiac's war itself we have full knowledge. Sevier was neither leader nor participant in any such marvellous feats as Mr. Gilmore describes; on the contrary, the skirmishes in which he may have been engaged were of such small importance that no record remains concerning them. Had Sevier done any such deeds all the colonies would have rung with his exploits, instead of their remaining utterly unknown for a hundred and twenty-five years. It is extraordinary that any author should be willing to put his name to such reckless misstatements, in what purports to be a history and not a book of fiction.

with the exception of George Rogers Clark, the greatest of the first generation of Trans-Alleghany pioneers.

Their followers were worthy of them. All alike were keenly alive to the disadvantages of living in a community where there was neither law *The* nor officer to enforce it. Accordingly, with *Settlers Organize* their characteristic capacity for combination, *a Govern-* so striking as existing together with the *ment.* equally characteristic capacity for individual self-help, the settlers determined to organize a government of their own. They promptly put their resolution into effect early in the spring of 1772, Robertson being apparently the leader in the movement.

They decided to adopt written articles of agreement, by which their conduct should be governed ; and these were known as the Articles of the Watauga Association. They formed a written constitution, the first ever adopted west of the mountains, or by a community composed of American-born freemen. It is this fact of the early independence and self-government of the settlers along the head-waters of the Tennessee that gives to their history its peculiar importance. They were the first men of American birth to establish a free and independent community on the continent. Even before this date, there had been straggling settlements of Pennsylvanians and Virginians along the head-waters of the Ohio ; but these settlements remained mere parts of the colonies behind them, and neither grew into a separate community, nor played a distinctive part in the growth of the west.

The first step taken by the Watauga settlers,[1] when they had determined to organize, was to meet in general convention, holding a kind of folk-thing, akin to the New England town-meeting. They then elected a representative assembly, a small parliament or " witanagemot," which met at Robertson's station. Apparently the freemen of each little fort or palisaded village, each blockhouse that was the centre of a group of detached cabins and clearings, sent a member to this first frontier legislature.[2] It consisted of thirteen representatives, who proceeded to elect from their number five—among them Sevier and Robertson— to form a committee or court, which should carry on the actual business of government, and should exercise both judicial and executive functions. This court had a clerk and a sheriff, or executive officer, who respectively recorded and enforced their decrees.

The Watauga Commonwealth.

The five members of this court, who are sometimes referred to as arbitrators, and sometimes as commissioners, had entire control of all matters affecting the common weal ; and all affairs in controversy were settled by the decision of a majority. They elected one of their number as chairman, he being also ex-officio chairman of the committee of thirteen ; and all their proceedings were noted for the prudence and moderation with which they behaved in their somewhat anomalous position. They were careful to avoid embroiling themselves with the neighboring

---

[1] The Watauga settlers and those of Carter's Valley were the first to organize ; the Nolichucky people came in later.

[2] Putnam, 30.

colonial legislatures; and in dealing with non-residents they made them give bonds to abide by their decision, thus avoiding any necessity of proceeding against their persons. On behalf of the community itself, they were not only permitted to control its internal affairs, but also to secure lands by making treaties with a foreign power, the Indians; a distinct exercise of the right of sovereignty. They heard and adjudicated all cases of difference between the settlers themselves; and took measures for the common safety. In fact the dwellers, in this little outlying frontier commonwealth, exercised the rights of full statehood for a number of years; establishing in true American style a purely democratic government with representative institutions, in which, under certain restrictions, the will of the majority was supreme, while, nevertheless, the largest individual freedom, and the utmost liberty of individual initiative were retained. The framers showed the American predilection for a written constitution or civil compact; and, what was more important, they also showed the common-sense American spirit that led them to adopt the scheme of government which should in the simplest way best serve their needs, without bothering their heads over mere high-sounding abstractions.[1]

The court or committee held their sessions at stated and regular times, and took the law of Vir-

---

[1] The original articles of the Watauga Association have been lost, and no copies are extant. All we know of the matter is derived from Haywood, Ramsey, and Putnam, three historians to whose praiseworthy industry Tennessee owes as much as Kentucky does to Marshall, Butler, and Collins. Ramsey, by the way, chooses rather inappropriate adjectives when he calls the government " paternal and patriarchal."

ginia as their standard for decisions. They saw to the recording of deeds and wills, settled all questions of Civil Gov- debt, issued marriage licenses, and carried ernment. on a most vigorous warfare against law-breakers, especially horse-thieves.[1] For six years their government continued in full vigor; then, in February, 1778, North Carolina having organized Washington County, which included all of what is now Tennessee, the governor of that State appointed justices of the peace and militia officers for the new county, and the old system came to an end. But Sevier, Robertson, and their fellow-committeemen were all members of the new court, and continued almost without change their former simple system of procedure and direct and expeditious methods of administering justice; as justices of the peace they merely continued to act as they acted while arbitrators of the Watauga Association, and in their summary mode of dealing with evil-doers paid a good deal more heed to the essence than to the forms of law. One record shows that a horse-thief was arrested on Monday, tried on Wednesday, and hung on Friday of the same week. Another deals with a claimant who, by his attorney, moved to be sworn into his office of clerk, "but the court swore in James Sevier, well knowing that said Sevier had been elected," and being evidently unwilling to waste their time hearing a contested election case when their minds were already made up as to the equity of the matter. They exercised the right of making suspicious indi-

[1] A very good account of this government is given in Allison's Address, pp. 5-8, and from it the following examples are taken.

viduals leave the county.[1] They also at times became censors of morals, and interfered with straight-forward effectiveness to right wrongs for which a more refined and elaborate system of jurisprudence would have provided only cumbersome and inadequate remedies. Thus one of their entries is to the effect that a certain man is ordered " to return to his family and demean himself as a good citizen, he having admitted in open court that he had left his wife and took up with an-other woman." From the character of the judges who made the decision, it is safe to presume that the delinquent either obeyed it or else promptly fled to the Indians for safety.[2] This fleeing to the Indians, by the way, was a feat often performed by the worst criminals—for the renegade, the man who had " painted his face " and deserted those of his own color, was a being as well known as he was abhorred and despised on the border, where such a deed was held to be the one unpardonable crime.

So much for the way in which the whites kept order among themselves. The second part of their task, the adjustment of their relations with their red neighbors, was scarcely less im-portant. Early in 1772 Virginia made a treaty with the Cherokee Nation, which established as the boundary between them a line running west from White Top Mountain in latitude

Treaty-Making with the Indians.

---

[1] A right the exercise of which is of course susceptible to great abuse, but, nevertheless, is often absolutely necessary to the well-being of a frontier community. In almost every case where I have personally known it exercised, the character of the individual ordered off justified the act.

[2] Allison's Address.

36° 30′.[1]   Immediately afterwards the agent[2] of the British Government among the Cherokees ordered the Watauga settlers to instantly leave their lands. They defied him, and refused to move; but feeling the insecurity of their tenure they deputed two commissioners, of whom Robertson was one, to make a treaty with the Cherokees. This was successfully accomplished, the Indians leasing to the associated settlers all the lands on the Watauga waters for the space of eight years, in consideration of about six thousand dollars' worth of blankets, paint, muskets, and the like.[3] The amount advanced was reimbursed to the men advancing it by the sale of the lands in small parcels to new settlers,[4] for the time of the lease.[5]

After the lease was signed, a day was appointed on which to hold a great race, as well as wrestling-matches and other sports, at Watauga. Not only many whites from the various settlements, but also a number of Indians, came to see or take part in the sports; and all went well until the evening, when some lawless men from Wolf Hills, who had been

[1] Ramsey, 109.   Putnam says 36° 35′.

[2] Alexander Cameron.

[3] Haywood, 43.

[4] Meanwhile Carter's Valley, then believed to lie in Virginia, had been settled by Virginians; the Indians robbed a trader's store, and indemnified the owners by giving them land, at the treaty of Sycamore Shoals. This land was leased in job lots to settlers, who, however, kept possession without paying when they found it lay in North Carolina.

[5] A similar but separate lease was made by the settlers on the Nolichucky, who acquired a beautiful and fertile valley in exchange for the merchandize carried on the back of a single pack-horse. Among the whites themselves transfers of land were made in very simple forms, and conveyed not the fee simple but merely the grantor's claim.

lurking in the woods round about,[1] killed an Indian, whereat his fellows left the spot in great anger.

The settlers now saw themselves threatened with a bloody and vindictive Indian war, and were plunged in terror and despair; yet they **Robertson's** were rescued by the address and daring of **Mission** Robertson. Leaving the others to build a **of Peace.** formidable palisaded fort, under the leadership of Sevier, Robertson set off alone through the woods and followed the great war trace down to the Cherokee towns. His mission was one of the greatest peril, for there was imminent danger that the justly angered savages would take his life. But he was a man who never rushed heedlessly into purposeless peril, and never flinched from a danger which there was an object in encountering. His quiet, resolute fearlessness doubtless impressed the savages to whom he went, and helped to save his life; moreover, the Cherokees knew him, trusted his word, and were probably a little overawed by a certain air of command to which all men that were thrown in contact with him bore witness. His ready tact and knowledge of Indian character did the rest. He persuaded the chiefs and warriors to meet him in council, assured them of the anger and sorrow with which all the Watauga people viewed the murder, which had undoubtedly been committed by some outsider, and wound up by declaring his determination to try to have the wrong-doer arrested and pun-

[1] Haywood says they were named Crabtree; Putnam hints that they had lost a brother when Boon's party was attacked and his son killed; but the attack on Boon did not take place till over a year after this time.

ished according to his crime. The Indians, already pleased with his embassy, finally consented to pass the affair over and not take vengeance upon innocent men. Then the daring backwoods diplomatist, well pleased with the success of his mission, returned to the anxious little community.

The incident, taken in connection with the plundering of a store kept by two whites in Holston Valley at the same time, and the unprovoked assault on Boon's party in Powell's Valley a year later, shows the extreme difficulty of preventing the worst men of each color from wantonly attacking the innocent. There was hardly a peaceable red or law-abiding white who could not recite injuries he had received from members of the opposite race; and his sense of the wrongs he had suffered, as well as the general frontier indifference to crimes committed against others, made him slow in punishing similar outrages by his own people. The Watauga settlers discountenanced wrong being done the Indians, and tried to atone for it, but they never hunted the offenders down with the necessary mercilessness that alone could have prevented a repetition of their offences. Similarly, but to an even greater degree, the good Indians shielded the bad.[1]

For several years after they made their lease with the Cherokees the men of the Watauga were not troubled by their Indian neighbors. They had

---

[1] Even La Rochefoucauld-Liancourt (8, 95), who loathed the backwoodsmen—few polished Europeans being able to see any but the repulsive side of frontier character, a side certainly very often prominent,—also speaks of the tendency of the worst Indians to go to the frontier to rob and murder.

to fear nothing more than a drought, a freshet, a forest fire, or an unusually deep snow-fall if hunting on the mountains in mid-winter. They lived Life on the in peace, hunting and farming, marrying, Watauga. giving in marriage, and rearing many healthy children. By degrees they wrought out of the stubborn wilderness comfortable homes, filled with plenty. The stumps were drawn out of the clearings, and other grains were sown besides corn. Beef, pork, and mutton were sometimes placed on the table, besides the more common venison, bear meat, and wild turkey. The women wove good clothing, the men procured good food, the log-cabins, if homely and rough, yet gave ample warmth and shelter. The families throve, and life was happy, even though varied with toil, danger, and hardship. Books were few, and it was some years before the first church,—Presbyterian, of course,—was started in the region.[1] The backwoods Presbyterians managed their church affairs much as they did their civil government: each congregation appointed a committee to choose ground, to build a meeting-house, to collect the minister's salary, and to pay all charges, by taxing the members proportionately for the same, the committee being required to turn in a full account, and receive instructions, at a general session or meeting held twice every year.[2]

Thus the Watauga folk were the first Americans

[1] Salem Church was founded (Allison, 8) in 1777, by Samuel Doak, a Princeton graduate, and a man of sound learning, who also at the same time started Washington College, the first real institution of learning south of the Alleghanies.

[2] "Annals of Augusta," 21.

who, as a separate body, moved into the wilderness
to hew out dwellings for themselves and their children, trusting only to their own shrewd heads, stout
hearts, and strong arms, unhelped and unhampered
by the power nominally their sovereign.[1] They built
up a commonwealth which had many successors;
they showed that the frontiersmen could do their
work unassisted; for they not only proved that they
were made of stuff stern enough to hold its own
against outside pressure of any sort, but they also
made it evident that having won the land they were
competent to govern both it and themselves. They
were the first to do what the whole nation has since
done. It has often been said that we owe all our
success to our surroundings; that any race with our
opportunities could have done as well as we have
done. Undoubtedly our opportunities have been
great; undoubtedly we have often and lamentably
failed in taking advantage of them. But what nation
ever has done all that was possible with the chances
offered it? The Spaniards, the Portuguese, and the
French, not to speak of the Russians in Siberia, have
all enjoyed, and yet have failed to make good use of,
the same advantages which we have turned to good
account. The truth is, that in starting a new nation
in a new country, as we have done, while there are
exceptional chances to be taken advantage of, there
are also exceptional dangers and difficulties to be
overcome. None but heroes can succeed wholly
in the work. It is a good thing for us at times to
compare what we have done with what we could

[1] See Appendix.

have done, had we been better and wiser ; it may
make us try in the future to raise our abilities to
the level of our opportunities.   Looked at absolutely, we must frankly acknowledge that we have
fallen very far short indeed of the high ideal we
should have reached.   Looked at relatively, it must
also be said that we have done better than any other
nation or race working under our conditions.

The Watauga settlers outlined in advance the
nation's work.   They tamed the rugged and shaggy
wilderness, they bid defiance to outside foes, and
they successfully solved the difficult problem of self-
government.

CHAPTER VIII.

LORD DUNMORE'S WAR, 1774.

On the eve of the Revolution, in 1774, the frontiers-men had planted themselves firmly among the Al-leghanies. Directly west of them lay the untenanted wilderness, traversed only by the war parties of the red men, and the hunting parties of both reds and whites. No settlers had yet penetrated it, and until they did so there could be within its borders no chance of race warfare, unless we call by that name the unchronicled and unending contest in which, now and then, some solitary white woodsman slew, or was slain by, his painted foe. But in the southwest and the northwest alike, the area of settlement already touched the home lands of the tribes, and hence the horizon was never quite free from the cloud of threatening Indian war; yet for the moment the southwest was at peace, for the Cherokees were still friendly.

It was in the northwest that the danger of collision was most imminent; for there the whites and Indians had wronged one another for a generation, and their interests were, at the time, clashing more directly than ever. Much the greater part of the western frontier was held or claimed by Virginia, whose royal governor was, at the time, Lord Dunmore.

War with the Indians Threatened.

He was an ambitious, energetic man, who held his allegiance as being due first to the crown, but who, nevertheless, was always eager to champion the cause of Virginia as against either the Indians or her sister colonies. The short but fierce and eventful struggle that now broke out was fought wholly by Virginians, and was generally known by the name of Lord Dunmore's war.

Virginia, under her charter, claimed that her boundaries ran across to the South Seas, to the Pacific Ocean. The king of Britain had graciously granted her the right to take so much of the continent as lay within these lines, provided she could win it from the Indians, French, and Spaniards; and provided also she could prevent herself from being ousted by the crown, or by some of the other colonies. A number of grants had been made with the like large liberality, and it was found that they sometimes conflicted with one another. The consequence was that while the boundaries were well marked near the coast, where they separated Virginia from the long-settled regions of Maryland and North Carolina, they became exceeding vague and indefinite the moment they touched the mountains. Even at the south this produced confusion, and induced the settlers of the upper Holston to consider themselves as Virginians, not Carolinians; but at the north the effect was still more confusing, and nearly resulted in bringing about an intercolonial war between Pennsylvania and Virginia.

The Virginians claimed all of extreme western Pennsylvania, especially Fort Pitt and the valley of the Monongahela, and, in 1774, proceeded boldly to exercise jurisdiction therein.[1] Indeed a strong party among the settlers favored the Virginian claim; whereas it would have been quite impossible to arouse anywhere in Virginia the least feeling in support of a similar claim on behalf of Pennsylvania. The borderers had a great contempt for the sluggish and timid government of the Quaker province, which was very lukewarm in protecting them in their rights—or, indeed, in punishing them when they did wrong to others. In fact, it seems probable that they would have declared for Virginia even more strongly, had it not been for the very reason that their feeling of independence was so surly as to make them suspicious of all forms of control; and they therefore objected almost as much to Virginian as Pennsylvanian rule, and regarded the outcome of the dispute with a certain indifference.[2]

Conflict with those of Pennsylvania.

For a time in the early part of 1774 there seemed quite as much likelihood of the Virginians being drawn into a fight with the Pennsylvanians as with the Shawnees. While the Pennsylvanian commissioners were trying to come to an agreement concerning the boundaries with Lord Dunmore, the representatives of the two contesting parties at Fort Pitt were on the verge of actual collision. The Earl's

[1] " American Archives," 4th series, Vol. I., p. 454. Report of Penn. Commissioners, June 27, 1774.

[2] Maryland was also involved, along her western frontier, in border difficulties with her neighbors ; the first we hear of the Cresap family is their having engaged in a real skirmish with the Pennsylvanian authorities. See also " Am. Arch.," IV., Vol. I., 547.

agent in the disputed territory was a Captain John
Conolly,[1] a man of violent temper and bad character.
He embodied the men favorable to his side as a sort
of Virginian militia, with which he not only menaced
both hostile and friendly Indians, but the adherents
of the Pennsylvanian government as well. He destroyed their houses, killed their cattle and hogs,
impressed their horses, and finally so angered them
that they threatened to take refuge in the stockade
at Fort Pitt, and defy him to open war,—although
even in the midst of these quarrels with Conolly their
loyalty to the Quaker State was somewhat doubtful.[2]

The Virginians were the only foes the western
Indians really dreaded; for their backwoodsmen
were of warlike temper, and had learned to   Use of the
fight effectively in the forest. The Indians   Term Long
styled them Long Knives; or, to be more   Knives.
exact, they called them collectively the "Big Knife."[3]
There have been many accounts given of the origin
of this name, some ascribing it to the long knives
worn by the hunters and backwoodsmen generally,
others to the fact that some of the noted Virginian
fighters in their early skirmishes were armed with
swords. At any rate the title was accepted by all
the Indians as applying to their most determined
foes among the colonists; and finally, after we had
become a nation, was extended so as to apply to
Americans generally.

[1] "Am. Arch.," IV., Vol. I., 394, 449, 469, etc. He was generally called
Dr. Conolly.

[2] See *do.*, 463, 471, etc., especially St. Clair's letters, *passim.*

[3] In most of the original treaties, "talks," etc., preserved in the Archives
of the State Department, where the translation is exact, the word " Big
Knife " is used.

The war that now ensued was not general. The
Six Nations, as a whole, took no part in it, while
Pennsylvania also stood aloof; indeed at one time it
was proposed that the Pennsylvanians and Iroquois
should jointly endeavor to mediate between the
combatants.[1] The struggle was purely between the
Virginians and the northwestern Indians.

The interests of the Virginians and Pennsylvanians
conflicted not only in respect to the ownership of the
land, but also in respect to the policy to be
pursued regarding the Indians. The former
were armed colonists, whose interest it was
to get actual possession of the soil;[2] whereas in
Pennsylvania the Indian trade was very important
and lucrative, and the numerous traders to the Indian
towns were anxious that the redskins should remain
in undisturbed enjoyment of their forests, and that
no white man should be allowed to come among
them; moreover, so long as they were able to make
heavy profits, they were utterly indifferent to the
well-being of the white frontiersmen, and in return
incurred the suspicion and hatred of the latter. The
Virginians accused the traders of being the main
cause of the difficulty,[3] asserting that they sometimes
incited the Indians to outrages, and always, even in
the midst of hostilities, kept them supplied with guns
and ammunition, and even bought from them the
horses that they had stolen on their plundering
expeditions against the Virginian border.[4] These
last accusations were undoubtedly justified, at least

The Pennsylvania Traders.

---

[1] Letter of John Penn, June 28, 1774. " Am. Arch.," IV., Vol. IV.
[2] " Am. Archives," *do.*, 465.   [3] *Do.*, 722.   [4] *Do.*, 872.

in great part, by the facts. The interests of the white trader from Pennsylvania and of the white settler from Virginia were so far from being identical that they were usually diametrically opposite.

The northwestern Indians had been nominally at peace with the whites for ten years, since the close of Bouquet's campaign. But Bouquet had inflicted a very slight punishment upon them, and in concluding an unsatisfactory peace had caused them to make but a partial reparation for the wrongs they had done.[1] They remained haughty and insolent, irritated rather than awed by an ineffective chastisement, and their young men made frequent forays on the frontier. Each of the ten years of nominal peace saw plenty of bloodshed. Recently they had been seriously alarmed by the tendency of the whites to encroach on the great hunting-grounds south of the Ohio[2]; for here and there hunters or settlers were already beginning to build cabins along the course of that stream. The cession by the Iroquois of these same hunting-grounds, at the treaty of Fort Stanwix, while it gave the whites a colorable title, merely angered the northwestern Indians. Half a century earlier they would hardly have dared dispute the power of the Six Nations to do what they chose with any land that could be reached by their war parties; but in 1774 they felt quite able to hold their own against their old oppressors, and had no

Outrages and Reprisals on the Frontier.

[1] "Am. Arch.," IV., Vol. I., p. 1015.

[2] McAfee MSS. This is the point especially insisted on by Cornstalk in his speech to the adventurers in 1773; he would fight before seeing the whites drive off the game.

intention of acquiescing in any arrangement the latter might make, unless it was also clearly to their own advantage.

In the decade before Lord Dunmore's war there had been much mutual wrong-doing between the northwestern Indians and the Virginian borderers; but on the whole the latter had occupied the position of being sinned against more often than that of sinning. The chief offence of the whites was that they trespassed upon uninhabited lands, which they forthwith proceeded to cultivate, instead of merely roaming over them to hunt the game and butcher one another. Doubtless occasional white men would murder an Indian if they got a chance, and the traders almost invariably cheated the tribesmen. But as a whole the traders were Indian rather than white in their sympathies, and the whites rarely made forays against their foes avowedly for horses and plunder, while the Indians on their side were continually indulging in such inroads. Every year parties of young red warriors crossed the Ohio to plunder the outlying farms, burn down the buildings, scalp the inmates, and drive off the horses.[1] Year by year the exasperation of the borderers grew greater and the tale of the wrongs they had to avenge longer.[2] Occasionally they took a brutal and ill-judged vengeance, which usually fell on innocent

[1] In the McAfee MSS., as already quoted, there is an account of the Shawnee war party, whom the McAfees encountered in 1773 returning from a successful horse-stealing expedition.

[2] "Am. Archives," IV., Vol. I., 872. Dunmore in his speech enumerates 19 men, women, and children who had been killed by the Indians in 1771, '72, and '73, and these were but a small fraction of the whole. "This was before a drop of Shawnee blood was shed."

Indians,[1] and raised up new foes for the whites. The savages grew continually more hostile, and in the fall of 1773 their attacks became so frequent that it was evident a general outbreak was at hand; eleven people were murdered in the county of Fincastle alone.[2] The Shawnees were the leaders in all these outrages; but the outlaw bands, such as the Mingos and Cherokees, were as bad, and parties of Wyandots and Delawares, as well as of the various Miami and Wabash tribes, joined them.

Thus the spring of 1774 opened with every thing ripe for an explosion. The Virginian borderers were fearfully exasperated, and ready to take vengeance upon any Indians, whether peaceful or hostile; while the Shawnees and Mingos, on their side, were arrogant and overbearing, and yet alarmed at the continual advance of the whites. The headstrong rashness of Conolly, who was acting as Lord Dunmore's lieutenant on the border, and who was equally willing to plunge into a war with Pennsylvania or the Shawnees, served as a firebrand to ignite this mass of tinder. The borderers were anxious for a war; and Lord Dunmore was not inclined to baulk them. He was ambitious of glory, and probably thought that in the midst of the growing difficulties between the mother country and the colonies, it would be good policy to distract the Virginians' minds by an Indian war, which, if he conducted it to a successful conclusion, might strengthen his own position.[3]

The Impending Outbreak.

[1] " Trans-Alleghany Pioneers," p. 262, gives an example that happened in 1772.

[2] "Am. Archives," IV., Vol. I. Letter of Col. Wm. Preston, Aug. 13, 1774.

[3] Many local historians, including Brantz Mayer (Logan and Cresap, p.

There were on the border at the moment three or four men whose names are so intimately bound up with Cresap and the history of this war, that they deserve a Greathouse. brief mention. One was Michael Cresap, a Maryland frontiersman, who had come to the banks of the Ohio with the purpose of making a home for his family.[1] He was of the regular pioneer type ; a good woodsman, sturdy and brave, a fearless fighter, devoted to his friends and his country ; but also, when his blood was heated, and his savage instincts fairly roused, inclined to regard any red man, whether hostile or friendly, as a being who should be slain on sight.

85), ascribe to the earl treacherous motives. Brantz Mayer puts it thus : " It was probably Lord Dunmore's desire to incite a war which would arouse and band the savages of the west, so that in the anticipated struggle with the united colonies the British home-interest might ultimately avail itself of these children of the forest as ferocious and formidable allies in the onslaught on the Americans." This is much too futile a theory to need serious discussion. The war was of the greatest advantage to the American cause ; for it kept the northwestern Indians off our hands for the first two years of the Revolutionary struggle ; and had Lord Dunmore been the far-seeing and malignant being that this theory supposes, it would have been impossible for him not also to foresee that such a result was absolutely inevitable. There is no reason whatever to suppose that he was not doing his best for the Virginians ; he deserved their gratitude ; and he got it for the time being. The accusations of treachery against him were afterthoughts, and must be set down to mere vulgar rancor, unless, at least, some faint shadow of proof is advanced. When the Revolutionary war broke out, however, the earl, undoubtedly, like so many other British officials, advocated the most outrageous measures to put down the insurgent colonists.

[1] See Brantz Mayer, p. 86, for a very proper attack on those historians who stigmatize as land-jobbers and speculators the perfectly honest settlers, whose encroachments on the Indian hunting-grounds were so bitterly resented by the savages. Such attacks are mere pieces of sentimental injustice. The settlers were perfectly right in feeling that they had a right to settle on the vast stretches of unoccupied ground, however wrong some of their individual deeds may have been. But Mayer, following Jacob's "Life of Cresap," undoubtedly paints his hero in altogether too bright colors.

Nor did he condemn the brutal deeds done by others on innocent Indians.

The next was a man named Greathouse, of whom it is enough to know that, together with certain other men whose names have for the most part, by a merciful chance, been forgotten,[1] he did a deed such as could only be committed by inhuman and cowardly scoundrels.

The other two actors in this tragedy were both Indians, and were both men of much higher stamp. One was Cornstalk, the Shawnee chief; a far-sighted seer, gloomily conscious of the impending ruin of his race, a great orator, a mighty warrior, a man who knew the value of his word and prized his honor, Cornstalk and who fronted death with quiet, disdainful and Logan. heroism; and yet a fierce, cruel, and treacherous savage to those with whom he was at enmity, a killer of women and children, whom we first hear of, in Pontiac's war, as joining in the massacre of unarmed and peaceful settlers who had done him no wrong, and who thought that he was friendly.[2] The other was Logan, an Iroquois warrior, who lived at that time away from the bulk of his people, but who was a man of note—in the loose phraseology of the border, a chief or headman—among the outlying parties of Senecas and Mingos, and the fragments of broken tribes that dwelt along the upper Ohio. He was a man of splendid appearance; over six feet high, straight as a spear-shaft, with a countenance as open

[1] Sappington, Tomlinson, and Baker were the names of three of his fellow-miscreants. See Jefferson MSS.

[2] At Greenbriar. See " Narrative of Captain John Stewart," an actor in the war.—*Magazine of American History*, Vol. I., p. 671.

as it was brave and manly,[1] until the wrongs he endured stamped on it an expression of gloomy ferocity. He had always been the friend of the white
man, and had been noted particularly for his kindness and gentleness to children. Up to this time he
had lived at peace with the borderers, for though
some of his kin had been massacred by them years
before, he had forgiven the deed — perhaps not
unmindful of the fact that others of his kin had
been concerned in still more bloody massacres of
the whites. A skilled marksman and mighty hunter, of commanding dignity, who treated all men
with a grave courtesy that exacted the same treatment in return, he was greatly liked and respected by
all the white hunters and frontiersmen whose friendship and respect were worth having; they admired
him for his dexterity and prowess, and they loved
him for his straightforward honesty, and his noble
loyalty to his friends. One of these old pioneer
hunters has left on record [2] the statement that he
deemed "Logan the best specimen of humanity he
ever met with, either white or red." Such was
Logan before the evil days came upon him.

Early in the spring the outlying settlers began
again to suffer from the deeds of straggling Indians.
Indians Be- Horses were stolen, one or two murders
gin their were committed, the inhabitants of the
Outrages. more lonely cabins fled to the forts, and
the backwoodsmen began to threaten fierce vengeance. On April 16th, three traders in the em-

---

[1] Loudon's " Indian Narratives," II., p. 223.
[2] See " American Pioneer," I., p. 189.

ploy of a man named Butler were attacked by some of the outlaw Cherokees, one killed, another wounded, and their goods plundered. Immediately after this Conolly issued an open letter, commanding the backwoodsmen to hold themselves in readiness to repel any attack by the Indians, as the Shawnees were hostile. Such a letter from Lord Dunmore's lieutenant amounted to a declaration of war, and there were sure to be plenty of backwoodsmen who would put a very liberal interpretation upon the order given them to repel an attack. Its effects were seen instantly. All the borderers prepared for war. Cresap was near Wheeling at the time, with a band of hunters and scouts, fearless men, who had adopted many of the ways of the redskins, in addition to their method of fighting. As soon as they received Conolly's letter they proceeded to declare war in the regular Indian style, calling a council, planting the war-post, and going through other savage ceremonies,[1] and eagerly waited for a chance to attack their foes.

Unfortunately the first stroke fell on friendly Indians. The trader, Butler, spoken of above, in order to recover some of the peltries of which he had been robbed by the Cherokees, had sent a canoe with two friendly Shawnees towards the place of the massacre. On the 27th Cresap and his followers ambushed these men near Captina, and killed and scalped them. Some of the better backwoodsmen strongly protested against this

Cresap Attacks Friendly Shawnees.

[1] Letter of George Rogers Clark, June 17, 1798. In Jefferson MSS., 5th Series, Vol. I. (preserved in Archives of State Department at Washington).

outrage [1]; but the mass of them were excited and angered by the rumor of Indian hostilities, and the brutal and disorderly side of frontier character was for the moment uppermost. They threatened to kill whoever interfered with them, cursing the "damned traders" as being worse than the Indians,[2] while Cresap boasted of the murder, and never said a word in condemnation of the still worse deeds that followed it.[3] The next day he again led out his men and attacked another party of Shawnees, who had been trading near Pittsburg, killed one and wounded two others, one of the whites being also hurt.[4]

Among the men who were with Cresap at this time was a young Virginian, who afterwards played a **George Rogers Clark.** brilliant part in the history of the west, who was for ten years the leader of the bold spirits of Kentucky, and who rendered the whole United States signal and effective service by one of his deeds in the Revolutionary war. This was George Rogers Clark, then twenty-one years old.[5] He was of good family, and had been fairly well educated, as education went in colonial days; but from his childhood he had been passionately fond of the wild roving life of the woods.

---

[1] Witness the testimony of one of the most gallant Indian fighters of the border, who was in Wheeling at the time ; letter of Col. Ebenezer Zane, February 4, 1800, in Jefferson MSS.

[2] Jefferson MSS. Deposition of John Gibson, April 4, 1800.

[3] *Do.* Deposition of Wm. Huston, April 19, 1798 ; also depositions of Samuel McKee, etc.

[4] "Am. Archives," IV., Vol. I., p. 468. Letter of Devereux Smith June 10, 1774, Gibson's letter, Also Jefferson MSS.

[5] *Historical Magazine*, I., p. 168. Born in Albemarle County, Va., November 19, 1752.

He was a great hunter; and, like so many other young colonial gentlemen of good birth and bringing up, and adventurous temper, he followed the hazardous profession of a backwoods surveyor. With chain and compass, as well as axe and rifle, he penetrated the far places of the wilderness, the lonely, dangerous regions where every weak man inevitably succumbed to the manifold perils encountered, but where the strong and far-seeing were able to lay the foundations of fame and fortune. He possessed high daring, unflinching courage, passions which he could not control, and a frame fitted to stand any strain of fatigue or hardship. He was a square-built, thick-set man, with high broad forehead, sandy hair, and unquailing blue eyes that looked out from under heavy, shaggy brows.[1]

Clark had taken part with Cresap in his assault upon the second party of Shawnees. On the following day the whole band of whites prepared to march off and attack Logan's camp at Yellow Creek, some fifty miles distant. After going some miles they began to feel ashamed of their mission; calling a halt, they discussed the fact that the camp they were preparing to attack, consisted exclusively of friendly Indians, and mainly of women and children; and forthwith abandoned their proposed trip and returned home. They were true borderers—brave, self-reliant, loyal to their friends, and good-hearted when their worst instincts were not suddenly aroused; but the sight of bloodshed maddened them as if they had been so many

[1] Military Journal of Major Ebenezer Denny, with an introductory memoir by William H. Denny (Publication of the Hist. Soc. of Penn.), Phil., 1860, p. 216.

wolves. Wrongs stirred to the depths their moody tempers, and filled them with a brutal longing for indiscriminate revenge. When goaded by memories of evil, or when swayed by swift, fitful gusts of fury, the uncontrolled violence of their passions led them to commit deeds whose inhuman barbarity almost equalled, though it could never surpass, that shown by the Indians themselves.[1]

But Logan's people did not profit by Cresap's change of heart. On the last day of April a small party of **Murder of** men, women, and children, including almost **Logan's** all of Logan's kin, left his camp and crossed **Kinsfolk.** the river to visit Greathouse, as had been their custom; for he made a trade of selling rum to the savages, though Cresap had notified him to stop. The whole party were plied with liquor, and became helplessly drunk, in which condition Greathouse and his associated criminals fell on and massacred them, nine souls in all.[2]   It was an inhuman and revolting

[1] The Cresap apologists, including even Brantz Mayer, dwell on Cresap's nobleness in *not* massacring Logan's family ! It was certainly to his credit that he did not do so, but it does not speak very well for him that he should even have entertained the thought. He was doubtless, on the whole, a brave, good-hearted man—quite as good as the average borderer ; but nevertheless apt to be drawn into deeds that were the reverse of creditable. Mayer's book has merit ; but he certainly paints Logan too black and Cresap too white, and (see Appendix) is utterly wrong as to Logan's speech. He is right in recognizing the fact that in the war, as a whole, justice was on the side of the frontiersmen.

[2] Devereux Smith's letter. Some of the evil-doers afterwards tried to palliate their misdeeds by stating that Logan's brother, when drunk, insulted a white man, and that the other Indians were at the time on the point of executing an attack upon them.   The last statement is self-evidently false ; for had such been the case, the Indians would, of course, never have let some of their women and children put themselves in the power of the whites, and get helplessly drunk ; and, anyhow, the allegations of such brutal and cowardly murderers are entirely unworthy of acceptance, unless backed up by outside evidence.

deed, which should consign the names of the perpetrators to eternal infamy.

At once the frontier was in a blaze, and the Indians girded themselves for revenge. The Mingos sent out runners to the other tribes, telling of the Wrath of butchery, and calling on all the red men to the Indians. join together for immediate and bloody vengeance.[1] They confused the two massacres, attributing both to Cresap, whom they well knew as a warrior[2]; and their women for long afterwards scared the children into silence by threatening them with Cresap's name as with that of a monster.[3] They had indeed been brutally wronged; yet it must be remembered that they themselves were the first aggressors. They had causelessly murdered and robbed many whites, and now their sins had recoiled on the heads of the innocent of their own race. The conflict could not in any event have been delayed long; the frontiersmen were too deeply and too justly irritated. These particular massacres, however discreditable to those taking part in them, were the occasions, not the causes, of the war; and though they cast a dark shade on the conduct of the whites, they do not relieve the red men from the charge of having committed earlier, more cruel, and quite as wanton outrages

Conolly, an irritable but irresolute man, was appalled by the storm he had helped raise. He meanly disclaimed all responsibility for Cresap's action,[4] and deposed him from his command of rangers; to which,

---

[1] Jefferson MSS., 5th Series, Vol. I. Heckewelder's letter.
[2] Jefferson MSS. Deposition of Col. James Smith, May 25, 1798.
[3] *Do.*, Heckewelder's letter.
[4] "Am. Archives," IV., Vol. I., p. 475.

however, he was soon restored by Lord Dunmore. Both the earl and his lieutenant, however, united in censuring severely Greathouse's deed.[1] Conolly, throughout May, held a series of councils with the Delawares and Iroquois, in which he disclaimed and regretted the outrages, and sought for peace.[2] To one of these councils the Delaware chief, Killbuck, with other warriors, sent a "talk" or "speech in writing"[3] disavowing the deeds of one of their own parties of young braves, who had gone on the war-path ; and another Delaware chief made a very sensible speech, saying that it was unfortunately inevitable that bad men on both sides should commit wrongs, and that the cooler heads should not be led away by acts due to the rashness and folly of a few. But the Shawnees showed no such spirit. On the contrary they declared for war outright, and sent a bold defiance to the Virginians, at the same time telling Conolly plainly that he lied. Their message is noteworthy, because, after expressing a firm belief that the Virginian leader could control his warriors, and stop the outrages if he wished, it added that the Shawnee head men were able to do the like with their own men when they required it. This last allegation took away all shadow of excuse from the Shawnees for not having stopped the excesses of which their young braves had been guilty during the past few years.

Though Conolly showed signs of flinching, his master the earl had evidently no thought of shrinking from the contest. He at once began actively to

Conolly's Fear. (margin note)

[1] *Do.*, p. 1015.   [2] *Do.*, p. 475.   [3] *Do.*, p. 418.

prepare to attack his foes, and the Virginians backed him up heartily, though the Royal Govern- **The Earl** ment, instead of supporting him, censured **Prepares** him in strong terms, and accused the whites **for War.** of being the real aggressors and the authors of the war.[1]

In any event, it would have been out of the question to avoid a contest at so late a date. Immediately after the murders in the end of April, the savages crossed the frontier in small bands. Soon all the back country was involved in the unspeakable horrors of a bloody Indian war, with its usual accompaniments of burning houses, tortured prisoners, and ruined families, the men being killed and the women and children driven off to a horrible captivity.[2] The Indians declared that they were not at war with Pennsylvania,[3] and the latter in return adopted an attitude of neutrality, openly disclaiming any share in the wrong that had been done, and assuring the Indians that it rested solely on the shoulders of the Virginians.[4] Indeed the Shawnees protected the Pennsylvania traders from some hostile Mingos, while the Pennsylvania militia shielded a party of Shawnees from some of Conolly's men [5]; and the Virginians, irritated by what they considered an abandonment of the white cause, were bent on

---

[1] *Do.*, p. 774. Letter of the Earl of Dartmouth, Sept. 10, 1774. A sufficient answer, by the way, to the absurd charge that Dunmore brought on the war in consequence of some mysterious plan of the Home Government to embroil the Americans with the savages. It is not at all improbable that the Crown advisers were not particularly displeased at seeing the attention of the Americans distracted by a war with the Indians; but this is the utmost that can be alleged.

[2] *Do.*, p. 808.   [3] *Do.*, p. 478.   [4] *Do.*, p. 506.   [5] *Do.*, p. 474.

destroying the Pennsylvania fur trade with the Indians.[1]   Nevertheless, some of the bands of young
braves who were out on the war-path failed to discriminate between white friends and foes, and a
number of Pennsylvanians fell victims to their desire for scalps and their ignorance or indifference as
to whom they were at war with.[2]

The panic along the Pennsylvania frontier was terrible ; the out settlers fled back to the interior across
Panic on the mountains, or gathered in numbers to de-
the Border. fend themselves.[3] On the Virginian frontier,
where the real attack was delivered, the panic was
more justifiable ; for terrible ravages were committed,
and the inhabitants were forced to gather together in
their forted villages, and could no longer cultivate their
farms, except by stealth.[4]   Instead of being cowed,
however, the backwoodsmen clamored to be led
against their foes, and made most urgent appeals for
powder and lead, of which there was a great
scarcity.[5]

The confusion was heightened by the anarchy in
which the government of the northwestern district
had been thrown in consequence of the quarrel concerning the jurisdiction. The inhabitants were doubtful as to which colony really had a right to their
allegiance, and many of the frontier officials were
known to be double-faced, professing allegiance to
both governments.[6]   When the Pennsylvanians
raised a corps of a hundred rangers there almost
ensued a civil war among the whites, for the Vir-

---

[1] *Do.*, p. 549.   [2] *Do.*, p. 471.   [3] *Do.*, pp. 435, 467, 602.
[4] *Do.*, pp. 405, 707.   [5] *Do.*, p. 808.   [6] *Do.*, p. 677.

ginians were fearful that the movement was really aimed against them.[1] Of course the march of events gradually forced most, even of the neutral Indians, to join their brethren who had gone on the war-path, and as an example of the utter confusion that reigned, the very Indians that were at war with one British colony, Virginia, were still drawing supplies from the British post of Detroit.[2]

Logan's rage had been terrible. He had changed and not for the better, as he grew older, becoming a sombre, moody man; worse than all, he had   **Logan's** succumbed to the fire-water, the curse of his   **Revenge.** race. The horrible treachery and brutality of the assault wherein his kinsfolk were slain made him mad for revenge; every wolfish instinct in him came to the surface. He wreaked a terrible vengeance for his wrongs; but in true Indian fashion it fell, not on those who had caused them, but on others who were entirely innocent. Indeed he did not know who had caused them. The massacres at Captina and Yellow Creek occurred so near together that they were confounded with each other; and not only the Indians but many whites as well[3] credited Cresap and Greathouse with being jointly responsible for both, and as Cresap was the most prominent, he was the one especially singled out for hatred.

Logan instantly fell on the settlement with a small band of Mingo warriors. On his first foray he took thirteen scalps, among them those of six children.[2] A party of Virginians, under a man named McClure, followed him: but he ambushed and defeated them,

---

[1] *Do.*, pp. 463, 467. [2] *Do.*, p. 684. [3] *Do.*, p. 435. [4] *Do.*, pp. 468, 546.

slaying their leader.[1] He repeated these forays
at least three times. Yet, in spite of his fierce
craving for revenge, he still showed many of the
traits that had made him beloved of his white
friends. Having taken a prisoner, he refused to
allow him to be tortured, and saved his life at the
risk of his own. A few days afterwards he suddenly
appeared to this prisoner with some gunpowder ink,
and dictated to him a note. On his next expedition
this note, tied to a war-club, was left in the house of
a settler, whose entire family was murdered. It was
a short document, written with ferocious directness,
as a kind of public challenge or taunt to the man
whom he wrongly deemed to be the author of his
misfortunes. It ran as follows :

" CAPTAIN CRESAP :
 " What did you kill my people on Yellow Creek for ?
The white people killed my kin at Conestoga, a great
while ago, and I thought nothing of that. But you killed
my kin again on Yellow Creek, and took my cousin
prisoner. Then I thought I must kill too ; and I have
been three times to war since ; but the Indians are not
angry, only myself.
 " *July* 21, 1774.   CAPTAIN JOHN LOGAN." [2]

There is a certain deliberate and blood-thirsty
earnestness about this letter which must have shown
the whites clearly, if they still needed to be shown,
what bitter cause they had to rue the wrongs that
had been done to Logan.

[1] *Do.*, p. 470.
[2] Jefferson MSS. Dep. of Wm. Robinson, February 28, 1800, and letter
from Harry Innes, March 2, 1799, with a copy of Logan's letter as made in
his note-book at the time.

The Shawnees and Mingos were soon joined by
many of the Delawares and outlying Iroquois, especially Senecas ; as well as by the Wyandots and   **Indian**
by large bands of ardent young warriors from   **Inroads.**
among the Algonquin tribes along the Miami, the Wabash, and the Lakes. Their inroads on the settlements
were characterized, as usual, by extreme stealth and
merciless ferocity. They stole out of the woods with
the silent cunning of wild beasts, and ravaged with
a cruelty ten times greater. They burned down the
lonely log-huts, ambushed travellers, shot the men as
they hunted or tilled the soil, ripped open the women
with child, and burned many of their captives at the
stake. Their noiseless approach enabled them to fall
on the settlers before their presence was suspected ;
and they disappeared as suddenly as they had come,
leaving no trail that could be followed. The charred
huts and scalped and mangled bodies of their victims were left as ghastly reminders of their visit, the
sight stirring the backwoodsmen to a frenzy of rage
all the more terrible in the end, because it was impo-
tent for the time being. Generally they made their
escape successfully ; occasionally they were beaten
off or overtaken and killed or scattered.

When they met armed woodsmen the fight was
always desperate. In May, a party of hunters and
surveyors, being suddenly attacked in the forest,
beat off their assailants and took eight scalps, though
with a loss of nine of their own number.[1] Moreover,
the settlers began to band together to make retaliatory inroads ; and while Lord Dunmore was busily

[1] " Am. Archives.," p. 373.

preparing to strike a really effective blow, he directed the frontiersmen of the northwest to under-

Counter-Strokes of the Backwoodsmen. take a foray, so as to keep the Indians employed. Accordingly, they gathered together, four hundred strong,[1] crossed the Ohio, in the end of July, and marched against a Shawnee town on the Muskingum. They had a brisk skirmish with the Shawnees, drove them back, and took five scalps, losing two men killed and five wounded. Then the Shawnees tried to ambush them, but their ambush was discovered, and they promptly fled, after a slight skirmish, in which no one was killed but one Indian, whom Cresap, a very active and vigorous man, ran down and slew with his tomahawk.[2] The Shawnee village was burned, seventy acres of standing corn were cut down, and the settlers returned in triumph. On the march back they passed through the towns of the peaceful Moravian Delawares, to whom they did no harm.

[1] Under a certain Angus MacDonald, *do.*, p. 722. They crossed the Ohio at Fish Creek, 120 miles below Pittsburg.

[2] "Am. Archives," IV., Vol. I., pp. 682, 684.

CHAPTER IX.

THE BATTLE OF THE GREAT KANAWHA ; AND LOGAN'S SPEECH, 1774.

MEANWHILE Lord Dunmore, having garrisoned the frontier forts, three of which were put under the orders of Daniel Boon, was making ready a formidable army with which to overwhelm the hostile Indians. It was to be raised, and to march, in two wings or divisions, each fifteen hundred strong, which were to join at the mouth of the Great Kanawha. One wing, the right or northernmost, was to be commanded by the earl in person; while the other, composed exclusively of frontiersmen living among the mountains west and southwest of the Blue Ridge, was entrusted to General Andrew Lewis. Lewis was a stalwart backwoods soldier, belonging to a family of famous frontier fighters, but though a sternly just and fearless man,[1] he does not appear to have had more than average qualifications to act as a commander of border troops when pitted against Indians.

The backwoodsmen of the Alleghanies felt that the quarrel was their own; in their hearts the desire for revenge burned like a sullen flame. The old men had passed their manhood with nerves tense from the

[1] Stewart's Narrative.

strain of unending watchfulness, and souls embittered by terrible and repeated disasters; the young men had been cradled in stockaded forts, round which there prowled a foe whose comings and goings were unknown, and who was unseen till the moment when the weight of his hand was felt. They had been helpless to avenge their wrongs, and now that there was at last a chance to do so, they thronged eagerly to Lewis' standard. The left wing or army assembled at the Great Levels of Greenbriar, and thither came the heroes of long rifle, tomahawk, and hunting-shirt, gathering from every stockaded hamlet, every lonely clearing and smoky hunter's camp that lay along the ridges from whose hollows sprang the sources of the Eastern and the Western Waters. They were not uniformed, save that they all wore the garb of the frontier hunter; but most of them were armed with good rifles, and were skilful woodsmen, and though utterly undisciplined, they were magnificent individual fighters.[1] The officers were clad and armed almost precisely like the rank and file, save that some of them had long swords girded to their waist-belts; they carried rifles, for, where the result of the contest depended mainly on the personal prowess of the individual fighter, the leader was expected literally to stand in the forefront of the battle, and to inspirit his followers by deeds as well as words.

Among these troops was a company of rangers who came from the scattered wooden forts of the Watauga and the Nolichucky. Both Sevier and

The Backwoods Levies Gather.

[1] "Am. Archiv." Col. Wm. Preston's letter, Sept. 28, 1774.

Robertson took part in this war, and though the former saw no fighting, the latter, who had the rank of sergeant, was more fortunate.

While the backwoods general was mustering his unruly and turbulent host of skilled riflemen, the English earl led his own levies, some fifteen hundred strong, to Fort Pitt.[1] Here he changed his plans, and decided not to try to join the other division, as he had agreed to do. This **Advance of the Earl's Army.** sudden abandonment of a scheme already agreed to and acted on by his colleague was certainly improper, and, indeed, none of the earl's movements indicated very much military capacity. However, he descended the Ohio River with a flotilla of a hundred canoes, besides keel-boats and pirogues,[2] to the mouth of the Hockhocking, where he built and garrisoned a small stockade. Then he went up the Hockhocking to the falls, whence he marched to the Scioto, and there entrenched himself in a fortified camp, with breastworks of fallen trees, on the edge of the Pickaway plains, not far from the Indian town of Old Chillicothe. Thence he sent out detachments that destroyed certain of the hostile towns. He had with him as scouts many men famous in frontier story, among them George Rogers Clark, Cresap, and Simon Kenton—afterwards the bane of every neighboring Indian tribe, and renowned all along the border for his deeds of desperate prowess, his wonderful adventures, and his hairbreadth escapes. Another, of a very different stamp, was Simon Girty, of evil fame, whom the

[1] *Do.*, p. 872.   [2] Doddridge, 235.

whole west grew to loathe, with bitter hatred, as "the white renegade." He was the son of a vicious Irish trader, who was killed by the Indians; he was adopted by the latter, and grew up among them, and his daring ferocity and unscrupulous cunning early made him one of their leaders.[1] At the moment he was serving Lord Dunmore and the whites; but he was by tastes, habits, and education a red man, who felt ill at ease among those of his own color. He soon returned to the Indians, and dwelt among them ever afterwards, the most inveterate foe of the whites that was to be found in all the tribes. He lived to be a very old man, and is said to have died fighting his ancient foes and kinsmen, the Americans, in our second war against the British.

But Lord Dunmore's army was not destined to strike the decisive blow in the contest. The great Shawnee **Cornstalk's** chief, Cornstalk, was as wary and able as he **Strategy.** was brave. He had from the first opposed the war with the whites[2]; but as he had been unable to prevent it, he was now bent on bringing it to a successful issue. He was greatly outnumbered; but he had at his command over a thousand painted and plumed warriors, the pick of the young men of the western tribes, the most daring braves to be found between the Ohio and the Great Lakes. His foes were divided, and he determined to strike first at

[1] See *Mag. of Am. Hist.*, XV., 256.

[2] De Haas, p. 161. He is a very fair and trustworthy writer; in particular, as regards Logan's speech and Cresap's conduct. It is to be regretted that Brantz Mayer, in dealing with these latter subjects, could not have approached them with the same desire to be absolutely impartial, instead of appearing to act solely as an advocate.

the one who would least suspect a blow, but whose ruin, nevertheless, would involve that of the other. If Lewis' army could be surprised and overwhelmed, the fate of Lord Dunmore's would be merely a question of days. So without delay, Cornstalk, crafty in council, mighty in battle, and swift to carry out what he had planned, led his long files of warriors, with noiseless speed, through leagues of trackless woodland to the banks of the Ohio.

The backwoodsmen who were to form the army of Lewis had begun to gather at the Levels of Greenbriar before the 1st of September, and by the 7th most of them were assembled. Altogether the force under Lewis consisted of four commands, as follows : a body of Augusta troops, under Col. Charles Lewis, a brother of the general's [1]; a body of Botetourt troops, under Col. William Fleming [2]; a small independent company, under Col. John Field; and finally the Fincastle men, from the Holston, Clinch, Watauga, and New River [3] settlements, under Col. William Christian. [4] One of Christian's captains was a stout old Marylander, of Welsh blood, named Evan Shelby ; and Shelby's son Isaac, [5] a stalwart, stern-visaged young man, who afterwards

Lewis' Army Gathers at Greenbriar.

[1] His eight captains were George Matthews, Alexander McClannahan, John Dickinson, John Lewis (son of William), Benjamin Harrison, William Paul, Joseph Haynes, and Samuel Wilson. Hale, " Trans-Alleghany Pioneers," p. 181.

[2] His seven captains were Matthew Arbuckle, John Murray, John Lewis (son of Andrew), James Robertson, Robert McClannahan, James Ward, and John Stewart (author of the Narrative).

[3] As the Kanawha was sometimes called.

[4] Whose five captains were Evan Shelby, Russell, Herbert, Draper, and Buford.

[5] Born December 11, 1750, near Hagerstown, Md.

played a very prominent part on the border, was a subaltern in his company, in which Robertson likewise served as a sergeant. Although without experience of drill, it may be doubted if a braver or physically finer set of men were ever got together on this continent.[1]

Among such undisciplined troops it was inevitable that there should be both delay and insubordination. Nevertheless they behaved a good deal better than their commander had expected; and he was much pleased with their cheerfulness and their eagerness for action. The Fincastle men, being from the remote settlements, were unable to get together in time to start with the others; and Col. Field grew jealous of his commander and decided to march his little company alone. The Indians were hovering around the camp, and occasionally shot at and wounded stragglers, or attempted to drive off the pack-horses.

The army started in three divisions. The bulk, consisting of Augusta men, under Col. Charles Lewis, marched on September 8th, closely followed by the Botetourt troops under Andrew Lewis himself.[2] Field, with his small company, started off on his own

[1] Letter of Col. Wm. Preston, September 28, 1774. "Am. Archives."

[2] Letter of one of Lord Dunmore's officers, November 21, 1774. "Am. Archives," IV., Vol. I., p. 1017. Hale gives a minute account of the route followed; Stewart says they started on the 11th.

With the journal of Floyd's expedition, mentioned on a previous page, I received MS. copies of two letters to Col. William Preston, both dated at Camp Union, at the Great Levels; one, of September 8th from Col. Andrew Lewis, and one of September 7th (9th?) from Col. William Christian.

Col. Lewis' letter runs in part: "From Augusta we have 600; of this county [Botetourt] about 400; Major Field is joined with 40. . . . I have had less Trouble with the Troops than I expected. . . . I received a letter from his Lordship last Sunday morning which was dated the 30th of

account; but after being out a couple of days, two of his scouts met two Indians, with the result that a man was killed on each side; after which, profiting by the loss, he swallowed his pride and made haste to join the first division. The Fincastle troops were delayed so long that most of them, with their commander, were still fifteen miles from the main body the day the battle was fought; but Captains Shelby and Russell, with parts of their companies, went on ahead of the others, and, as will be seen, joined Lewis in time to do their full share of the fighting. Col.

August at Old Towns, which I take to be Chresops; he then I am told had Col. Stephens and Major Conolly at his Elbow as might easily be discovered by the Contents of his Letter which expressed his Lordship's warmest wishes that I would with all the troops from this Quarter join him at the mouth of the little Kanaway; I wrote his Lordship that it was not in my power to alter our rout. . . . The Indians wounded a man within two miles of us . . . and wounded another; from this we may expect they will be picking about us all the March." He states that he has more men than he expected, and will therefore need more provisions, and that he will leave some of his poorest troops to garrison the small fort.

Col. Christian's letter states that the Augusta men took with them 400 pack-horses, carrying 54,000 pounds of flour, and 108 beeves; they started "yesterday"; Field marched "this evening"; Fleming and his 450 Botetourt men, with 200 pack-horses, "are going next Monday." Field had brought word that Dunmore expected to be at the mouth of the Great Kanawha "some days after the 20th." Some Indians had tried to steal a number of pack-horses, but had been discovered and frightened off.

Christian was very much discontented at being bidden to stay behind until he could gather 300 men, and bring up the rear; he expresses his fear that his men will be much exasperated when they learn that they are to stay behind, and reiterates: "I would not for all I am worth be behind crossing the Ohio and that we should miss lending our assistance." Field brought an account of McDonald's fight (see *ante*, p. 216); he said the whites were 400 and the Indians but 30 strong, that the former had 4 men killed and 6 wounded; the Indians but 3 or 4 killed and 1 captured, and their town was burnt. The number of the Shawnees and their allies was estimated at 1,200 warriors that could be put into one battle. The 400 horses that had started with the Augusta men were to return as fast as they could (after reaching the embarkment point, whence the flour was carried in canoes).

Christian himself only reached the Levels on the afternoon of the day the Augusta men had marched. He was burning with desire to distinguish himself, and his men were also very eager to have a share in the battle; and he besought Lewis to let him go along with what troops he had. But he was refused permission, whereat he was greatly put out.

Lewis found he had more men than he expected, and so left some of the worst troops to garrison the small forts. Just before starting he received a letter from the Earl advising, but not commanding, a change in their plans; to this he refused to accede, and was rather displeased at the proposal, attributing it to the influence of Conolly, whom the backwoods leaders were growing to distrust. There is not the slightest reason to suppose, however, that he then, or at any time during the campaign, suspected the Earl of treachery; nor did the latter's conduct give any good ground for such a belief. Nevertheless, this view gained credit among the Virginians in later years, when they were greatly angered by the folly and ferocity of Lord Dunmore's conduct during the early part of the Revolutionary war, and looked at all his past acts with jaundiced eyes.[1]

[1] When the Revolutionary war broke out the Earl not only fought the revolted colonists with all legitimate weapons, but tried to incite the blacks to servile insurrection, and sent agents to bring his old foes, the red men of the forest, down on his old friends, the settlers. He encouraged piratical and plundering raids, and on the other hand failed to show the courage and daring that are sometimes partial offsets to ferocity. But in this war, in 1774, he conducted himself with great energy in making preparations, and showed considerable skill as a negotiator in concluding the peace, and apparently went into the conflict with hearty zest and good will. He was evidently much influenced by Conolly, a very weak adviser, however; and his whole course betrayed much vacillation, and no generalship.

Lewis' troops formed a typical backwoods army, both officers and soldiers. They wore fringed hunting-shirts, dyed yellow, brown, white, and even red; quaintly carved shot-bags and powder-horns hung from their broad ornamented belts; they had fur caps or soft hats, moccasins, and coarse woollen leggings reaching half-way up the thigh.[1] Each carried his flint-lock, his tomahawk, and scalping-knife. They marched in long files with scouts or spies thrown out in front and on the flanks, while axe-men went in advance to clear a trail over which they could drive the beef cattle, and the pack-horses, laden with provisions, blankets, and ammunition. They struck out straight through the trackless wilderness, making their road as they went, until on the 21st of the month[2] they reached the Kanawha, at the mouth of Elk Creek. Here they halted to build dug-out canoes; and about this time were overtaken by the companies of Russell and Shelby. On October 1st[3] they started to descend the river in twenty-seven canoes, a portion of the army marching down along the Indian trail, which followed the base of the hills, instead of the river bank, as it was thus easier to cross the heads of the creeks and ravines.[4]

They reached the mouth of the river on the 6th,[5]

March of the Back-woodsmen.

[1] Smyth's "Tour," II., p. 179.   [2] "Am. Archives," p. 1017.

[3] *Do.* Stewart says they reached the mouth of the Kanawha on Oct. 1st; another account says Sept. 30th; but this is an error, as shown both by the "Am. Archives" and by the Campbell MSS.   [4] Hale, 182.

[5] Campbell MSS. Letter of Isaac Shelby to John Shelby, Oct. 16, 1774. A portion of this letter, unsigned, was printed in "Am. Archives," p. 1016, and in various newspapers (even at Belfast; see Hale, p. 187, who thinks it was written by Captain Arbuckle). As it is worth preserving and has never been printed in full I give it in the Appendix.

and camped on Point Pleasant, the cape of land jut-
ting out between the Ohio and the Kanawha.   As a
They Camp consequence the bloody fight that ensued is
at Point sometimes called the battle of Point Pleas-
Pleasant. ant, and sometimes the battle of the Great
Kanawha.   Hitherto the Indians had not seriously
molested Lewis' men, though they killed a settler
right on their line of march, and managed to drive
off some of the bullocks and pack-horses.[1]

The troops, though tired from their journey, were
in good spirits, and eager to fight.   But they were
impatient of control, and were murmuring angrily
that there was favoritism shown in the issue of beef.
Hearing this, Lewis ordered all the poorest beeves to
be killed first; but this merely produced an explosion of discontent, and large numbers of the men in
mutinous defiance of the orders of their officers began
to range the woods, in couples, to kill game.   There
was little order in the camp,[2] and small attention was
paid to picket and sentinel duty; the army, like a
body of Indian warriors, relying for safety mainly
upon the sharp-sighted watchfulness of the individual members and the activity of the hunting parties.

On the 9th Simon Girty[3] arrived in camp bring-

---

[1] Stewart's Narrative.

[2] Smyth, II., p. 158.   He claims to have played a prominent part in the
battle.   This is certainly not so, and he may not have been present at all;
at least Col. Stewart, who was there and was acquainted with every one of
note in the army, asserts positively that there was no such man along; nor
has any other American account ever mentioned him.   His military knowledge was nil, as may be gathered from his remark, made when the defeats of
Braddock and Grant were still recent, that British regulars with the bayonet
were best fitted to oppose Indians.

[3] Some accounts say that he was accompanied by Kenton and McCulloch;
others state that no messenger arrived until after the battle.   But this is cer-

ing a message from Lord Dunmore, which bade Lewis meet him at the Indian towns near the Pickaway plains. Lewis was by no means pleased at the change, but nevertheless prepared to break camp and march next morning. He had with him at this time about eleven hundred men.[1]

His plans, however, were destined to be rudely forestalled, for Cornstalk, coming rapidly through the forest, had reached the Ohio. That very night the Indian chief ferried his men across the river on rafts, six or eight miles above the forks,[2] and by dawn was on the point of hurling his whole force, of nearly a thousand warriors,[3] on the camp of his slumbering foes. *Cornstalk's Indians Attack Them.*

Before daylight on the 10th small parties of hunters had, as usual, left Lewis' camp. Two of these men, from Russell's company, after having gone somewhat over a mile, came upon a large party of Indians; one was killed, and the survivor ran back at full speed to give the alarm, telling

tainly wrong. Shelby's letter shows that the troops learned the governor's change of plans before the battle.

[1] "Am. Archives," IV., Vol. I., p. 1017; and was joined by Col. Christian's three hundred the day after the battle.

[2] Campbell MSS. Letter of Col. William Preston (presumably to Patrick Henry), Oct. 31, 1774. As it is interesting and has never been published, I give it in the Appendix.

[3] Many of the white accounts make their number much greater, without any authority; Shelby estimates it at between eight hundred and one thousand. Smith, who generally gives the Indian side, says that on this occasion they were nearly as numerous as the whites. Smyth, who bitterly hates the Americans, and always belittles their deeds, puts the number of Indians at nine hundred; he would certainly make it as small as possible. So the above estimate is probably pretty near the truth, though it is of course impossible to be accurate. At any rate, it was the only important engagement fought by the English or Americans against the northwestern Indians in which there was a near approach to equality of force.

those in camp that he had seen five acres of ground covered with Indians as thick as they could stand.[1]

Battle of the Great Kanawha. Almost immediately afterwards two men of Shelby's company, one being no less a person than Robertson himself and the other Valentine, a brother of John Sevier, also stumbled upon the advancing Indians; being very wary and active men, they both escaped, and reached camp almost as soon as the other.

Instantly the drums beat to arms,[2] and the backwoodsmen,—lying out in the open, rolled in their blankets,—started from the ground, looked to their flints and priming, and were ready on the moment. The general, thinking he had only a scouting party to deal with, ordered out Col. Charles Lewis and Col. Fleming, each with one hundred and fifty men. Fleming had the left, and marched up the bank of the Ohio, while Lewis, on the right, kept some little distance inland. They went about half a mile.[3] Then, just before sunrise, while it was still dusk, the men in camp, eagerly listening, heard the reports of three guns, immediately succeeded by a clash like a peal of thin thunder, as hundreds of rifles rang out together. It was evident that the attack was serious and Col. Field was at once despatched to the front with two hundred men.[4]

---

[1] Campbell MSS. Shelby's letter. Their names were Mooney and Hickman; the latter was killed. Most historians have confused these two men with the two others who discovered the Indians at almost the same time.

[2] " Am. Archives," IV., Vol, I., p. 1017.

[3] *Do.*, p. 1017. Letter from Stanton, Virginia, Nov. 4, 1774, says ⅔ of a mile ; Shelby says ¼ of a mile.

[4] *Do.*, Letter of Nov. 17th.

He came only just in time. At the first fire both of the scouts in front of the white line had been killed. The attack fell first, and with especial fury, on the division of Charles Lewis, who himself was mortally wounded at the very outset; he had not taken a tree,[1] but was in an open piece of ground, cheering on his men, when he was shot. He stayed with them until the line was formed, and then walked back to camp unassisted, giving his gun to a man who was near him. His men, who were drawn up on the high ground skirting Crooked Run,[2] began to waver, but were rallied by Fleming, whose division had been attacked almost simultaneously, until he too was struck down by a bullet. The line then gave way, except that some of Fleming's men still held their own on the left in a patch of rugged ground near the Ohio. At this moment, however, Colonel Field came up and restored the battle, while the backwoodsmen who had been left in camp also began to hurry up to take part in the fight. General Lewis at last, fully awake to the danger, began to fortify the camp by felling timber so as to form a breastwork running across the point from the Ohio to the Kanawha. This work should have been done before; and through attending to it Lewis was unable to take any personal part in the battle.

Meanwhile the frontiersmen began to push back their foes, led by Col. Field. The latter himself, however, was soon slain ; he was at the time behind

---

[1] The frontier expression for covering one's self behind a tree-trunk.

[2] A small stream running into the Kanawha near its mouth. **De Haas**, p. 151.

a great tree, and was shot by two Indians on his
right, while he was trying to get a shot at another
on his left, who was distracting his attention by
mocking and jeering at him.[1] The command then
fell on Captain Evan Shelby, who turned his company over to the charge of his son, Isaac. The troops
fought on steadily, undaunted by the fall of their
leaders, while the Indians attacked with the utmost
skill, caution, and bravery. The fight was a succession of single combats, each man sheltering himself
behind a stump, or rock, or tree-trunk, the superiority
of the backwoodsmen in the use of the rifle being
offset by the superiority of their foes in the art of
hiding and of shielding themselves from harm. The
hostile lines, though about a mile and a quarter in
length, were so close together, being never more than
twenty yards apart, that many of the combatants
grappled in hand-to-hand fighting, and tomahawked
or stabbed each other[2] to death. The clatter of the
rifles was incessant, while above the din could be
heard the cries and groans of the wounded, and the
shouts of the combatants, as each encouraged his own
side, or jeered savagely at his adversaries. The cheers
of the whites mingled with the appalling war-whoops
and yells of their foes. The Indians also called out
to the Americans in broken English, taunting them,
and asking them why their fifes were no longer
whistling—for the fight was far too close to permit
of any such music. Their headmen walked up and
down behind their warriors, exhorting them to go in
close, to shoot straight, and to bear themselves well

[1] Campbell MSS. Preston's letter.
[2] "Am. Archives." Letter of November 4, 1774.

in the fight [1]; while throughout the action the whites opposite Cornstalk could hear his deep, sonorous voice as he cheered on his braves, and bade them "be strong, be strong." [2]

About noon the Indians tried to get round the flank of the whites, into their camp; but this movement was repulsed, and a party of the Americans [3] followed up their advantage, and running along the banks of the Kanawha out-flanked the enemy in turn. The Indians being pushed very hard now began to fall back, the best fighters covering the retreat, while the wounded were being carried off; although,—a rare thing in Indian battles—they were pressed so close that they were able to bear away but a portion of their dead. The whites were forced to pursue with the greatest caution; for those of them who advanced heedlessly were certain to be ambushed and receive a smart check. Finally, about one o'clock, the Indians, in their retreat, reached a very strong position, where the underbrush was very close and there were many fallen logs and steep banks. Here they stood resolutely at bay, and the whites did not dare attack them in such a stronghold. So the action came almost to an end; though skirmishing went on until about an hour before sunset, the Indians still at times taunting their foes and calling out to them that they had eleven hundred men as well as the whites, and that to-morrow they were going to be two thousand strong. [4] This was only bravado, however; they had suffered too heavily to renew the

[1] Campbell MSS. Preston's letter.　　　[2] Stewart's Narrative.
[3] Led by Isaac Shelby, James Stewart, and George Matthews.
[4] Campbell MSS. Preston's letter.

attack, and under cover of darkness they slipped away, and made a most skilful retreat, carrying all their wounded in safety across the Ohio. The exhausted Americans, having taken a number of scalps, as well as forty guns, and many tomahawks[1] and some other plunder,[2] returned to their camp.

The battle had been bloody as well as stubborn. The whites, though the victors, had suffered more than their foes, and indeed had won only because it was against the entire policy of Indian warfare to suffer a severe loss, even if a victory could be gained thereby. Of the whites, some seventy-five men had been killed or mortally wounded, and one hundred and forty severely or slightly wounded,[3] so that they lost a fifth of their whole number. The Indians had not lost much more than half as many; about forty warriors were killed outright or died of their wounds.[4]

---

[1] "Am. Archives." Letter of November 4, 1774. It is doubtful if Logan was in this fight; the story about Cornstalk killing one of his men who flinched may or may not be true.

[2] Hale, 199; the plunder was afterwards sold at auction for £74 4s. 6d.

[3] These are the numbers given by Stewart; but the accounts vary greatly. Monette ("Valley of the Mississippi,") says 87 killed and 141 wounded. The letters written at the time evidently take no account of any but the badly wounded. Shelby thus makes the killed 55, and the wounded (including the mortally hurt) 68. Another account ("Am. Archives," p. 1017) says 40 men killed and 96 wounded, 20 odd of whom were since dead; whilst a foot-note to this letter enumerates 53 dead outright, and 87 wounded, "some of whom have since died." It is evidently impossible that the slightly wounded are included in these lists; and in all probability Stewart's account is correct, as he was an eye-witness and participant.

[4] Twenty-one were scalped on the field; the bodies of 12 more were afterwards found behind logs or in holes where they had been lain, and 8 eventually died of their wounds. (See "American Archives," Smith, Hale, De Haas, etc.) Smith, who wrote from the Indian side, makes their loss only 28; but this apparently does not include the loss of the western Indians, the allies of the Shawnees, Mingos, and Delawares.

Among the Indians no chief of importance was slain; whereas the Americans had seventeen officers killed or wounded, and lost in succession their second, third, and fourth in command. The victors buried their own dead and left the bodies of the vanquished to the wolves and ravens. At midnight, after the battle, Col. Christian and his Fincastle men reached the ground.

The battle of the Great Kanawha was a purely American victory, for it was fought solely by the backwoodsmen themselves. Their immense superiority over regular troops in such contests can be readily seen when their triumph on this occasion is compared with the defeats previously suffered by Braddock's grenadiers and Grant's highlanders, at the hands of the same foes. It was purely a soldiers' battle, won by hard individual fighting; there was no display of generalship, except on Cornstalk's part.[1] It was the most closely contested of any battle ever fought with the northwestern Indians; and it was the only victory gained over a large body of them by a force but slightly superior in numbers.[2] Both because of the character of the fight itself, and because of the results that flowed from it, it is worthy of being held in especial remembrance.

[1] Smyth, the Englishman, accuses Lewis of cowardice, an accusation which deserves no more attention than do the similar accusations of treachery brought against Dunmore. Brantz Mayer speaks in very hyperbolic terms of the " relentless Lewis," and the " great slaughter " of the Indians.

[2] Wayne won an equally decisive victory, but he outnumbered his foes three to one. Bouquet, who was almost beaten, and was saved by the provincial rangers, was greatly the superior in force, and suffered four times the loss he inflicted. In both cases, especially that of Bouquet, the account of the victor must be received with caution where it deals with the force and loss of the vanquished. In the same way Shelby and the other reporters of the Kanawha fight stated that the Indians lost more heavily than the whites.

Lewis left his sick and wounded in the camp at the Point, protected by a rude breastwork, and with **March** an adequate guard. With the remainder **to the** of his forces, over a thousand strong, he **Pickaway** crossed the Ohio, and pushed on to the **Plains.** Pickaway plains. When but a few miles from the earl's encampment he was met by a messenger informing him that a treaty of peace was being negotiated with the Indians.[1] The backwoodsmen, flushed with success, and angry at their losses, were eager for more bloodshed; and it was only with difficulty that they were restrained, and were finally induced to march homewards, the earl riding down to them and giving his orders in person. They grumbled angrily against the earl for sending them back, and in later days accused him of treachery for having done so; but his course was undoubtedly proper, for it would have been very difficult to conclude peace in the presence of such fierce and unruly auxiliaries.

The spirit of the Indians had been broken by their defeat. Their stern old chief, Cornstalk, alone remained with unshaken heart, resolute to bid defiance to his foes and to fight the war out to the bitter end. But when the council of the headmen and war-chiefs

[1] The stories of how Lewis suspected the earl of treachery, and of how the backwoodsmen were so exasperated that they wished to kill the latter, may have some foundation; but are quite as likely to be pure inventions, made up after the Revolutionary war. In De Haas, "The American Pioneer," etc., can be found all kinds of stories, some even told by members of the Clark and Lewis families, which are meant to criminate Dunmore, but which make such mistakes in chronology—placing the battle of Lexington in the year of the Kanawha fight, asserting that peace was not made till the following spring, etc.—that they must be dismissed offhand as entirely untrustworthy.

was called it became evident that his tribesmen would
not fight, and even his burning eloquence could not
goad the warriors into again trying the   The In-
hazard of battle. They listened unmoved   dians Sue
and in sullen silence to the thrilling and   for Peace.
impassioned words with which he urged them to
once more march against the Long Knives, and if
necessary to kill their women and children, and
then themselves die fighting to the last man. At
last, when he saw he could not stir the hearts of
his hearers he struck his tomahawk into the war-
post and announced that he himself would go and
make peace. At that the warriors broke silence,
and all grunted out approvingly, ough! ough! ough!
and then they instantly sent runners to the earl's
army to demand a truce.[1]

Accordingly, with all his fellow-chiefs, he went to
Lord Dunmore's camp, and there entered into a treaty.
The crestfallen Indians assented to all the   Treaty
terms the conquerors proposed. They agreed   of Peace.
to give up all the white prisoners and stolen horses
in their possession, and to surrender all claim to the
lands south of the Ohio, and they gave hostages as an
earnest of their good-faith.[2] But their chief spokes-
man, Cornstalk, while obliged to assent to these
conditions, yet preserved through all the proceedings
a bearing of proud defiance that showed how little
the fear of personal consequences influenced his own
actions. At the talks he addressed the white leader
with vehement denunciation and reproach, in a tone

---

[1] Stewart's Narrative.
[2] " Am. Archives," IV. St. Clair's letter, Dec. 4, 1774. Also Jefferson
MSS. Dep. of Wm. Robinson, etc.

that seemed rather that of a conqueror than of one of the conquered. Indeed, he himself was not conquered; he felt that his tribesmen were craven, but he knew that his own soul feared nothing. The Virginians, who, like their Indian antagonists, prized skill in oratory only less than skill in warfare, were greatly impressed by the chieftain's eloquence, by his command of words, his clear, distinct voice, his peculiar emphasis, and his singularly grand and majestic, and yet graceful, bearing; they afterwards said that his oratory fully equalled that of Patrick Henry himself.[1]

Every prominent chief but one came to the council. The exception was Logan, who remained apart in the Mingo village, brooding over his wrongs, and the vengeance he had taken. His fellows, when questioned about his absence, answered that he was like a mad dog, whose bristles were still up, but that they were gradually falling; and when he was entreated to be present at the meeting he responded that he was a warrior, not a councillor, and would not come. The Mingos, because they failed to appear at the treaty, had their camp destroyed and were forced to give hostages, as the Delawares and Shawnees had done,[2] and Logan himself finally sullenly acquiesced in, or at least ceased openly to oppose, the peace.

But he would not come in person to Lord Dunmore; so the earl was obliged to communicate with him through a messenger, a frontier veteran [3] named

[1] See De Haas, 162.

[2] "Am. Archives," IV., Vol. I., pp. 1013, 1226.

[3] John Gibson, afterwards a general in the army of the United States. See Appendix.

John Gibson, who had long lived among the Indians and knew thoroughly both their speech and their manners.[1] To this messenger Logan was   **Logan's** willing to talk. Taking him aside, he sud-   **Speech.** denly addressed him in a speech that will always retain its place as perhaps the finest outburst of savage eloquence of which we have any authentic record. The messenger took it down in writing, translating it literally,[2] and, returning to camp, gave it to Lord Dunmore. The earl then read it, in open council, to the whole backwoods army, including Cresap, Clark, and the other scouts. The speech, when read, proved to be no message of peace, nor an acknowledgment of defeat, but instead, a strangely pathetic recital of his wrongs, and a fierce and exulting justification of the vengeance he had taken. It ran as follows:

"I appeal to any white man to say if ever he entered Logan's cabin hungry and he gave him not meat; if ever he came cold and naked and he clothed him not? During the course of the last long and bloody war, Logan remained idle in his camp, an advocate for peace. Such was my love for the whites that my countrymen pointed as I passed and said, 'Logan is the friend of the white man.' I had even thought to have lived with you, but for the injuries of one man. Colonel Cresap, the last spring, in cold blood and unprovoked, murdered all the relations of Logan, not even sparing my women and

---

[1] Jefferson MSS. Statements of John Gibson, etc.; there is some uncertainty as to whether Logan came up to Gibson at the treaty and drew him aside, or whether the latter went to seek the former in his wigwam.

[2] Jefferson Papers (State Department MSS.), 5-1-4. Statement of Col. John Gibson to John Anderson, an Indian trader at Pittsburg, in 1774. Anderson had asked him if he had not himself added somewhat to the speech; he responded that he had not, that it was a literal translation or transcription of Logan's words.

children. There runs not a drop of my blood in the veins of any living creature. This called on me for revenge. I have sought it. I have killed many. I have fully glutted my vengeance. For my country I rejoice at the beams of peace; but do not harbor a thought that mine is the joy of fear. Logan never felt fear. He will not turn on his heel to save his life. Who is there to mourn for Logan? Not one."

The tall frontiersmen, lounging in a circle round about, listened to the reading of the speech with eager interest; rough Indian haters though they were, they were so much impressed by it that in the evening it was a common topic of conversation over their camp fires, and they continually attempted to rehearse it to one another.[1] But they knew that Greathouse, not Cresap, had been the chief offender in the murder of Logan's family; and when the speech was read, Clark, turning round, jeered at and rallied Cresap as being so great a man that the Indians put every thing on his shoulders; whereat, Cresap, much angered, swore that he had a good mind to tomahawk Greathouse for the murder.[2]

The speech could not have been very satisfactory to the earl; but at least it made it evident that Logan did not intend to remain on the war-path; and so Lord Dunmore marched home with his hostages. On the homeward march, near the mouth of the River Hockhocking, the officers of the army held a notable meeting. They had followed the British earl to battle; but they were Americans, in

[1] Jefferson MSS. Affidavits of Andrew Rogers, Wm. Russell, and others who were present.
[2] Clark's letter.

warm sympathy with the Continental Congress, which was then in session. Fearful lest their countrymen might not know that they were at one with them in the struggle of which the shadow was looming up with ever increasing blackness, they passed resolutions which were after-

The Army Passes Resolutions.

wards published. Their speakers told how they had lived in the woods for three months, without hearing from the Congress at Philadelphia, nor yet from Boston, where the disturbances seemed most likely to come to a head. They spoke of their fear lest their countrymen might be misled into the belief that this numerous body of armed men was hostile or indifferent to the cause of America; and proudly alluded to the fact that they had lived so long without bread or salt, or shelter at night, and that the troops they led could march and fight as well as any in the world. In their resolutions they professed their devotion to their king, to the honor of his crown, and to the dignity of the British empire; but they added that this devotion would only last while the king deigned to rule over a free people, for their love for the liberty of America outweighed all other considerations, and they would exert every power for its defence, not riotously, but when regularly called forth by the voice of their countrymen.

They ended by tendering their thanks to Lord Dunmore for his conduct. He was also warmly thanked by the Virginia Legislature, as well as by the frontiersmen of Fincastle,[1] and he fully deserved their gratitude.

[1] See De Haas, 167.

The war had been ended in less than six months' time; and its results were of the utmost importance. **Results of** It had been very successful. In Brad-**the War.** dock's war, the borderers are estimated to have suffered a loss of fifty souls for every Indian slain; in Pontiac's war, they had learned to defend themselves better, and yet the ratio was probably as ten to one [1]; whereas in this war, if we consider only males of fighting age, it is probable that a good deal more than half as many Indians as whites were killed, and even including women and children, the ratio would not rise to more than three to one. Certainly, in all the contests waged against the northwestern Indians during the last half of the eighteenth century there was no other where the whites inflicted so great a relative loss on their foes. Its results were most important. It kept the northwestern tribes quiet for the first two years of the Revolutionary struggle; and above all it rendered possible the settlement of Kentucky, and therefore the winning of the West. Had it not been for Lord Dunmore's war, it is more than likely that when the colonies achieved their freedom they would have found their western boundary fixed at the Alleghany Mountains.[2]

Nor must we permit our sympathy for the foul wrongs of the two great Indian heroes of the contest to blind us to the fact that the struggle was precipitated, in the first place, by the outrages of the red

[1] These are Smith's estimates, derived largely from Indian sources. They are probably excessive, but not very greatly so.

[2] It is difficult to understand why some minor historians consider this war as fruitless.

men, not the whites; and that the war was not only inevitable, but was also in its essence just and righteous on the part of the borderers. Even the unpardonable and hideous atrocity of the murder of Logan's family, was surpassed in horror by many of the massacres committed by the Indians about the same time. The annals of the border are dark and terrible.

Among the characters who played the leaders' parts in this short and tragic drama of the backwoods few came to much afterwards. Cresap died a brave Revolutionary soldier. Of Greathouse we know nothing; we can only hope that eventually the Indians scalped him. Conolly became a virulent tory, who yet lacked the power to do the evil that he wished. Lewis served creditably in the Revolution; while at its outbreak Lord Dunmore was driven from Virginia and disappears from our ken. Proud, gloomy Logan never recovered from the blow that had been dealt him; he drank deeper and deeper, and became more and more an implacable, moody, and blood-thirsty savage, yet with noble qualities that came to the surface now and then. Again and again he wrought havoc among the frontier settlers; yet we several times hear of his saving the lives of prisoners. Once he saved Simon Kenton from torture and death, when Girty, moved by a rare spark of compassion for his former comrade, had already tried to do so and failed. At last he perished in a drunken brawl by the hand of another Indian.

Cornstalk died a grand death, but by an act of

Fates of the Actors in the Struggle.

cowardly treachery on the part of his American foes; it is one of the darkest stains on the checkered pages of frontier history. Early in 1777 he came into the garrison at Point Pleasant to explain that, while he was anxious to keep at peace, his tribe were bent on going to war; and he frankly added that of course if they did so he should have to join them. He and three other Indians, among them his son and the chief Redhawk, who had also been at the Kanawha battle, were detained as hostages. While they were thus confined in the fort a member of a company of rangers was killed by the Indians near by; whereupon his comrades, headed by their captain,[1] rushed in furious anger into the fort to slay the hostages. Cornstalk heard them rushing in, and knew that his hour had come; with unmoved countenance he exhorted his son not to fear, for it was the will of the Great Spirit that they should die there together; then, as the murderers burst into the room, he quietly rose up to meet them, and fell dead pierced by seven or eight bullets. His son and his comrades were likewise butchered, and we have no record of any more infamous deed.

Though among the whites, the men who took prominent parts in the struggle never afterwards made any mark, yet it is worth noting that all the aftertime leaders of the west were engaged in some way in Lord Dunmore's war. Their fates were various. Boon led the vanguard of the white advance across the mountains, wandered his life long

---

[1] John Hall; it is worth while preserving the name of the ringleader in so brutal and cowardly a butchery. See Stewart's Narrative.

through the wilderness, and ended his days, in extreme old age, beyond the Mississippi, a backwoods hunter to the last. Shelby won laurels at King's Mountain, became the first governor of Kentucky, and when an old man revived the memories of his youth by again leading the western men in battle against the British and Indians. Sevier and Robertson were for a generation the honored chiefs of the southwestern people. Clark, the ablest of all, led a short but brilliant career, during which he made the whole nation his debtor. Then, like Logan, he sank under the curse of drunkenness,—often hardly less dangerous to the white borderer than to his red enemy,—and passed the remainder of his days in ignoble and slothful retirement.

CHAPTER X.

LORD DUNMORE's war, waged by Americans for the good of America, was the opening act in the drama whereof the closing scene was played at Yorktown. It made possible the twofold character of the Revolutionary war, wherein on the one hand the Americans won by conquest and colonization new lands for their children, and on the other wrought out their national independence of the British king. Save for Lord Dunmore's war we could not have settled beyond the mountains until after we had ended our quarrel with our kinsfolk across the sea. It so cowed the northern Indians that for two or three years they made no further organized effort to check the white advance. In consequence, the Kentucky pioneers had only to contend with small parties of enemies until time had been given them to become so firmly rooted in the land that it proved impossible to oust them. Had Cornstalk and his fellow-chiefs kept their hosts unbroken, they would undoubtedly have swept Kentucky clear of settlers in 1775,—as was done by the mere rumor of their hostility the preceding summer. Their defeat gave the opportunity for Boon to settle Kentucky, and therefore for Robertson to settle Middle Tennessee, and for Clark to con-

quer Illinois and the Northwest; it was the first in
the chain of causes that gave us for our western frontier in 1783 the Mississippi and not the Alleghanies.

As already mentioned, the speculative North Carolinian Henderson had for some time been planning
the establishment of a proprietary colony beyond the
mountains, as a bold stroke to reëstablish his ruined
fortunes; and early in 1775, as the time seemed
favorable, he proceeded to put his venturous scheme
into execution. For years he had been in close
business relations with Boon; and the latter had
attempted to lead a band of actual settlers to Kentucky in 1773. Naturally, when Henderson wished
to fix on a place wherein to plant his colony, Henderson
he chose the beautiful land which the rumor **and Boon.**
of Boon's discovery had rendered famous all along the
border; and equally naturally he chose the pioneer
hunter himself to act as his lieutenant and as the
real leader of the expedition. The result of the
joint efforts of these two men was to plant in Kentucky a colony of picked settlers, backed by such
moral and material support as enabled them to maintain themselves permanently in the land. Boon had
not been the first to discover Kentucky, nor was he
the first to found a settlement therein [1]; but it was
his exploration of the land that alone bore lasting
fruit, and the settlement he founded was the first
that contained within itself the elements of perma-
nence and growth.

[1] The first permanent settlement was Harrodsburg, then called Harrodstown, founded in 1774, but soon abandoned, and only permanently
occupied on March 18, 1775, a fortnight before Boon began the erection
of his fort.

Of course, as in every other settlement of inland America, the especial point to be noticed is the individual initiative of the different settlers. Neither the royal nor the provincial governments had any thing to do with the various colonies that were planted almost simultaneously on the soil of Kentucky. Different and Independent Settlements in Kentucky. Each little band of pioneers had its own leaders, and was stirred by its own motives. All had heard, from different sources, of the beauty and fertility of the land, and as the great danger from the Indians was temporarily past, all alike went in to take possession, not only acting without previous agreement, but for the most part being even in ignorance of one another's designs. Yet the dangers surrounding these new-formed and far-off settlements were so numerous, and of such grave nature, that they could hardly have proved permanent had it not been for the comparatively well-organized settlement of Boon, and for the temporary immunity which Henderson's treaty purchased from the southern Indians.

The settlement of Kentucky was a much more adventurous and hazardous proceeding than had been the case with any previous westward extension of population from the old colonies; because Kentucky, instead of abutting on already settled districts, was an island in the wilderness, separated by two hundred miles of unpeopled and almost impassable forest from even the extreme outposts of the seacoast commonwealths. Hitherto every new settlement had been made by the simple process of a portion of the backwoods pioneers being thrust out in advance of the others, while, nevertheless, keeping in touch with them, and having their rear covered, as it were, by the already colonized country. Now, for the first time, a new community of pioneers sprang up, isolated in the heart of the wilderness, and thrust far beyond the uttermost limits of the old colonies, whose solid mass lay along the Atlantic seaboard. The vast belt of mountainous woodland that lay between was as complete a barrier as if it had been a broad arm of the ocean. The first American incomers to Kentucky were for several years almost cut off from the bulk of their fellows beyond the forest-clad mountains; much as, thirteen centuries before, their forebears, the first English settlers in Britain, had been cut off from the rest of the low-Dutch folk who continued to dwell on the eastern coast of the German Ocean.

Henderson and those associated with him in his scheme of land speculation began to open negotiations with the Cherokees as soon as the victory of the Great Kanawha for the moment lessened the danger to be apprehended from the northwestern Indians. **The Treaty of the Sycamore Shoals.** In October, 1774, he and Nathaniel Hart, one of his partners in the scheme, journeyed to the Otari towns, and made their proposals. The Indians proceeded very cautiously, deputing one of their number, a chief called the Carpenter, to return with the two white envoys, and examine the goods they proposed to give in exchange. To this Henderson made no objection; on the contrary, it pleased him, for he was anxious to get an indisputable Indian title to the proposed new colony. The Indian delegate made a favorable report in January, 1775; and then the Overhill Cherokees were bidden to assemble at the Sycamore Shoals of the Watauga. The order was issued by the head-chief, Oconostota, a very old man, renowned for the prowess he had shown in former years when warring against the English. On the 17th of March, Oconostota and two other chiefs, the Raven and the Carpenter, signed the Treaty of the Sycamore Shoals, in the presence and with the assent of some twelve hundred of their tribe, half of them warriors; for all who could had come to the treaty grounds. Henderson thus obtained a grant of all the lands lying along and between the Kentucky and the Cumberland rivers. He promptly named the new colony Transylvania. The purchase money was 10,000 pounds of lawful English money; but, of course, the payment was made mainly in merchandise, and not specie. It took a number of days before the treaty was finally concluded; no rum was allowed to be sold, and there was little drunkenness, but herds of beeves were driven in, that the Indians might make a feast.

The main opposition to the treaty was made by a chief named Dragging Canoe, who continued for years to be the most inveterate foe of the white race to be found among the Cherokees. On the second day of the talk he spoke strongly against granting the Americans what they asked, pointing out, in words of glowing eloquence, how the Cherokees, who had once owned the land down to the sea, had been steadily driven back by the whites until they

had reached the mountains, and warning his comrades that they must now put a stop at all hazards
to further encroachments, under penalty of seeing
the loss of their last hunting-grounds, by which
alone their children could live. When he had finished his speech he abruptly left the ring of speakers, and the council broke up in confusion. The
Indian onlookers were much impressed by what he
said; and for some hours the whites were in dismay
lest all further negotiations should prove fruitless.
It was proposed to get the deed privately; but to
this the treaty-makers would not consent, answering
that they cared nothing for the treaty unless it was
concluded in open council, with the full assent of all
the Indians. By much exertion Dragging Canoe was
finally persuaded to come back; the council was re-
sumed next day, and finally the grant was made
without further opposition. The Indians chose their
own interpreter; and the treaty was read aloud and
translated, sentence by sentence, before it was signed,
on the fourth day of the formal talking.

The chiefs undoubtedly knew that they could
transfer only a very imperfect title to the land they
thus deeded away. Both Oconostota and Dragging
Canoe told the white treaty-makers that the land
beyond the mountains, whither they were going, was
a " dark ground," a " bloody ground "; and warned
them that they must go at their own risk, and not
hold the Cherokees responsible, for the latter could
no longer hold them by the hand. Dragging Canoe
especially told Henderson that there was a black
cloud hanging over the land, for it lay in the path

of the northwestern Indians—who were already at war with the Cherokees, and would surely show as little mercy to the white men as to the red. Another old chief said to Boon : " Brother, we have given you a fine land, but I believe you will have much trouble in settling it." What he said was true, and the whites were taught by years of long warfare that Kentucky was indeed what the Cherokees called it, a dark and bloody ground.[1]

After Henderson's main treaty was concluded, the Watauga Association entered into another, by which they secured from the Cherokees, for 2,000 pounds sterling, the lands they had already leased.

As soon as it became evident that the Indians would consent to the treaty, Henderson sent Boon

---

[1] The whole account of this treaty is taken from the Jefferson MSS., 5th Series, Vol. VIII. ; " a copy of the proceedings of the Virginia Convention, from June 15 to November 19, 1777, in relation to the Memorial of Richard Henderson, and others " ; especially from the depositions of James Robertson, Isaac Shelby, Charles Robertson, Nathaniel Gist, and Thomas Price, who were all present. There is much interesting matter aside from the treaty ; Simon Girty makes depositions as to Braddock's defeat and Bouquet's fight ; Lewis, Croghan, and others show the utter vagueness and conflict of the Indian titles to Kentucky, etc., etc. Though the Cherokees spoke of the land as a " dark " or " bloody " place or ground, it does not seem that by either of these terms they referred to the actual meaning of the name Kentucky. One or two of the witnesses tried to make out that the treaty was unfairly made ; but the bulk of the evidence is overwhelmingly the other way.

Haywood gives a long speech made by Oconostota against the treaty ; but this original report shows that Oconostota favored the treaty from the outset, and that it was Dragging Canoe who spoke against it. Haywood wrote fifty years after the event, and gathered many of his facts from tradition ; probably tradition had become confused, and reversed the position of the two chiefs. Haywood purports to give almost the exact language Oconostota used ; but when he is in error even as to who made the speech, he is exceedingly unlikely to be correct in any thing more than its general tenor.

ahead witn a company of thirty men to clear a trail from the Holston to the Kentucky.[1] This, the first regular path opened into the wilderness, was   **Boon** long called Boon's trace, and became forever   **Goes to** famous in Kentucky history as the Wilder-   **Kentucky.** ness Road, the track along which so many tens of thousands travelled while journeying to their hoped-for homes in the bountiful west. Boon started on March 10th with his sturdy band of rifle-bearing axe-men, and chopped out a narrow bridle-path—a pony trail, as it would now be called in the west. It led over Cumberland Gap, and crossed Cumberland, Laurel, and Rockcastle rivers at fords that were swimming deep in the time of freshets. Where it went through tall, open timber, it was marked by blazes on the tree trunks, while a regular path was cut and trodden out through the thickets of underbrush and the dense canebrakes and reed-beds.

After a fortnight's hard work the party had almost reached the banks of the Kentucky River, and deemed that their chief trials were over. But half an hour before daybreak on the morning of the 25th, as they lay round their smouldering camp-fires, they were attacked by some Indians, who killed two of them and wounded a third ; the others sprang to arms at once, and stood their ground without suffering further loss or damage till it grew light, when the Indians silently drew off.[2] Continuing his course,

---

[1] Then sometimes called the Louisa ; a name given it at first by the English explorers, but by great good-fortune not retained.

[2] Collins, II., 498. Letter of Daniel Boon, April 1, 1775. Collins has done good work for Kentucky history, having collected a perfect mass of materials of every sort. But he does not discriminate between facts of un-

Boon reached the Kentucky River, and on April 1st began to build Boonsborough, on an open plain where there was a lick with two sulphur springs.

Meanwhile other pioneers, as hardy and enterprising as Boon's companions, had likewise made up their Indians minds that they would come in to possess Attack the the land; and in bands or small parties they Settlers. had crossed the mountains or floated down the Ohio, under the leadership of such men as Harrod, Logan,[1] and the McAfees.[2] But hardly had they built their slight log-cabins, covered with brush or bark, and broken ground for the corn-planting, when some small Indian war-parties, including that which had attacked Boon's company, appeared among them. Several men were "killed and sculped," as Boon phrased it; and the panic among the rest was very great, insomuch that many forthwith set out to return. Boon was not so easily daunted; and he at once sent a special messenger to hurry forward the main body under Henderson, writing to the latter with quiet resolution and much good sense:

"My advice to you, sir, is to come or send as soon as possible. Your company is desired greatly, for the people are very uneasy, but are willing to stay and venture their lives with you, and now is the time to flusterate

doubted authenticity, and tales resting on the idlest legend; so that he must be used with caution, and he is, of course, not to be trusted where he is biassed by the extreme rancor of his political prejudices. Of the Kentucky historians, Marshall is by far the most brilliant, and Mann Butler the most trustworthy and impartial. Both are much better than Collins.

[1] Benjamin Logan; there were many of the family in Kentucky. It was a common name along the border; the Indian chief Logan had been named after one of the Pennsylvania branch.

[2] McAfee MSS.

[frustrate?] the intentions of the Indians, and keep the country whilst we are in it.   If we give way to them now, it will ever be the case." [1]

Henderson had started off as soon as he had finished the treaty.   He took wagons with him, but was obliged to halt and leave them **The** in Powell's Valley, for beyond that even **Journey** so skilful a pathfinder and road-maker as **of Henderson's** Boon had not been able to find or make **Company.** a way passable for wheels.[2]   Accordingly, their goods and implements were placed on pack-horses, and the company started again.[3]   Most fortunately a full account of their journey has been kept; for among Henderson's followers at this time was a man named William Calk, who jotted down in his diary the events of each day.[4]   It is a short record, but as amusing as it is instructive; for the writer's mind was evidently as vigorous as his language was terse and untrammelled.   He was with a small party, who were going out as partners; and his journal is a faithful record of all things, great or small, that at the time impressed him.   The opening entry contains the information that "Abram's dog's leg got broke by Drake's dog."   The owner of the latter beast, by the way, could not have been a pleasant companion on a trip of this sort, for else-

[1] Boon's letter.
[2] Richard Henderson's " Journal of an Expedition to Cantucky in 1775 " (Collins).
[3] April 5th.
[4] It is printed in the Filson Club publications ; see " The Wilderness Road," by Thomas Speed, Louisville, Ky., 1886 ; one of the best of an excellent series.

where the writer, who, like most backwoodsmen, appreciated cleanliness in essentials, records with evident disfavor the fact that "Mr. Drake Bakes bread without washing his hands." Every man who has had the misfortune to drive a pack-train in thick timber, or along a bad trail, will appreciate keenly the following incident, which occurred soon after the party had set out for home :

"I turned my hors to drive before me and he got scard ran away threw Down the Saddel Bags and broke three of our powder goards and Abram's beast Burst open a walet of corn and lost a good Deal and made a turrabel flustration amongst the Reast of the Horses Drake's mair run against a sapling and noct it down we cacht them all again and went on and lodged at John Duncan's."

Another entry records the satisfaction of the party when at a log fort (before getting into the wilderness) they procured some good loaf-bread and good whisky.

They carried with them seed-corn [1] and "Irish tators" to plant, and for use on the journey had bacon, and corn-meal which was made either into baked corn-dodgers or else into johnny-cakes, which were simply cooked on a board beside the fire, or else perhaps on a hot stone or in the ashes. The meal had to be used very sparingly; occasionally a beef was killed, out of the herd of cattle that accompanied the emigrants; but generally they lived on the game they shot—deer, turkeys, and, when they

---

[1] It is not necessary to say that "corn" means maize; Americans do not use the word in the sense in which it is employed in Britain.

got to Kentucky, buffaloes. Sometimes this was killed as they travelled; more often the hunters got it by going out in the evening after they had pitched camp.

The journey was hard and tiresome. At times it rained; and again there were heavy snow-storms, in one of which an emigrant got lost, and only found his way to camp by the help of a pocket-compass. The mountains were very steep, and it was painfully laborious work to climb them, while chopping out a way for the pack-train. At night a watch had to be kept for Indians. It was only here and there that the beasts got good grazing. Sometimes the horses had their saddles turned while struggling through the woods. But the great difficulty came in crossing the creeks, where the banks were rotten, the bottom bad, or the water deep; then the horses would get mired down and wet their packs, or they would have to be swum across while their loads were ferried over on logs. One day, in going along a creek, they had to cross it no less than fifty times, by "very bad foards."

On the seventh of April they were met by Boon's runner, bearing tidings of the loss occasioned by the Indians; and from that time on they met parties of would-be settlers, who, panic-struck by the sudden forays, were fleeing from the country. Henderson's party kept on with good courage, and persuaded quite a number of the fugitives to turn back with them. Some of these men who were thus leaving the country were not doing so because of fright; for many, among them the McAffees, had not brought out their families, but had simply come to clear the ground, build cabins, plant corn, and turn some branded cattle loose in the woods, where they were certain to thrive well, winter and summer, on the nourishing cane and wild pea-vine. The men then intended to go back to the settlements and bring out their wives and children, perhaps not till the following year; so that things were in a measure prepared for them, though they were very apt to find that the cattle had been stolen by the Indians, or had strayed too far to be recovered.[1]

The bulk of those fleeing, however, were simply frightened out of the country. There seems no reason to doubt[2] that the establishment of the **The Founding of Boonsborough Saves Kentucky.** strong, well-backed settlement of Boonsborough was all that prevented the abandonment of Kentucky at this time; and when such was the effect of a foray by small and scattered war parties of Indians from tribes nominally at peace with us,[3] it can easily be imagined how hopeless it would have been to have tried to settle the land had there still been in existence a strong hostile confederacy such as that

[1] McAfee MSS. Some of the McAfees returned with Henderson.

[2] Boon's letter, Henderson's journal, Calk's diary, McAfee's autobiography all mention the way in which the early settlers began to swarm out of the country in April, 1775. To judge from their accounts, if the movement had not been checked instantly the country would have been depopulated in a fortnight, exactly as in 1774.

[3] It must be remembered that the outrages of the Indians this year in Kentucky were totally unprovoked; they were on lands where they did not themselves dwell, and which had been regularly ceded to the whites by all the tribes—Iroquois, Shawnees, Cherokees, etc.—whom the whites could possibly consider as having any claim to them. The wrath of the Kentuckians against all Indians is easily understood.

presided over by Cornstalk. Beyond doubt the restless and vigorous frontiersmen would ultimately have won their way into the coveted western lands; yet had it not been for the battle of the Great Kanawha, Boon and Henderson could not, in 1775, have planted their colony in Kentucky; and had it not been for Boon and Henderson, it is most unlikely that the land would have been settled at all until after the Revolutionary war, when perhaps it might have been British soil. Boon was essentially a type, and possesses his greatest interest for us because he represents so well the characteristics as well as the life-work of his fellow backwoodsmen; still, it is unfair not to bear in mind also the leading part he played and the great services he rendered to the nation.

The incomers soon recovered from the fright into which they had been thrown by the totally unexpected Indian attack; but the revengeful anger it excited in their breasts did not pass away. They came from a class already embittered by long warfare with their forest foes; they hoarded up their new wrongs in minds burdened with the memories of countless other outrages; and it is small wonder that repeated and often unprovoked treachery at last excited in them a fierce and indiscriminate hostility to all the red-skinned race. They had come to settle on ground to which, as far as it was possible, the Indian title had been by fair treaty extinguished. They ousted no Indians from the lands they took; they had had neither the chance nor the wish to them-

Anger Excited by the Indians.

selves do wrong; in their eyes the attack on the part of the Indians was as wanton as it was cruel; and in all probability this view was correct, and their assailants were actuated more by the desire for scalps and plunder than by resentment at the occupation of hunting grounds to which they could have had little claim. In fact, throughout the history of the discovery and first settlement of Kentucky, the original outrages and murders were committed by the Indians on the whites, and not by the whites on the Indians. In the gloomy and ferocious wars that ensued, the wrongs done by each side were many and great.

Henderson's company came into the beautiful Kentucky country in mid-April, when it looked its best:
Henderson Reaches Boonsborough. the trees were in leaf, the air heavy with fragrance, the snowy flowers of the dogwood whitened the woods, and the banks of the streams burned dull crimson with the wealth of red-bud blossoms. The travellers reached the fort that Boon was building on the 20th of the month, being welcomed to the protection of its wooden walls by a volley from twenty or thirty rifles. They at once set to with a will to finish it, and to make it a strong place of refuge against Indian attacks. It was a typical forted village, such as the frontiersmen built everywhere in the west and southwest during the years that they were pushing their way across the continent in the teeth of fierce and harassing warfare; in some features it was not unlike the hamlet-like " tun " in which the forefathers of these same pioneers dwelt, long centu-

ries before, when they still lived by the sluggish waters of the lower Rhine, or had just crossed to the eastern coast of Britain.[1]

The fort was in shape a parallelogram, some two hundred and fifty feet long and half as wide. It was more completely finished than the majority of its kind, though little or no iron was used in its construction. At each corner was a two-storied loop-holed block-house to act as a bastion. The stout log-cabins were arranged in straight lines, so that their outer sides formed part of the wall, the spaces between them being filled with a high stockade, made of heavy squared timbers thrust upright into the ground, and bound together within by a horizontal stringer near the top. They were loop-holed like the block-houses. The heavy wooden gates, closed with stout bars, were flanked without by the block-houses and within by small windows cut in the nearest cabins. The houses had sharp, sloping roofs, made of huge clapboards, and these great wooden slabs were kept in place by long poles, bound with withes to the rafters. In case of dire need each cabin was separately defensible. When danger threatened, the cattle were kept in the open space in the middle.

The Settlers Build Forts.

Three other similar forts or stations were built about the same time as Boonsborough, namely: Harrodstown, Boiling Springs, and St. Asaphs, better known as Logan's Station, from its founder's name   These all lay to the southwest, some thirty

---

[1] When the block-house and palisade enclosed the farm of a single settler the " tun," in its still earlier sense, was even more nearly reproduced.

odd miles from Boonsborough. Every such fort or station served as the rallying-place for the country round about, the stronghold in which the people dwelt during time of danger; and later on, when all danger had long ceased, it often remained in changed form, growing into the chief town of the district. Each settler had his own farm besides, often a long way from the fort, and it was on this that he usually intended to make his permanent home. This system enabled the inhabitants to combine for defence, and yet to take up the large tracts of four to fourteen hundred acres,[1] to which they were by law entitled. It permitted them in time of peace to live well apart, with plenty of room between, so that they did not crowd one another—a fact much appreciated by men in whose hearts the spirit of extreme independence and self-reliance was deeply ingrained. Thus the settlers were scattered over large areas, and, as elsewhere in the southwest, the county and not the town became the governmental unit. The citizens even of the smaller governmental divisions acted through representatives, instead of directly, as in the New England town-meetings.[2] The centre of county government was of course the county court-house.

[1] Four hundred acres were gained at the price of $2.50 per 100 acres, by merely building a cabin and raising a crop of corn ; and every settler with such a " cabin right " had likewise a preëmption right to 1,000 acres adjoining, for a cost that generally approached forty dollars a hundred.

[2] In Mr. Phelan's scholarly " History of Tennessee," pp. 202–204, etc., there is an admirably clear account of the way in which Tennessee institutions (like those of the rest of the Southwest) have been directly and without a break derived from English institutions ; whereas many of those of New England are rather pre-Normanic revivals, curiously paralleled in England as it was before the Conquest.

Henderson, having established a land agency at Boonsborough, at once proceeded to deed to the Transylvania colonists entry certificates of surveys of many hundred thousand acres. Most of the colonists were rather doubtful whether these certificates would ultimately prove of any value, and preferred to rest their claims on their original cabin rights; a wise move on their part, though in the end the Virginia Legislature confirmed Henderson's sales in so far as they had been made to actual settlers. All the surveying was of course of the very rudest kind. Only a skilled woodsman could undertake the work in such a country; and accordingly much of it devolved on Boon, who ran the lines as well as he could, and marked the trees with his own initials, either by powder or else with his knife.[1] The State could not undertake to make the surveys itself, so it authorized the individual settler to do so. This greatly promoted the rapid settlement of the country, making it possible to deal with land as a commodity, and outlining the various claims; but the subsequent and inevitable result was that the sons of the settlers reaped a crop of endless confusion and litigation.

It is worth mentioning that the Transylvania company opened a store at Boonsborough. Powder and lead, the two commodities most in demand, were sold respectively for $2.66⅔ and 16⅔ cents per pound. The payment was rarely made in coin; and how high the above prices were may be gathered from the fact that ordinary labor was credited at 33⅓ cents per day

---

[1] Boon's deposition, July 29, 1795.

while fifty cents a day was paid for ranging, hunting, and working on the roads.[1]

Henderson immediately proceeded to organize the government of his colony, and accordingly issued a call for an election of delegates to the Legislature of Transylvania, each of the four stations mentioned above sending members.

The Transylvania Legislature.

The delegates, seventeen in all, met at Boonsborough and organized the convention on the 23d of May. Their meetings were held without the walls of the fort, on a level plain of white clover, under a grand old elm. Beneath its mighty branches a hundred people could without crowding find refuge from the noon-day sun; 't was a fit council-house for this pioneer legislature of game hunters and Indian fighters.[2]

These weather-beaten backwoods warriors, who held their deliberations in the open air, showed that they had in them good stuff out of which to build a free government. They were men of genuine force of character, and they behaved with a dignity and wisdom that would have well become any legislative body. Henderson, on behalf of the proprietors of Transylvania, addressed them, much as a crown governor would have done. The portion of his address dealing with the destruction of game is worth noting. Buffalo, elk, and deer had abounded immediately round Boonsborough when the settlers first arrived, but the slaughter had been so great

[1] Mann Butler, p. 31.

[2] Henderson's Journal. The beauty of the elm impressed him very greatly. According to the list of names eighteen, not seventeen, members were elected; but apparently only seventeen took part in the proceedings.

that even after the first six weeks the hunters began to find some difficulty in getting any thing without going off some fifteen or twenty miles. However, stray buffaloes were still killed near the fort once or twice a week.[1] Calk in his journal quoted above, in the midst of entries about his domestic work— such as, on April 29th "we git our house kivered with bark and move our things into it at Night and Begin housekeeping," and on May 2d, "went and sot in to clearing for corn,"—mentions occasionally killing deer and turkey; and once, while looking for a strayed mare, he saw four "bofelos." He wounded one, but failed to get it, with the luck that generally attended backwoods hunters when they for the first time tried their small-bore rifles against these huge, shaggy-maned wild cattle.

As Henderson pointed out, the game was the sole dependence of the first settlers, who, most of the time, lived solely on wild meat, even the parched corn having been exhausted; and without game the new-comers could not have stayed in the land a week.[2] Accordingly he advised the enactment of game-laws; and he was especially severe in his comments upon the "foreignors" who came into the country merely to hunt, killing off the wild beasts, and taking their skins and furs away, for the benefit of persons not concerned in the settlement. This last point is curious as showing how instantly and naturally the colonists succeeded not only to the lands of the In-

[1] Henderson's Journal.

[2] " Our game, the only support of life amongst many of us, and without which the country would be abandoned ere to-morrow." Henderson's address.

dians, but also to their habits of thought; regarding intrusion by outsiders upon their hunting-grounds with the same jealous dislike so often shown by their red-skinned predecessors.

Henderson also outlined some of the laws he thought it advisable to enact, and the Legislature followed his advice. They provided for courts of law, for regulating the militia, for punishing criminals, fixing sheriffs' and clerks' fees, and issuing writs of attachment.[1]   One of the members was a clergyman : owing to him a law was passed forbidding profane swearing or Sabbath-breaking; a puritanic touch which showed the mountain rather than the seaboard origin of the men settling Kentucky.   The three remaining laws the Legislature enacted were much more characteristic, and were all introduced by the two Boons—for Squire Boon was still the companion of his brother. As was fit and proper, it fell to the lot of the greatest of backwoods hunters to propose a scheme for game protection, which the Legislature immediately adopted; and his was likewise the " act for preserving the breed of horses,"— for, from the very outset, the Kentuckians showed the love for fine horses and for horse-racing which has ever since distinguished them.   Squire Boon was the author of a law " to protect the range "; for the preservation of the range or natural pasture over which the branded horses and cattle of the pioneers ranged at will, was as necessary to the welfare of the stock as the preservation of the game was to the

[1] Journal of the Proceedings of the House of Delegates or Representatives of the Colony of Transylvania.

welfare of the men. In Kentucky the range was excellent, abounding not only in fine grass, but in cane and wild peas, and the animals grazed on it throughout the year. Fires sometimes utterly destroyed immense tracts of this pasture, causing heavy loss to the settlers; and one of the first cares of pioneer legislative bodies was to guard against such accidents.

It was likewise stipulated that there should be complete religious freedom and toleration for all sects. This seems natural enough now, but in the eighteenth century the precedents were the other way. Kentucky showed its essentially American character in nothing more than the diversity of religious belief among the settlers from the very start. They came almost entirely from the back-woods mountaineers of Virginia, Pennsylvania, and North Carolina, among whom the predominant faith had been Presbyterianism; but from the beginning they were occasionally visited by Baptist preachers,[1] whose creed spread to the borders sooner than Methodism; and among the original settlers of Harrodsburg were some Catholic Marylanders.[2] The first service ever held in Kentucky was by a clergyman of the Church of England, soon after Henderson's arrival; but this was merely owing to the presence of Henderson himself, who, it must be remembered, was not in the least a backwoods product. He stood completely isolated from the other

---

[1] Possibly in 1775, certainly in 1776; MS. autobiography of Rev. Wm. Hickman. In Durrett's library.

[2] "Life of Rev. Charles Nerinckx," by Rev. Camillus P. Maes, Cincinnati, 1880, p. 67.

immigrants during his brief existence as a pioneer, and had his real relationship with the old English founders of the proprietary colonies, and with the more modern American land speculators, whose schemes are so often mentioned during the last half of the eighteenth century. Episcopacy was an exotic in the backwoods; it did not take real root in Kentucky till long after that commonwealth had emerged from the pioneer stage.

When the Transylvanian Legislature dissolved, never to meet again, Henderson had nearly finished playing his short but important part in the founding of Kentucky. He was a man of the seacoast regions, who had little in common with the backwoodsmen by whom he was surrounded; he came from a comparatively old and sober community, and he could not grapple with his new associates; in his journal he alludes to them as a set of scoundrels who scarcely believed in God or feared the devil. A British friend [1] of his, who at this time visited the settlement, also described the pioneers as being a lawless, narrow-minded, unpolished, and utterly insubordinate set, impatient of all restraint, and relying in every difficulty upon their individual might; though he grudgingly admitted that they were frank, hospitable, energetic, daring, and possessed of much common-sense. Of course it was hopeless to expect that such bold spirits, as they conquered the wilderness, would be content to hold it even at a small quit-rent from Henderson. But the latter's colony

The Collapse of the Transylvania Colony.

[1] Smyth, p. 330.

was toppled over by a thrust from without before it had time to be rent in sunder by violence from within.

Transylvania was between two millstones. The settlers revolted against its authority, and appealed to Virginia; and meanwhile Virginia, claiming the Kentucky country, and North Carolina as mistress of the lands round the Cumberland, proclaimed the purchase of the Transylvanian proprietors null and void as regards themselves, though valid as against the Indians. The title conveyed by the latter thus enured to the benefit of the colonies; it having been our policy, both before and since the Revolution, not to permit any of our citizens to individually purchase lands from the savages.

Lord Dunmore denounced Henderson and his acts; and it was in vain that the Transylvanians appealed to the Continental Congress, asking leave to send a delegate thereto, and asserting their devotion to the American cause; for Jefferson and Patrick Henry were members of that body, and though they agreed with Lord Dunmore in nothing else, were quite as determined as he that Kentucky should remain part of Virginia. So Transylvania's fitful life flickered out of existence; the Virginia Legislature in 1778, solemnly annulling the title of the company, but very properly recompensing the originators by the gift of two hundred thousand acres.[1] North Carolina pursued a precisely similar course; and Henderson, after the collapse of his colony, drifts out of history.

[1] Gov. James T. Morehead's "address" at Boonsborough, in 1840 (Frankfort, Ky., 1841).

Boon remained to be for some years one of the Kentucky leaders. Soon after the fort at Boonsborough was built, he went back to North Carolina for his family, and in the fall returned, bringing out a band of new settlers, including twenty-seven "guns"—that is, rifle-bearing men,—and four women, with their families, the first who came to Kentucky, though others shortly followed in their steps.[1] A few roving hunters and daring pioneer settlers also came to his fort in the fall; among them, the famous scout, Simon Kenton, and John Todd,[2] a man of high and noble character and well-trained mind, who afterwards fell by Boon's side when in command at the fatal battle of Blue Licks. In this year also Clark[3] and Shelby[4] first came to Kentucky; and many other men whose names became famous in frontier story, and whose sufferings and long wanderings, whose strength, hardihood, and fierce daring, whose prowess as Indian fighters and killers of big game, were told by the firesides of Kentucky to generations born when the elk and the buffalo had vanished from her borders as completely as the red Indian himself. Each leader gathered round him a little party of men, who helped him build the fort which was to be the stronghold of the district. Among the earliest of these

[1] *Do.*, p. 51.   Mrs. Boon, Mrs. Denton, Mrs. McGarry, Mrs. Hogan ; all were from the North Carolina backwoods ; their ancestry is shown by their names.   They settled in Boonsborough and Harrodsburg.

[2] Like Logan he was born in Pennsylvania, of Presbyterian Irish stock. He had received a good education.

[3] Morehead, p. 52.

[4] Shelby's MS. autobiography, in Durrett's Library at Louisville.

town-builders were Hugh McGarry, James Harrod, and Benjamin Logan. The first named was a coarse, bold, brutal man, always clashing with his associates (he once nearly shot Harrod in a dispute over work). He was as revengeful and foolhardy as he was daring, but a natural leader in spite of all. Soon after he came to Kentucky his son was slain by Indians while out boiling sugar from the maples ; and he mercilessly persecuted all redskins for ever after. Harrod and Logan were of far higher character, and superior to him in every respect. Like so many other backwoodsmen, they were tall, spare, athletic men, with dark hair and grave faces. They were as fearless as they were tireless, and were beloved by their followers. Harrod finally died alone in the wilderness, nor was it ever certainly known whether he was killed by Indian or white man, or perchance by some hunted beast. The old settlers always held up his memory as that of a man ever ready to do a good deed, whether it was to run to the rescue of some one attacked by Indians, or to hunt up the strayed plough-horse of a brother settler less skilful as a woodsman ; yet he could hardly read or write. Logan was almost as good a woodsman and individual fighter, and in addition was far better suited to lead men. He was both just and generous. His father had died intestate, so that all of his property by law came to Logan, who was the eldest son ; but the latter at once divided it equally with his brothers and sisters. As soon as he came to Kentucky he rose to leadership, and remained for many years among the foremost of the commonwealth founders.

All this time there penetrated through the sombre forests faint echoes of the strife the men of the sea-coast had just begun against the British king. The rumors woke to passionate loyalty the hearts of the pioneers; and a roaming party of hunters, when camped on a branch [1] of the Elkhorn, by the hut of one of their number, named McConnell, called the spot Lexington, in honor of the memory of the Massachusetts minute-men, about whose death and victory they had just heard. [2]

By the end of 1775 the Americans had gained firm foothold in Kentucky. Cabins had been built and clearings made ; there were women and children in the wooden forts, cattle grazed on the range, and two or three hundred acres of corn had been sown and reaped. There were perhaps some three hundred men in Kentucky, a hardy, resolute, strenuous band. They stood shoulder to shoulder in the wilderness, far from all help, surrounded by an overwhelm-ing number of foes. Each day's work was fraught with danger as they warred with the wild forces from which they wrung their living. Around them on every side lowered the clouds of the impending death struggle with the savage lords of the neighbor-ing lands.

These backwoodsmen greatly resembled one an-other ; their leaders were but types of the rank and

---

[1] These frontiersmen called a stream a " run," " branch," " creek," or " fork," but never a " brook," as in the northeast.

[2] " History of Lexington," G. W. Ranck, Cincinnati, 1872, p. 19. The town was not permanently occupied till four years later.

file, and did not differ so very widely from them;
yet two men stand out clearly from their fellows.
Above the throng of wood-choppers, game-hunters,
and Indian fighters loom the sinewy figures of **Daniel
Boon and George Rogers Clark.**

CHAPTER XI.

IN THE CURRENT OF THE REVOLUTION—THE SOUTHERN BACKWOODSMEN OVERWHELM THE CHEROKEES, 1776.

THE great western drift of our people began almost at the moment when they became Americans, and ceased to be merely British colonists. They crossed the great divide which sundered the springs of the seaboard rivers from the sources of the western waters about the time that American citizens first publicly acted as American freemen, knit together by common ties, and with interests no longer akin to those of the mother country. The movement which was to make the future nation a continental power was begun immediately after the hitherto separate colonies had taken the first step towards solidification. While the communities of the seacoast were yet in a fever heat from the uprising against the stamp tax, the first explorers were toiling painfully to Kentucky, and the first settlers were building their palisaded hamlets on the banks of the Watauga. The year that saw the first Continental Congress saw also the short, grim tragedy of Lord Dunmore's war. The early battles of the Revolution were fought while Boon's comrades were laying the foundations of their commonwealth.

Hitherto the two chains of events had been only
remotely connected; but in 1776, the year of the
Declaration of Independence, the struggle   The
between the king and his rebellious sub- Westerners
jects shook the whole land, and the men of Drawn into
the western border were drawn headlong   of the
into the full current of revolutionary war- Revolution.
fare. From that moment our politics became national, and the fate of each portion of our country
was thenceforth in some sort dependent upon the
welfare of every other. Each section had its own
work to do; the east won independence while the
west began to conquer the continent. Yet the deeds
of each were of vital consequence to the other.
Washington's Continentals gave the west its freedom; and took in return for themselves and their
children a share of the land that had been conquered
and held by the scanty bands of tall backwoodsmen.

The backwoodsmen, the men of the up-country,
were, as a whole, ardent adherents of the patriot or
American side. Yet there were among them many
loyalists or tories; and these tories included in their
ranks much the greatest portion of the vicious and the
disorderly elements. This was the direct reverse of
what obtained along portions of the seaboard, where
large numbers of the peaceable, well-to-do people
stood loyally by the king. In the up-country, however, the Presbyterian Irish, with their fellows of
Calvinistic stock and faith, formed the back-bone of
the moral and order-loving element; and the Presbyterian Irish [1] were almost to a man staunch and

---

[1] Mr. Phelan, in his "History of Tennessee," deserves especial praise
for having so clearly understood the part played by the Scotch-Irish.

furious upholders of the Continental Congress. Naturally, the large bands of murderers, horse-thieves, Civil War and other wild outlaws, whom these grim on the friends of order hunted down with merciless Border. severity, were glad to throw in their lot with any party that promised revenge upon their foes. But of course there were lawless characters on both sides; in certain localities where the crop of jealousies, always a rank backwoods growth, had been unusually large, and had therefore produced long-standing and bitter feuds,[1] the rival families espoused opposite sides from sheer vindictive hatred of one another. As a result, the struggle in the backwoods between tories and whigs, king's-men and congress-men,[2] did not merely turn upon the questions everywhere at stake between the American and British parties. It was also in part a fight between the law-abiding and the lawless, and in part a slaking of savage personal animosities, wherein the borderers glutted their vengeance on one another. They exercised without restraint the right of private warfare, long abandoned in more civilized regions. It was natural that such a contest should be waged with appalling ferocity.

Nevertheless this very ferocity was not only inevitable, but it was in a certain sense proper; or, at least, even if many of its manifestations were blamable, the spirit that lay behind them was right. The backwoodsmen were no sentimentalists; they were grim, hard, matter-of-fact men, engaged all

---

[1] The Campbell MSS. contain allusions to various such feuds, and accounts of the jealousies existing not only between families, but between prominent members of the same family.

[2] See Milfort, Smyth, etc., as well as the native writers.

their lives long in an unending struggle with hostile forces, both human and natural; men who in this struggle had acquired many unamiable qualities, but who had learned likewise to appreciate at their full value the inestimable virtues of courage and common-sense. The crisis demanded that they should be both strong and good; but, above all things, it demanded that they should be strong. Weakness would have ruined them. It was needful that justice should stand before mercy; and they could no longer have held their homes, had they not put down their foes, of every kind, with an iron hand. They did not have many theories; but they were too genuinely liberty-loving not to keenly feel that their freedom was jeopardized as much by domestic disorder as by foreign aggression.

The tories were obnoxious under two heads: they were the allies of a tyrant who lived beyond the sea, and they were the friends of anarchy at home. They were felt by the frontiersmen to be criminals rather than ordinary foes. They included in their ranks the mass of men who had been guilty of the two worst frontier crimes—horse-stealing and murder; and their own feats were in the eyes of their neighbors in no way distinguishable from those of other horse-thieves and murderers. Accordingly the backwoodsmen soon grew to regard toryism as merely another crime; and the courts sometimes executed equally summary justice on tory, desperado, and stock-thief, holding each as having forfeited his life." [1]

[1] Executions for " treason," murder, and horse-stealing were very common. For an instance where the three crimes were treated alike as deserving the death penalty the perpetrators being hung, see Calendar of Virginia State Papers, Vol. III., p. 361.

The backwoodsmen were engaged in a threefold contest. In the first place, they were occasionally, but not often, opposed to the hired British and German soldiers of a foreign king. Next, they were engaged in a fierce civil war with the tories of their own number. Finally, they were pitted against the Indians, in the ceaseless border struggle of a rude, vigorous civilization to overcome an inevitably hostile savagery. The regular British armies, marching to and fro in the course of their long campaigns on the seaboard, rarely went far enough back to threaten the frontiersmen; the latter had to do chiefly with tories led by British chiefs, and with Indians instigated by British agents.

Soon after the conflict with the revolted colonists became one of arms as well as one of opinions the **Indian** British began to rouse the Indian tribes to **Hostilities.** take their part. In the northwest they were at first unsuccessful; the memory of Lord Dunmore's war was still fresh in the minds of the tribes beyond the Ohio, and they remained for the most part neutral. The Shawnees continued even in 1776 to send in to the Americans white prisoners collected from among their outlying bands, in accordance with the terms of the treaty entered into on the Pickaway plains.[1]

But the southwestern Indians were not held in check by memories of recent defeat, and they were alarmed by the encroachments of the whites. Although the Cherokees had regularly ceded to the

---

[1] " American Archives," 4th Series, Vol. VI., p. 541. But parties of young braves went on the war-path from time to time.

Watauga settlers their land, they still continued jealous of them; and both Creeks and Cherokees were much irritated at the conduct of some of the lawless Georgian frontiersmen.[1] The colonial authorities tried to put a stop to this lawlessness, and one of the chief offenders was actually seized and hung in the presence of two Indians.[2] This had a momentary effect on the Creeks, and induced them for the time being to observe a kind of nominal neutrality, though they still furnished bodies of warriors to help the British and Cherokees.[3]

The latter, however, who were the nearest neighbors of the Americans, promptly took up the tomahawk at the bidding of the British. The royal agents among these southern Indians had so far successfully[4] followed the perfectly cold-blooded though perhaps necessary policy of exciting the tribes to war with one another, in order that they might leave the whites at peace; but now, as they officially reported to the British commander, General Gage, they deemed this course no longer wise, and, instead of fomenting, they endeavored to allay, the strife between the Chickasaws and Creeks, so as to allow the latter to turn their full strength against the Georgians.[5] At the same time every effort was made to induce the Cherokees to rise,[6] and they were

[1] *Do.*, Vol III., p. 790.   [2] *Do.*, Vol. VI., p. 1228.

[3] See Milfort, pp. 46, 134, etc.

[4] "American Archives," 4th Series, Vol. I., p. 1094, for example of fight between Choctaws and Creeks.

[5] *Do.*, Vol. IV., p. 317. Letter of Agent John Stuart to General Gage, St. Augustine, Oct. 3, 1775.

[6] State Department MSS. No. 71, Vol. II., p. 189. Letter of David Taitt, Deputy Superintendent (of British) in Creek Nation.

promised gunpowder, blankets, and the like [1] although some of the promised stores were seized by the Americans while being forwarded to the Indians.[2]

In short, the British were active and successful in rousing the war spirit among Creeks, Cherokees, Chocktaws, and Chickasaws, having nu-

The British Incite the Indians to War.

merous agents in all these tribes.[3] Their success, and the consequent ravages of the Indians, maddened the American frontiersmen upon whom the blow fell, and changed their resentment against the British king into a deadly and lasting hatred, which their sons and grandsons inherited. Indian warfare was of such peculiar atrocity that the employment of Indians as allies forbade any further hope of reconciliation. It is not necessary to accept the American estimate of the motives inspiring the act in order to sympathize fully with the horror and anger that it aroused among the frontiersmen. They saw their homes destroyed, their wives outraged, their children captured, their friends butchered and tortured wholesale by Indians armed with British weapons, bribed by British gold, and obeying the orders of British agents and commanders. Their stormy anger was not likely to be allayed by the consideration that Congress also had at first made some effort to enlist Indians in the patriot forces, nor were they apt to bear in mind the fact that the British, instead

---

[1] "American Archives," Vol. III., p. 218, August 21, 1775.

[2] *Do.*, p. 790 September 25, 1775.

[3] State Department MSS., No. 51, Vol. II., p. 17 (volume of "Intercepted Letters"). Letters of Andrew Rainsford, John Mitchell, and Alex. McCullough, to Rt. Hon. Lord George Germain.

of being abnormally cruel, were in reality less so than our former French and Spanish opponents.[1]

Looking back it is easy to see that the Indians were the natural foes of the American people, and therefore the natural allies of the British Government. They had constantly to fear the advance of the Americans, while from the fur traders, Indian agents, and army officers who alone represented Britain, they had nothing but coveted treasures of every kind to expect. They seemed tools forged for the hands of the royal commanders, whose own people lay far beyond the reach of reprisals in kind ; and it was perhaps too much to expect that in that age such tools should not be used.[2] We had less temptation to employ them, less means wherewith to pay them, and more cause to be hostile to and dread them ; and moreover our skirts are not quite clear in the matter, after all, for we more than once showed a tendency to bid for their support.

But, after all is said, the fact remains that we have to deal, not with what, under other circumstances, the Americans *might* have done, but with what the British actually *did;* and for this there can be many apologies, but no sufficient excuse.   When the com-

---

[1] No body of British troops in the Revolution bore such a dark stain on its laurels as the massacre at Fort William Henry left on the banners of Montcalm ; even the French, not to speak of the Spaniards and Mexicans, were to us far more cruel foes than the British, though generally less formidable.   In fact the British, as conquerors and rulers in America, though very disagreeable, have not usually been either needlessly cruel nor (relatively speaking) unjust, and compare rather favorably with most other European nations.

[2] Though it must be remembered that in our own war with Mexico we declined the proffered—and valuable—aid of the Comanches.

missioners to the southern Indians wrote to Lord George Germain, "we have been indefatigable in our endeavors to keep up a constant succession of parties of Indians to annoy the rebels,"[1] the writers must have well known, what the king's ministers should also have made it their business to know, that the war-parties whom they thus boasted of continually sending against the settlements directed their efforts mainly, indeed almost exclusively, not against bodies of armed men, but against the husbandmen as they unsuspectingly tilled the fields, and against the women and children who cowered helplessly in the log-cabins. All men knew that the prisoners who fell into Indian hands, of whatever age or sex, often suffered a fate hideous and revolting beyond belief and beyond description. Such a letter as that quoted above makes the advisers of King George the Third directly responsible for the manifold and frightful crimes of their red allies.

It is small wonder that such a contest should have roused in the breasts of the frontiersmen not only ruthless and undying abhorrence of the Indians, but also a bitterly vindictive feeling of hostility towards Great Britain ; a feeling that was all-powerful for a generation afterwards, and traces of which linger even to the present day. Moreover, the Indian forays, in some ways, damaged the loyalist cause. The savages had received strict instructions not to molest any of the king's friends[2] ; but they were far too intent on plunder and rapine to discriminate

---

[1] State Department MSS. "Intercepted Letters," Pensacola, July 12, 1779.   [2] *Do.*

between whig and tory. Accordingly their ravages
drove the best tories, who had at first hailed the
Indian advance with joy, into the patriot ranks,[1]
making the frontier almost solidly whig; save for
the refugees, who were willing to cast in their lot
with the savages.

While the Creeks were halting and considering,
and while the Choctaws and Chickasaws were being
visited by British emissaries, the Chero-   **The**
kees flung themselves on the frontier folk.   **Cherokees**
They had been short of ammunition; but **Go to War.**
when the British agents[2] sent them fifty horse-loads[3]
by a pack-train that was driven through the Creek
towns, they no longer hesitated. The agents showed
very poor generalship in making them rise so early,
when there were no British troops in the southern
States,[4] and when the Americans were consequently
unhampered and free to deal with the Indians.
Had the rising been put off until a British army
was in Georgia, it might well have proved successful.

The Cherokee villages stood in that cluster of
high mountain chains which mark the ending of
the present boundaries of Georgia and both Carolinas. These provinces lay east and southeast of
them. Directly north were the forted villages of
the Watauga pioneers, in the valley of the upper
Tennessee, and beyond these again, in the same val-

---

[1] " Am. Archives," 5th Series, I., 610.

[2] Stuart and Cameron ; the latter dwelt among them, and excited them
to war.

[3] " Am. Archives," 5th Series, III., 649.

[4] The only British attempt made at that time against the southern colonies was in too small force, and failed.

ley, the Virginian outpost settlements. Virginia, North and South Carolina, and Georgia were alike threatened by the outbreak, while the Watauga people were certain to be the chief sufferers. The Cherokees were so near the settlements that their incursions were doubly dangerous. On the other hand, there was not nearly as much difficulty in dealing them a counter-blow as in the case of the northern Indians, for their towns lay thickly together and were comparatively easy of access. Moreover, they were not rated such formidable fighters. By comparing Lord Dunmore's war in 1774 with this struggle against the Cherokees in 1776, it is easy to see the difference between a contest against the northern and one against the southern tribes. In 1776 our Indian foes were more numerous than in 1774, for there were over two thousand Cherokee warriors—perhaps two thousand five hundred,— assisted by a few Creeks and tories; they were closer to the frontier, and so their ravages were more serious; but they did not prove such redoubtable foes as Cornstalk's warriors, their villages were easier reached, and a more telling punishment was inflicted.

The Cherokees had been showing signs of hostility for some time. They had murdered two Virginians the previous year[1]; and word was brought to the settlements, early in the summer of '76, that they were undoubtedly preparing for war, as they were mending guns, making moccasins and beating flour for the march.[2]   In June their ravages began.[3]

[1] "American Archives," 4th Series, Vol. III., p. 1112.

[2] *Do.*, 5th Series, Vol. I., p. 111.

[3] *Do.*, 4th Series, Vol. VI., p. 1229.

The Otari, or Overhill Cherokees, had sent runners to the valley towns, asking their people to wait until all were ready before marching, that the settlements might be struck simultaneously; but some of the young braves among the lower towns could not be restrained, and in consequence the outlying settlers of Georgia and the Carolinas were the first to be assailed.

The main attack was made early in July, the warriors rushing down from their upland fastnesses in fierce and headlong haste, the different bands marching north, east, and southeast at the same moment. From the Holston to the Tugelou, from southwestern Virginia to northwestern Georgia, the back-county settlements were instantly wrapped in the sudden horror of savage warfare.

The Watauga people, the most exposed of all, received timely warning from a friendly squaw, [1] to whom the whites ever after showed respect and gratitude. They at once began to prepare for the stroke; and in all the western world of woodsmen there were no men better fitted for such a death grapple. They still formed a typical pioneer community; and their number had been swelled from time to time by the arrival of other bold and restless spirits. Their westernmost settlement this year was in Carter's valley; where four men had cleared a few acres of corn-land, and had hunted buffalo for their winter's meat. [2]

The Watauga Settlers Attacked.

---

[1] Her name was Nancy Ward. Campbell MSS., Haywood, etc.
[2] Ramsey, 144. The buffalo were killed (winter of 1775–1776) twelve miles northeast of Carter's valley.

As soon as they learned definitely that the Otari
warriors, some seven hundred in number, were
marching against them, they took refuge in their
wooden forts or stations. Among the most important of these were the one at Watauga, in which
Sevier and Robertson held command, and another
known as Eaton's Station,[1] placed just above the
forks of the Holston. Some six miles from the latter, near the Long Island or Big Island of the Holston, lay quite a large tract of level land, covered
with an open growth of saplings, and known as the
Island flats.

The Indians were divided into several bands ;
some of their number crossed over into Carter's valley, and after ravaging it, passed on up the Clinch.
The settlers at once gathered in the little stockades ;
those who delayed were surprised by the savages,
and were slain as they fled, or else were captured,
perhaps to die by torture,—men, women, and children alike. The cabins were burnt, the grain destroyed, the cattle and horses driven off, and the
sheep and hogs shot down with arrows ; the Indians carried bows and arrows for this express purpose, so as to avoid wasting powder and lead. The
bolder war-parties, in their search for scalps and
plunder, penetrated into Virginia a hundred miles
beyond the frontier,[2] wasting the country with tomahawk and brand up to the Seven-Mile Ford. The

---

[1] Haywood and his followers erroneously call it Heaton's ; in the Campbell MSS., as well as the "Am. Archives," 5th Series, I., p. 464, it is called
Eaton's or Amos Eaton's. This is contemporary authority. Other forts
were Evan Shelby's, John Shelby's, Campbell's, the Wommack Fort, etc.

[2] "Am. Archives," 5th Series, I., 973.

roads leading to the wooden forts were crowded
with settlers, who, in their mortal need of hurry,
had barely time to snatch up a few of the household
goods, and, if especially lucky, to mount the women
and children on horses; as usual in such a flight,
there occurred many deeds of cowardly selfishness,
offset by many feats of courage and self-sacrifice.
Once in the fort, the backwoodsmen often banded
into parties, and sallied out to fall on the Indians.
Sometimes these parties were worsted; at other
times they overcame their foes either by ambush or
in fair fight.   One such party from the Wolf Hills
fort killed eleven Indian warriors; and on their return they hung the scalps of their slain foes, as tro-
phies of triumph, from a pole over the fort gate.[1]
They were Bible-readers in this fort, and they had
their Presbyterian minister with them, having organized a special party to bring in the books he had left
in his cabin; they joined in prayer and thanksgiving
for their successes; but this did not hinder them
from scalping the men they killed.   They were too
well-read in the merciless wars of the Chosen People
to feel the need of sparing the fallen; indeed they
would have been most foolish had they done so; for
they were battling with a heathen enemy more ruthless and terrible than ever was Canaanite or Philistine.

The two largest of the invading Indian bands[2]
moved, one by way of the mountains, to fall on the

---

[1] " American Pioneers," I., 534. Letter of Benjamin Sharp, who was
in the fort at the time as a boy fourteen years old.

[2] Many writers speak as if all the Indians were in these two bands, which
was not so.   It is impossible to give their numbers exactly ; probably each
contained from 150 to 300 warriors.

Watauga fort and its neighbors, and the other, led by the great war chief, Dragging Canoe, to lay waste the country guarded by Eaton's Station.

The white scouts—trained woodsmen, whose lives had been spent in the chase and in forest warfare—
The Settlers Gather at Eaton's Station. kept the commanders or headmen of the forts well informed of the Indian advance. As soon as it was known what part was really threatened, runners were sent to the settlements near by, calling on the riflemen to gather at Eaton's Station; whither they accordingly came in small bodies, under their respective militia captains.[1]

No man was really in command; the senior captain exercised a vague kind of right of advice over the others, and the latter in turn got from their men such obedience as their own personal influence was able to procure. But the levy, if disorderly, was composed of excellent marksmen and woodsmen, sinewy, hardy, full of fight, and accustomed to act together. A council was held, and it was decided not to stay cooped up in the fort, like turkeys in a pen, while the Indians ravaged the fields and burnt the homesteads, but to march out at once and break the shock by a counter-stroke.

Accordingly, on the morning of the twentieth of July, they filed out of the fort, one hundred and seventy strong, and bent their steps towards the Island Flats. Well versed in woodland warfare, the

---

[1] James Thompson, James Shelby, William Buchanan, John Campbell, William Cocke, and Thomas Madison. See their letter of August 2, 1776, "Am. Archives," 5th Series, I., 464. Haywood, relying on tradition, says five companies gathered; he is invaluable as an authority, but it must be kept in mind that he often relies on traditional statement.

frontier riflemen marched as well as fought on a system of their own, much more effective for this purpose than the discipline of European regulars.   The
men of this little levy walked strung out in Indian
file, in two parallel lines,[1] with scouts in front, and
flankers on each side.   Marching thus they could
not be surprised, and were ready at any moment to
do battle with the Indians, in open order and taking
shelter behind the trees; while regulars, crowded
together, were helpless before the savages whom the
forest screened from view, and who esteemed it an
easy task to overcome any number of foes if gathered
in a huddle.[2]

When near the Flats the whites, walking silently
with moccasined feet, came suddenly on a party
of twenty Indians, who, on being attacked, fled in
the utmost haste, leaving behind ten of their bundles
—for the southern warriors carried with them, when
on the war-path, small bundles containing their few
necessaries.

After this trifling success a council was held, and,
as the day was drawing to a close, it was decided to
return to the fort.   Some of the men were dissatisfied
with the decision, and there followed an incident as
characteristic in its way as was the bravery with
which the battle was subsequently fought.   The discontented soldiers expressed their feelings freely,
commenting especially upon the supposed lack of
courage on the part of one of the captains.   The lat-

[1] The report of the six captains says "two divisions"; from Haywood
we learn that the two divisions were two lines, evidently marching side by
side, there being a right line and a left line.

[2] See James Smith, *passim*.

ter, after brooding over the matter until the men had begun to march off the ground towards home, suddenly halted the line in which he was walking, and proceeded to harangue the troops in defence of his own reputation. Apparently no one interfered to prevent this remarkable piece of military self-justification ; the soldiers were evidently accustomed openly to criticise the conduct of their commanders, while the latter responded in any manner they saw fit. As soon as the address was over, and the lines once more straightened out, the march was renewed in the original order; and immediately afterwards the scouts brought news that a considerable body of Indians, misled by their retreat, was running rapidly up to assail their rear.[1]

The right file was promptly wheeled to the right and the left to the left, forming a line of battle a quarter of a mile long, the men taking advantage of the cover when possible. There was at first some confusion and a momentary panic, which was instantly quelled, the officers and many of the men joining to encourage and rally the few whom the suddenness of the attack rendered faint-hearted. The Otari warriors, instead of showing the usual Indian caution, came running on at headlong speed, believing that the whites were fleeing in terror ; while still some three hundred yards off [2] they raised the warwhoop and charged without halting, the foremost

---

[1] Among the later Campbell MSS. are a number of copies of papers containing traditional accounts of this battle. They are mostly very incorrect, both as to the numbers and losses of the Indians and whites, and as to the battle itself very little help can be derived from them.

[2] Campbell MSS.

chiefs hallooing out that the white men were running, and to come on and scalp them. They were led by Dragging Canoe himself, and were formed very curiously, their centre being cone-shaped, while their wings were curved outward ; apparently they believed the white line to be wavering and hoped to break through its middle at the same time that they outflanked it, trusting to a single furious onset instead of to their usual tactics.[1] The result showed their folly. The frontiersmen on the right and left scattered out still farther, so that their line could not be outflanked ; and waiting coolly till the Otari were close up, the whites fired into them. The long rifles cracked like four-horse whips ; they were held in skilful hands, many of the assailants fell, and the rush was checked at once. A short fight at close quarters ensued here and there along the line, Dragging Canoe was struck down and severely wounded, and then the Indians fled in the utmost confusion, every man for himself. Yet they carried off their wounded and perhaps some of their dead. The whites took thirteen scalps, and of their own number but four were seriously hurt ; they also took many guns and much plunder.

In this battle of the Island Flats[2] the whites were slightly superior[3] in number to their foes ; and

[1] Campell MSS.
[2] Tennessee historians sometimes call it the battle of Long Island ; which confuses it with Washington's defeat of about the same date.
[3] The captains' report says the Indians were " not inferior " in numbers ; they probably put them at a maximum. Haywood and all later writers greatly exaggerate the Indian numbers ; as also their losses, which are commonly placed at " over 40," " 26 being left dead on the

they won without difficulty, inflicting a far heavier loss than they received. In this respect it differs markedly from most other Indian fights of the same time; and many of its particulars render it noteworthy. Moreover, it had a very good effect, cheering the frontiersmen greatly, and enabling them to make head against the discouraged Indians.

On the same day the Watauga fort [1] was attacked by a large force at sunrise. It was crowded with women and children,[2] but contained only forty or fifty men. The latter, however, were not only resolute and well-armed, but were also on the alert to

ground." In reality only 13 were so left; but in the various skirmishes on the Watauga about this time, from the middle of July to the middle of August, the backwoodsmen took in all 26 scalps, and one prisoner ("American Archives," 5th Series, I., 973). This is probably the origin of the "26 dead" story; the "over 40" being merely a flourish. Ramsey gives a story about Isaac Shelby rallying the whites to victory, and later writers of course follow and embellish this; but Shelby's MS. autobiography (see copy in Col. Durrett's library at Louisville) not only makes no mention of the battle, but states that Shelby was at this time in Kentucky; he came back in August or September, and so was hundreds of miles from the place when the battle occurred. Ramsey gives a number of anecdotes of ferocious personal encounters that took place during the battle. Some of them are of very doubtful value—for instance that of the man who killed six of the most daring Indians himself (the total number killed being only thirteen), and the account of the Indians all retreating when they saw another of their champions vanquished. The climax of absurdity is reached by a recent writer, Mr. Kirke, who, after embodying in his account all the errors of his predecessors and adding several others on his own responsibility, winds up by stating that "two hundred and ten men under Sevier and [Isaac] Shelby. . . . beat back . . . fifteen thousand Indians." These numbers can only be reached by comparing an exaggerated estimate of all the Cherokees, men, women, and children, with the white men encountered by a very small proportion of the red warriors in the first two skirmishes. Moreover, as already shown, Shelby was nowhere near the scene of conflict, and Sevier was acting as Robertson's subaltern.

[1] Another fort, called Fort Lee, had been previously held by Sevier but had been abandoned; see Phelan, p. 42.

[2] "American Archives," 5th Series, I., 973; 500 women and children.

guard against surprise; the Indians were discovered as they advanced in the gray light, and were at once beaten back with loss from the loop- **The Wa-** holed stockade. Robertson commanded in **tauga Fort** the fort, Sevier acting as his lieutenant. **Besieged.** Of course, the only hope of assistance was from Virginia, North Carolina being separated from the Watauga people by great mountain chains; and Sevier had already notified the officers of Fincastle that the Indians were advancing. His letter was of laconic brevity, and contained no demand for help; it was merely a warning that the Indians were undoubtedly about to start, and that "they intended to drive the country up to New River before they returned"—so that it behooved the Fincastle men to look to their own hearthsides. Sevier was a very fearless, self-reliant man, and doubtless felt confident that the settlers themselves could beat back their assailants. His forecast proved correct; for the Indians, after maintaining an irregular siege of the fort for some three weeks, retired, almost at the moment that parties of frontiersmen came to the rescue from some of the neighboring forts. [1]

While the foe was still lurking about the fort the people within were forced to subsist solely on parched corn; and from time to time some of them became so irritated by the irksome monotony of their confinement, that they ventured out heedless of the danger. Three or four of them were killed by

---

[1] Campbell MSS. Haywood says that the first help came fron Evan Shelby; Col. Russell, at Eaton's Station proving dilatory. In the Campbell MSS. are some late letters written by sons of the Captain Campbell who took part in the Island Flats fight, denying this statement.

the Indians, and one boy was carried off to one of
their towns, where he was burnt at the stake; while
a woman who was also captured at this time was
only saved from a like fate by the exertions of the
same Cherokee squaw already mentioned as warning
the settlers. Tradition relates that Sevier, now a
young widower, fell in love with the woman he
soon afterwards married during the siege. Her
name was Kate Sherrill. She was a tall girl, brown-
haired, comely, lithe and supple "as a hickory sapling." One day while without the fort she was
almost surprised by some Indians. Running like a
deer, she reached the stockade, sprang up so as to
catch the top with her hands, and drawing herself
over, was caught in Sevier's arms on the other side;
through a loop-hole he had already shot the head-
most of her pursuers.

Soon after the baffled Otari retreated from Robertson's fort the other war parties likewise left the
settlements. The Watauga men together
**The War-
Parties
Retreat
from the
Watauga.** with the immediately adjoining Virginian
frontiersmen had beaten back their foes
unaided, save for some powder and lead
they had received from the older settlements; and moreover had inflicted more loss than
they suffered. [1] They had made an exceedingly vigorous and successful fight.

The outlying settlements scattered along the

---

[1] "American Archives," 5th Series, I., 973. Of the Watauga settlers
eighteen men, two women, and several children had been killed; two or
three were taken captive. Of the Indians twenty-six were scalped;
doubtless several others were slain. Of course these figures only apply to
the Watauga neighborhood.

western border of the Carolinas and Georgia had
been attacked somewhat earlier; the Cherokees from
the lower towns, accompanied by some Creeks and
Tories, beginning their ravages in the last
days of June.[1] A small party of Georgians had, just previously, made a sudden
march into the Cherokee country. They
were trying to capture the British agent
Cameron, who, being married to an Indian wife, dwelt
in her town, and owned many negroes, horses, and
cattle. The Cherokees, who had agreed not to interfere, broke faith and surprised the party, killing some
and capturing others who were tortured to death.[2]

The Geor-
gian and
Carolinian
Frontiers
Ravaged.

The frontiers were soon in a state of wild panic;
for the Cherokee inroad was marked by the usual
features. Cattle were driven off, houses burned,
plantations laid waste, while the women and children
were massacred indiscriminately with the men.[3] The
people fled from their homes and crowded into the
stockade forts; they were greatly hampered by the
scarcity of guns and ammunition, as much had been
given to the troops called down to the coast by
the war with Britain. All the southern colonies
were maddened by the outbreak; and prepared for
immediate revenge, knowing that if they were quick
they would have time to give the Cherokees a good
drubbing before the British could interfere.[4] The
plan was that they should act together, the Virginians
invading the Overhill country at the same time that

[1] *Do.*, p. 611.
[2] " History of Georgia," Hugh McCall, Savannah, 1816, p. 76.
[3] "Am. Archives," 5th Series, I., 610.
[4] *Do.*, 4th Series, VI., 1228.

the forces from North and South Carolina and Georgia destroyed the valley and lower towns. Thus the Cherokees would be crushed with little danger. It proved impossible, however, to get the attacks made quite simultaneously.

The back districts of North Carolina suffered heavily at the outset; however, the inhabitants showed that they were able to take care of themselves. The Cherokees came down the Catawba murdering many people; but most of the whites took refuge in the little forts, where they easily withstood the Indian assaults. General Griffith Rutherford raised a frontier levy and soon relieved the besieged stations. He sent word to the provincial authorities that if they could only get powder and lead the men of the Salisbury district were alone quite capable of beating off the Indians, but that if it was intended to invade the Cherokee country he must also have help from the Hillsborough men.[1] He was promised assistance, and was told to prepare a force to act on the offensive with the Virginians and South Carolinians.

Before he could get ready the first counter-blow had been struck by Georgia and South Carolina. Georgia

Georgia's Share in the Struggle. was the weakest of all the colonies, and the part it played in this war was but trifling. She was threatened by British cruisers along the coast, and by the Tories of Florida; and there was constant danger of an uprising of the black slaves, who outnumbered the whites. The vast herds of cattle and great rice plantations of the

---

[1] *Do.*, 5th Series, I., 613.

south offered a tempting bait to every foe. Tories were numerous in the population, while there were incessant bickerings with the Creeks, frequently resulting in small local wars, brought on as often by the faithlessness and brutality of the white borderers as by the treachery and cruelty of the red. Indeed the Indians were only kept quiet by presents, it being an unhappy feature of the frontier troubles that while lawless whites could not be prevented from encroaching on the Indian lands, the Indians in turn could only be kept at peace with the law-abiding by being bribed.[1]

Only a small number of warriors invaded Georgia. Nevertheless they greatly harassed the settlers, capturing several families and fighting two or three skirmishes with varying results.[2] By the middle of July Col. Samuel Jack[3] took the field with a force of two hundred rangers, all young men, the old and infirm being left to guard the forts. The Indians fled as soon as he had embodied his troops, and towards the end of the month he marched against one or two of their small lower towns, which he burned, destroying the grain and driving off the cattle. No resistance was offered, and he did not lose a man.

The heaviest blow fell on South Carolina, where the Cherokees were led by Cameron himself, accompanied by most of his tories. Some of his warriors

---

[1] *Do.*, 5th Series, I., 7, and III., 649. The Georgia frontiersmen seem to have been peculiarly brutal in their conduct to the Creeks ; but the latter were themselves very little, if at all, better.

[2] McCall ; five families captured ; in three skirmishes eight whites were killed and six Indian scalps taken.

[3] McCall ; the Tennessee historians erroneously assign the command to Col. McBury.

came from the lower towns that lay along the Tugelou and Keowee, but most were from the middle towns, **South** in the neighborhood of the Tellico, and **Carolina** from the valley towns that lay well to the **Suffers** westward of these, among the mountains, **Most.** along the branches of the Hiawassee and Chattahoochee rivers. Falling furiously on the scattered settlers, they killed them or drove them into the wooden forts, ravaging, burning, and murdering as elsewhere, and sparing neither age nor sex. Col. Andrew Williamson was in command of the western districts, and he at once began to gather together a force, taking his station at Picken's Fort, with forty men, on July 3d.[1] It was with the utmost difficulty that he could get troops, guns, or ammunition ; but his strenuous and unceasing efforts were successful, and his force increased day by day. It is worth noting that these lowland troops were for the most part armed with smooth-bores, unlike the rifle-bearing mountaineers. As soon as he could muster a couple of hundred men,[2] he left the fort and advanced towards the Indians, making continual halts,[3] so as to allow the numerous volunteers that were flocking to his standard to reach him. At the same time the Americans were much encouraged by the repulse of an assault made just before daylight on one of the forts.[4] The attacking party was some two hundred strong, half of them being white men, naked and painted like the Indi-

[1] "View of South Carolina," John Drayton, Charleston, 1802, p. 231. A very good book.

[2] More exactly two hundred and twenty-two, on the 8th of July.

[3] E. g., at Hogskin Creek and Barker's Creek.

[4] Lyndley's Fort, on Rayborn Creek.

ans; but after dark, on the evening before the attack, a band of one hundred and fifty American militia, on their way to join Williamson, entered the fort. The assault was made before dawn; it was promptly repulsed, and at daybreak the enemy fled, having suffered some loss; thirteen of the tories were captured, but the more nimble Indians escaped.

By the end of July, Williamson had gathered over eleven hundred militia[1] (including two small rifle companies), and advanced against the Indian towns, sending his spies and scouts before him. On the last day of the month he made a rapid night march, with three hundred and fifty horsemen, to surprise Cameron, who lay with a party of tories and Indians, encamped at Oconoree Creek, beyond the Cherokee town of Eseneka, which commanded the ford of the river Keowee. The cabins and fenced gardens of the town lay on both sides of the river. Williamson had been told by his prisoners that the hither bank was deserted, and advanced heedlessly, without scouts or flankers. In consequence he fell into an ambush, for when he reached the first houses, hidden Indians suddenly fired on him from front and flank. Many horses, including that of the commander, were shot down, and the startled troops began a disorderly retreat, firing at random. Col. Hammond rallied about twenty of the coolest, and ordering them to reserve their fire, he charged the fence from behind which the heaviest hostile fire came. When up to it, they shot into the

First Campaign Against the Cherokees.

[1] Eleven hundred and fifty-one, of whom one hundred and thirty were riflemen. He was camped at Twenty-threeMile Creek.

dark figures crouching behind it, and jumping over charged home. The Indians immediately fled, leaving one dead and three wounded in the hands of the whites. The action was over; but the by-no-means-reassured victors had lost five men mortally and thirteen severely wounded, and were still rather nervous. At daybreak Williamson destroyed the houses near by, and started to cross the ford. But his men, in true militia style, had become sulky and mutinous, and refused to cross, until Col. Hammond swore he would go alone, and plunged into the river, followed by three volunteers, whereupon the whole army crowded after. The revulsions in their feelings was instantaneous; once across they seemed to have left all fear as well as all prudence behind. On the hither side there had been no getting them to advance; on the farther there was no keeping them together, and they scattered everywhere. Luckily the Indians were too few to retaliate; and besides the Cherokees were not good marksmen, using so little powder in their guns that they made very ineffective weapons. After all the houses had been burned, and some six thousand bushels of corn, besides peas and beans, destroyed, Williamson returned to his camp. Next day he renewed his advance, and sent out detachments against all the other lower towns, utterly destroying every one by the middle of August, although not without one or two smart skirmishes.[1] His troops were very much elated, and

---

[1] At Tomassee, where he put to flight a body of two or three hundred warriors, he lost eight killed and fifteen wounded, and at Tugelou, four wounded. Besides these two towns, he also destroyed Soconee, Keowee, Ostatay, Chehokee, Eustustie, Sugaw Town, and Brass Town.

only the lack of provisions prevented his marching against the middle towns. As it was, he retired to refit, leaving a garrison of six hundred men at Eseneka, which he christened Fort Rutledge. This ended the first stage of the retaliatory campaign, undertaken by the whites in revenge for the outbreak. The South Carolinians, assisted slightly by a small independent command of Georgians, who acted separately, had destroyed the lower Cherokee towns, at the same time that the Watauga people repulsed the attack of the Overhill warriors.

The second and most important movement was to be made by South Carolina, North Carolina, and Virginia jointly, each sending a column of two thousand men,[1] the two former against the middle and valley, the latter against the Overhill towns. If the columns acted together the Cherokees would be overwhelmed by a force three times the number of all their warriors. The plan succeeded well, although the Virginia division was delayed so that its action, though no less effective, was much later than that of the others, and though the latter likewise failed to act in perfect unison.

Second Campaign against the Cherokees.

Rutherford and his North Carolinians were the first to take the field.[2] He had an army of two thousand gunmen, besides pack-horsemen and men

---

[1] All militia of course, with only the training they had received on the rare muster days; but a warlike set, utterly unlike ordinary militia, and for woodland work against savages in many respects much superior to European regulars. This campaign against the Cherokees was infinitely more successful than that waged in 1760 against the same foe by armies of grenadiers and highlanders.

[2] That is, after the return of the South Carolinians from their destruction of the lower towns.

to tend the drove of bullocks, together with a few
Catawba Indians,—a total of twenty-four hundred.[1]
On September 1st he left the head of the Catawba,[2]
and the route he followed was long known by the
name of Rutherford's trace. There was not a tent in
his army, and but very few blankets; the pack-horses
carried the flour, while the beef was driven along on
the hoof. Officers and men alike wore homespun
hunting-shirts trimmed with colored cotton; the cloth
was made from hemp, tow, and wild-nettle bark.

He passed over the Blue Ridge at Swananoa Gap,
crossed the French Broad at the Warriors' Ford, and
then went through the mountains[3] to the middle
towns, a detachment of a thousand men making a
forced march in advance. This detachment was
fired at by a small band of Indians from an ambush,
and one man was wounded in the foot; but no
further resistance was made, the towns being abandoned.[4] The main body coming up, parties of
troops were sent out in every direction, and all of
the middle towns were destroyed. Rutherford had
expected to meet Williamson at this place, but the
latter did not appear, and so the North Carolina
commander determined to proceed alone against the
valley towns along the Hiawassee. Taking with him
only nine hundred picked men, he attempted to cross
the rugged mountain chains which separated him from
his destination; but he had no guide, and missed the

[1] "Historical Sketches or North Carolina," John H. Wheeler, Phil.,
1851, p. 383.

[2] "Am. Archives," 5th Series, Vol. II., p. 1235.

[3] Up Hominy Creek, across the Pigeon, up Richland Creek, across
Tuckaseigee River, over Cowee Mount.

[4] "Am. Archives," 5th Series, II., p. 1235.

regular pass—a fortunate thing for him, as it afterwards turned out, for he thus escaped falling into an
ambush of five hundred Cherokees who were encamped along it.[1]   After in vain trying to penetrate
the tangle of gloomy defiles and wooded peaks, he
returned to the middle towns at Canucca on September 18th.   Here he met Williamson, who had just
arrived, having been delayed so that he could not
leave Fort Rutledge until the 13th.[2]   The South Carolinians, two thousand strong, had crossed the Blue
Ridge near the sources of the Little Tennessee.

While Rutherford rested [3] Williamson, on the 19th,
pushed on through Noewee pass, and fell into the
ambush which had been laid for the former.   The
pass was a narrow, open valley, walled in by steep
and lofty mountains.   The Indians waited until the
troops were struggling up to the outlet, and then
assailed them with a close and deadly fire.   The surprised soldiers recoiled and fell into confusion; and
they were for the second time saved from disaster by
the gallantry of Colonel Hammond, who with voice
and action rallied them, endeavoring to keep them
firm while a detachment was sent to clamber up the
rocks and outflank the Indians.   At the same time
Lieutenant Hampton got twenty men together, out
of the rout, and ran forward, calling out: "Loaded

---

[1] *Do.*

[2] Drayton.   There was a good deal of jealousy between the two armies
and their reports conflict on some points.

[3] There is some conflict in the accounts of the destruction of the valley
towns; after carefully comparing the accounts in the "American Archives,"
Drayton, White, Ramsey, etc., I believe that the above is substantially accurate.   However it is impossible to reconcile all of the accounts of the
relative order of Rutherford's and Williamson's marches.

guns advance, empty guns fall down and load." Being joined by some thirty men more he pushed desperately upwards. The Indians fled from the shock; and the army thus owed its safety solely to two gallant officers. Of the whites seventeen were killed and twenty-nine wounded [1]; they took fourteen scalps. [2]

Although the distance was but twenty odd miles, it took Williamson five days of incredible toil before he reached the valley towns. The troops showed the utmost patience, clearing a path for the pack-train along the sheer mountain sides and through the dense, untrodden forests in the valleys. The trail often wound along cliffs where a single misstep of a pack-animal resulted in its being dashed to pieces. But the work, though fatiguing, was healthy; it was noticed that during the whole expedition not a man was laid up for any length of time by sickness.

Rutherford joined Williamson immediately afterwards, and together they utterly laid waste the valley towns; and then, in the last week of September, started homewards. All the Cherokee settlements west of the Appalachians had been destroyed from the face of the earth, neither crops nor cattle being left; and most of the inhabitants were obliged to take refuge with the Creeks.

Rutherford reached home in safety, never having experienced any real resistance; he had lost but three men in all. He had killed twelve Indians, and had captured nine more, besides seven whites and

[1] Drayton; the "Am. Archives" say only twelve killed and twenty wounded. In another skirmish at Cheowee three South Carolinians were killed.

[2] "Am. Archives," 5th Series, II., p. 1235.

four negroes.   He had also taken piles of deerskins,
a hundred-weight of gunpowder and twenty-five
hundred pounds of lead; and, moreover, had wasted
and destroyed to his heart's content.[1]

Williamson, too, reached home without suffering
further damage, entering Fort Rutledge on October
7th.   In his two expeditions he had had ninety-four
men killed and wounded, but he had done much more
harm than any one else to the Indians.   It was said
the South Carolinians had taken seventy-five scalps[2];
at any rate, the South Carolina Legislature had offered
a reward of £75 for every warrior's scalp, as well as
£100 for every Indian, and £80 for every tory or
negro, taken prisoner.[3]   But the troops were for-
bidden to sell their prisoners as slaves—not a need-
less injunction, as is shown by the fact that when it
was issued there had already been at least one case
in Williamson's own army where a captured Indian
was sold into bondage.

The Virginian troops had meanwhile been slowly
gathering at the Great Island of the Holston, under
Colonel William Christian, preparatory to The March
assaulting the Overhill Cherokees.   While   of the
they were assembling the Indians threat- Virginians.
ened them from time to time; once a small party of
braves crossed the river and killed a soldier near
the main post of the army, and also killed a settler; a day or two later another war-party slipped
by towards the settlements, but on being pursued
by a detachment of militia faced about and re-

[1] *Do.*

[2] *Do.*, p. 990 ; Drayton puts the total Cherokee loss at two hundred.

[3] *Do.*, Vol. III., p. 33.

turned to their town.[1] On the first of October the army started, two thousand strong,[2] including some troops from North Carolina, and all the gunmen who could be spared from the little stockaded hamlets scattered along the Watauga, the Holston, and the Clinch. Except a small force of horse-riflemen the men were on foot, each with tomahawk, scalping-knife, and long, grooved flint-lock; all were healthy, well equipped, and in fine spirits, driving their pack-horses and bullocks with them. Characteristically enough a Presbyterian clergyman, following his backwoods flock, went along with this expedition as chaplain. The army moved very cautiously, the night encampments being made behind breastworks of felled timbers. There was therefore no chance for a surprise; and their great inferiority in number made it hopeless for the Cherokees to try a fair fight. In their despair they asked help from the Creeks; but the latter replied that they had plucked the thorn of warfare from their (the Creeks') foot, and were welcome to keep it.[3]

The Virginians came steadily on[4] until they reached the Big Island of the French Broad.[5] Here the Cherokees had gathered their warriors, and they

[1] These two events took place on September 26th and 29th; "Am. Archives," 5th Series, Vol. II., p. 540. Ramsey is thus wrong in saying no white was killed on this expedition.

[2] McAfee MSS.; one of the McAfees went along and preserved a rough diary of dates.

[3] "History of Virginia," John Burke (continued by L. H. Girardin), Petersburg, 1816, p. 176.

[4] After camping a few days at Double Springs, the head-waters of Lick Creek, to let all the Watauga men come up.

[5] They sent spies in advance. The trail led through forests and marshy canebrakes; across Nolichucky, up Long Creek and down Dunplin Creek to the French Broad. Haywood and Ramsey.

sent a tory trader across with a flag of truce. Christian well knowing that the Virginians greatly outnumbered the Indians, let the man go through his camp at will,[1] and sent him back with word that the Cherokee towns were doomed, for that he would surely march to them and destroy them. That night he left half of his men in camp, lying on their arms by the watch-fires, while with the others he forded the river below and came round to surprise the Indian encampment from behind ; but he found that the Indians had fled, for their hearts had become as water, nor did they venture at any time, during this expedition, to molest the white forces. Following them up, Christian reached the towns early in November,[2] and remained two weeks, sending out parties to burn the cabins and destroy the stores of corn and potatoes. The Indians[3] sent in a flag to treat for peace, surrendering the horses and prisoners they had taken, and agreeing to fix a boundary and give up to the settlers the land they already had, as well as some additional territory. Christian made peace on these terms and ceased his ravages, but he excepted the town of Tuskega, whose people had burned alive the boy taken captive at Watauga. This town he reduced to ashes.

Nor would the chief Dragging Canoe accept peace at all; but gathering round him the fiercest and most unruly of the young men, he left the rest of the tribe and retired to the Chickamauga fastnesses.

When the preliminary truce had been made Christian marched his forces homeward, and disbanded them a fortnight before Christmas, leaving a

---

[1] McAfee MSS.   [2] Nov. 5th. *Do.*   [3] Nov. 8th. *Do.*

garrison at Holston, Great Island. During the ensuing spring and summer peace treaties were definitely concluded between the Upper Cherokees and Virginia and North Carolina at the Great Island of the Holston,[1] and between the Lower Cherokees and South Carolina and Georgia at De Witt's Corners. The Cherokees gave up some of their lands; of the four seacoast provinces South Carolina gained most, as was proper, for she had done and suffered most.[2]

The Watauga people and the westerners generally were the real gainers by the war. Had the Watauga settlements been destroyed, they would no longer have covered the Wilderness Road to Kentucky; and so Kentucky must perforce have been abandoned. But the followers of Robertson and Sevier stood stoutly for their homes; not one of them fled over the mountains. The Cherokees had been so roughly handled that for several years they did not again go to war as a body; and this not only gave the settlers a breathing time, but also enabled them to make themselves so strong that when the struggle was renewed they could easily hold their own. The war was thus another and important link in the chain of events by which the west was won; and had any link in the chain snapped during these early years, the peace of 1783 would probably have seen the trans-Alleghany country in the hands of a non-American power.

[1] The boundary then established between the Cherokees and Watauga people was known as Brown's Line.

[2] As a very rough guess after a careful examination of all the authorities, it may be said that in this war somewhat less than two hundred Indians were slain, all warriors. The loss of the whites in war was probably no greater; but it included about as many more women and children. So that perhaps two or three times as many whites as Indians were killed, counting in every one.

CHAPTER XII.

GROWTH AND CIVIL ORGANIZATION OF KENTUCKY, 1776.

By the end of 1775 Kentucky had been occupied by those who were permanently to hold it. Stout-hearted men, able to keep what they had **Permanent** grasped moved in, and took with them their **Settlers** wives and children. There was also of **Come in.** course a large shifting element, composing, indeed, the bulk of the population: hunters who came out for the season; "cabinners," or men who merely came out to build a cabin and partially clear a spot of ground, so as to gain a right to it under the law; surveyors, and those adventurers always to be found in a new country, who are too restless, or too timid, or too irresolute to remain.

The men with families and the young men who intended to make permanent homes formed the heart of the community, the only part worth taking into account. There was a steady though thin stream of such immigrants, and they rapidly built up around them a life not very unlike that which they had left behind with their old homes. Even in 1776 there was marrying and giving in marriage, and children were born in Kentucky. The new-comers had to settle in forts, where the young men and maidens had many chances for courtship. They married early, and were as fruitful as they were hardy.[1] Most of these marriages were civil contracts, but some may have been solemnized by clergymen, for the commonwealth received from the outset occasional visits from ministers.

These ministers belonged to different denominations, but all were sure of a hearing. The backwoods-**Religion of the Settlers.** men were forced by their surroundings to exercise a grudging charity towards the various forms of religious belief entertained among themselves—though they hated and despised French and Spanish Catholics. When off in the wilderness they were obliged to take a man for what he did, not for what he thought. Of course there were instances to the contrary, and there is an amusing and authentic story of two hunters, living alone and far from any settlement, who quarrelled because one was a Catholic and the other a Protestant. The seceder took up his abode in a hollow tree within speaking distance of his companion's cabin. Every day on arising they bade each other good-morning; but not another word passed between them for the many months during which they saw no other white face.[2] There was a single serious and important, albeit only partial, exception to this general rule of charity. After the outbreak of the Revolution, the Kentuckians, in common with other backwoodsmen, grew to thoroughly dislike one

[1] Imlay, p. 55, estimated that from natural increase the population of Kentucky doubled every fifteen years,—probably an exaggeration.
[2] Hale's "Trans-Alleghany Pioneers," p. 251.

religious body which they already distrusted; this was the Church of England, the Episcopal Church. They long regarded it as merely the persecuting ecclesiastical arm of the British Government. Such of them as had been brought up in any faith at all had for the most part originally professed some form of Calvinism; they had very probably learnt their letters from a primer which in one of its rude cuts represented John Rogers at the stake, surrounded by his wife and seven children, and in their after lives they were more familiar with the "Pilgrim's Progress" than with any other book save the Bible; so that it was natural for them to distrust the successors of those who had persecuted Rogers and Bunyan.[1]   Still, the border communities were, as times then went very tolerant in religious matters; and of course most of the men had no chance to display, or indeed to feel, sectarianism of any kind, for they had no issue to join, and rarely a church about which to rally.

By the time Kentucky was settled the Baptists had begun to make headway on the frontier, at the expense of the Presbyterians. The rough democracy of the border welcomed a sect which was itself essentially democratic. To many of the backwoodsmen's prejudices, notably their sullen and narrow hostility towards all rank, whether or not based on merit and learning, the Baptists' creed appealed strongly. Where their preachers obtained foothold, it was made a matter of reproach to the Presby-

---

[1] " Pioneer Life in Kentucky," Daniel Drake, Cincinnati, 1870, p. 196 (an invaluable work).

terian clergymen that they had been educated in early life for the ministry as for a profession. The love of liberty, and the defiant assertion of equality, so universal in the backwoods, and so excellent in themselves, sometimes took very warped and twisted forms, notably when they betrayed the backwoodsmen into the belief that the true democratic spirit forbade any exclusive and special training for the professions that produce soldiers, statesmen, or ministers.

The fact that the Baptist preachers were men exactly similar to their fellows in all their habits

Baptist Preachers Visit Kentucky. of life, not only gave them a good standing at once, but likewise enabled them very early to visit the farthest settlements, travelling precisely like other backwoodsmen; and once there, each preacher, each earnest professor, doing bold and fearless missionary work, became the nucleus round which a little knot of true believers gathered. Two or three of them made short visits to Kentucky during the first few years of its existence. One, who went thither in the early spring of 1776, kept a journal of his trip.[1] He travelled over the Wilderness Road with eight other men. Three of them were Baptists like himself, who prayed every night; and their companions, though they did not take part in the praying, did not interrupt it. Their journey through the melancholy and silent wilderness resembled in its incidents the countless other similar journeys that were made at that time and later.

---

[1] MS. autobiography of Rev. William Hickman. He was born in Virginia, February 4, 1747. A copy in Col. Durrett's library at Louisville, Ky.

They suffered from cold and hunger and lack of shelter ; they became footsore and weary, and worn out with driving the pack-horses. On the top of the lonely Cumberland Mountains they came upon the wolf-eaten remains of a previous traveller, who had recently been killed by Indians. At another place they met four men returning—cowards, whose hearts had failed them when in sight of the promised land. While on the great Indian war-trail they killed a buffalo, and thenceforth lived on its jerked meat. One night the wolves smelt the flesh, and came up to the camp-fire ; the strong hunting-dogs rushed out with clamorous barking to drive them away, and the sudden alarm for a moment made the sleepy way-farers think that roving Indians had attacked them. When they reached Crab Orchard their dangers were for the moment past ; all travellers grew to regard with affection the station by this little grove of wild apple-trees. It is worthy of note that the early set-tlers loved to build their homes near these natural orchards, moved by the fragrance and beauty of the bloom in spring.[1]

The tired Baptist was not overpleased with Har-rodstown, though he there listened to the preaching of one of his own sect.[2] He remarked "a poor town it was in those days," a couple of rows of smoky cabins, tenanted by dirty women and ragged children, while the tall, unkempt frontiersmen lounged about in greasy hunting-shirts, breech-clouts, leggings, and

[1] There were at least three such "Crab-Orchard" stations in Virginia, Kentucky, and Tennessee. The settlers used the word "crab" precisely as Shakespeare does.

[2] A Mr. Finley. Hickman MS.

moccasins. There was little or no corn until the crops were gathered, and, like the rest, he had to learn to eat wild meat without salt. The settlers, —as is always the case in frontier towns where the people are wrapped up in their own pursuits and rivalries, and are obliged to talk of one another for lack of outside interests,—were divided by bickering, gossiping jealousies; and at this time they were quarrelling as to whether the Virginian cabin-rights or Henderson's land-grants would prove valid. As usual, the zealous Baptist preacher found that the women were the first to "get religion," as he phrased it. Sometimes their husbands likewise came in with them; at other times they remained indifferent. Often they savagely resented their wives and daughters being converted, visiting on the head of the preacher an anger that did not always find vent in mere words; for the backwoodsmen had strong, simple natures, powerfully excited for good or evil, and those who were not God-fearing usually became active and furious opponents of all religion.

It is curious to compare the description of life in a frontier fort as given by this undoubtedly prejudiced observer with the equally prejudiced, but golden- instead of sombre-hued, reminiscences of frontier life, over which the pioneers lovingly lingered in their old age. To these old men the long-vanished stockades seemed to have held a band of brothers, who were ever generous, hospitable, courteous, and fearless, always ready to help one another, never envious, never flinching from any foe.[1] Neither account

Different Types Among the Settlers.

[1] McAfee MSS.

is accurate; but the last is quite as near the truth as the first. On the border, as elsewhere, but with the different qualities in even bolder contrast, there was much both of good and bad, of shiftless viciousness and resolute honesty. Many of the hunters were mere restless wanderers, who soon surrendered their clearings to small farming squatters, but a degree less shiftless than themselves; the latter brought the ground a little more under cultivation, and then likewise left it and wandered onwards, giving place to the third set of frontiersmen, the steady men who had come to stay. But often the first hunters themselves stayed and grew up as farmers and landed proprietors.[1] Many of the earliest pioneers, including most of their leaders, founded families, which took root in the land and flourish to this day, the children, grandchildren, and great-grandchildren of the old-time Indian fighters becoming Congressmen and judges, and officers in the regular army and in the Federal and Confederate forces during the civil war.[2] In fact the very first comers to a wild and dangerous country are apt to be men with fine qualities of heart and head; it is not until they have partly tamed the land that the scum of the frontier drifts into it.[3]

In 1776, as in after years, there were three routes that were taken by immigrants to Kentucky. One

[1] McAfee MSS.

[2] Such was the case with the Clarks, Boons, Seviers, Shelbys, Robertsons, Logans, Cockes, Crocketts, etc.; many of whose descendants it has been my good-fortune personally to know.

[3] This is as true to-day in the far west as it was formerly in Kentucky and Tennessee; at least to judge by my own experience in the Little Missouri region, and in portions of the Kootenai, Cœur d'Alêne, and Bighorn countries.

led by backwoods trails to the Greenbriar settlements, and thence down the Kanawha to the Ohio [1]; but the

Three Routes to Kentucky. travel over this was insignificant compared to that along the others. The two really important routes were the Wilderness Road, and that by water, from Fort Pitt down the Ohio River. Those who chose the latter way embarked in roughly built little flat-boats at Fort Pitt, if they came from Pennsylvania, or else at the old Redstone Fort on the Monongahela, if from Maryland or Virginia, and drifted down with the current. Though this was the easiest method, yet the danger from Indians was so very great that most immigrants, the Pennsylvanians as well as the Marylanders, Virginians, and North Carolinians,[2] usually went overland by the Wilderness

The Wilderness Road. Road. This was the trace marked out by Boon, which to the present day remains a monument to his skill as a practical surveyor and engineer. Those going along it went on foot, driving their horses and cattle. At the last important frontier town they fitted themselves out with pack-saddles; for in such places two of the leading indus-

[1] McAfee MSS. See also "Trans-Alleghany Pioneers," p. 111. As Mr. Hale points out, this route, which was travelled by Floyd, Bullitt, the McAfees, and many others, has not received due attention, even in Colonel Speed's invaluable and interesting "Wilderness Road."

[2] Up to 1783 the Kentucky immigrants came from the backwoods of Pennsylvania, Maryland, Virginia, and North Carolina, and were of almost precisely the same character as those that went to Tennessee. See Imlay, p. 168. At the close of the Revolutionary war, Tennessee and Kentucky were almost alike in population. But after that time the population of Kentucky rapidly grew varied, and the great immigration of upper-class Virginians gave it a peculiar stamp of its own. By 1796, when Logan was defeated for governor, the control of Kentucky had passed out of the hands of the pioneers; whereas in Tennessee the old Indian fighters continued to give the tone to the social life of the State, and remained in control until they died.

tries were always those of the pack-saddle maker and the artisan in deer leather. When there was need, the pioneer could of course make a rough pack-saddle for himself, working it up from two forked branches of a tree. If several families were together, they moved slowly in true patriarchal style. The elder boys drove the cattle, which usually headed the caravan; while the younger children were packed in crates of hickory withes and slung across the backs of the old quiet horses, or else were seated safely between the great rolls of bedding that were carried in similar fashion. The women sometimes rode and sometimes walked, carrying the babies. The men, rifle on shoulder, drove the pack-train, while some of them walked spread out in front, flank, and rear, to guard against the savages.[1] A tent or brush lean-to gave cover at night. Each morning the men packed the animals while the women cooked breakfast and made ready the children. Special care had to be taken not to let the loaded animals brush against the yellow-jacket nests, which were always plentiful along the trail in the fall of the year; for in such a case the vicious swarms attacked man and beast, producing an immediate stampede, to the great detriment of the packs.[2] In winter the fords and mountains often became impassable, and trains were

[1] McAfee MSS. Just as the McAfee family started for Kentucky, the wife of one of their number, George, was confined. The others had to leave her; but at the first long halt the husband hurried back, only to meet his wife on the way; for she had ridden after them just three days after her confinement, taking her baby along.

[2] "Pioneer Biography," James McBride (son of a pioneer who was killed by the Indians in 1789 in Kentucky), p. 183, Cincinnati, 1869. One of the excellent series published by Robert Clarke & Co., to whom American historians owe a special and unique debt of gratitude.

kept in one place for weeks at a time, escaping starvation only by killing the lean cattle; for few deer
at that season remained in the mountains.

Both the water route and the wilderness road were
infested by the savages at all times, and whenever
there was open war the sparsely settled regions from
which they started were likewise harried. When
the northwestern tribes threatened Fort Pitt and
Fort Henry—or Pittsburg and Wheeling, as they
were getting to be called,—they threatened one
of the two localities which served to cover the communications with Kentucky; but it was far more
serious when the Holston region was menaced, because the land travel was at first much the more
important.

The early settlers of course had to suffer great
hardship even when they reached Kentucky. The
Hardships only two implements the men invariably
Endured by carried were the axe and rifle, for they
the Early were almost equally proud of their skill
Settlers. as warriors, hunters, and wood-choppers.
Next in importance came the sickle or scythe. The
first three tasks of the pioneer farmer were to build
a cabin, to make a clearing—burning the brush, cutting down the small trees, and girdling the large—
and to plant corn. Until the crop ripened he hunted
steadily, and his family lived on the abundant game,
save for which it would have been wholly impossible to have settled Kentucky so early. If it was
winter-time, however, all the wild meat was very
lean and poor eating, unless by chance a bear was
found in a hollow tree, when there was a royal feast,

the breast of the wild turkey serving as a substitute
for bread.[1]   If the men were suddenly called away
by an Indian inroad, their families sometimes had to
live for days on boiled tops of green nettles.[2]   Naturally the children watched the growth of the tasselled
corn with hungry eagerness until the milky ears were
fit for roasting.   When they hardened, the grains
were pounded into hominy in the hominy-block, or
else ground into meal in the rough hand-mill, made
of two limestones in a hollow sycamore log.   Until
flax could be grown the women were obliged to be
content with lint made from the bark of dead nettles.
This was gathered in the spring-time by all the people of a station acting together, a portion of the men
standing guard while the rest, with the women and
children, plucked the dead stalks.   The smart girls
of Irish ancestry spun many dozen cuts of linen from
this lint, which was as fine as flax but not so strong.[3]

Neither hardship nor danger could render the
young people downhearted, especially when several
families, each containing grown-up sons
and daughters, were living together in
almost every fort.   The chief amusements
were hunting and dancing.   There being
no permanent ministers, even the gloomy Calvinism
of some of the pioneers was relaxed.   Long afterwards one of them wrote, in a spirit of quaint
apology, that " dancing was not then considered
criminal,"[4] and that it kept up the spirits of the
young people, and made them more healthy and
happy ; and recalling somewhat uneasily the merri-

*Amuse-
ments and
Explora-
tions.*

---

[1] McAfee MSS.   [2] McBride, II., 197.   [3] McAfee MSS.   [4] *Do.*

ment in the stations, in spite of the terrible and interminable Indian warfare, the old moralist felt obliged to condemn it, remarking that, owing to the lack of ministers of the gospel, the impressions made by misfortune were not improved.

Though obliged to be very careful and to keep their families in forts, and in spite of a number of them being killed by the savages,[1] the settlers in 1776 were able to wander about and explore the country thoroughly,[2] making little clearings as the basis of " cabin claims," and now and then gathering into stations which were for the most part broken up by the Indians and abandoned.[3] What was much more important, the permanent settlers in the well-established stations proceeded to organize a civil government.

They by this time felt little but contempt for the Henderson or Transylvania government. Having **The Har-** sent a petition against it to the provincial **rodstown** authorities, they were confident that what **Conven-** faint shadow of power it still retained **tion.** would soon vanish; so they turned their attention to securing a representation in the Virginia convention. All Kentucky was still considered as a

[1] Morehead, App. Floyd's letter.

[2] They retained few Indian names ; Kentucky in this respect differing from most other sections of the Union. The names were either taken from the explorers, as Floyd's Fork ; or from some natural peculiarity, as the Licking, so called from the number of game licks along its borders ; or else they commemorated some incident. On Dreaming Creek Boon fell asleep and dreamed he was stung by yellow-jackets. The Elkhorn was so named because a hunter, having slain a monstrous bull elk, stuck up its horns on a pole at the mouth. At Bloody Run several men were slain. Eagle Branch was so called because of the many bald eagles round it. See McAfee MSS.   [3] Marshall, 45.

part of Fincastle County, and the inhabitants were therefore unrepresented at the capital. They determined to remedy this; and after due proclamation, gathered together at Harrodstown early in June, 1776. During five days an election was held, and two delegates were chosen to go to Williamsburg, then the seat of government.

This was done at the suggestion of Clark, who, having spent the winter in Virginia had returned to Kentucky in the spring. He came out alone   **Clark** and on foot, and by his sudden appearance   **Comes to** surprised the settlers not a little. The first   **Kentucky.** to meet him was a young lad,[1] who had gone a few miles out of Harrodstown to turn some horses on the range. The boy had killed a teal duck that was feeding in a spring, and was roasting it nicely at a small fire, when he was startled by the approach of a fine soldierly man, who hailed him: "How do you do my little fellow? What is your name? Ar'n't you afraid of being in the woods by yourself?" The stranger was evidently hungry, for on being invited to eat he speedily finished the entire duck; and when the boy asked his name he answered that it was Clark, and that he had come out to see what the brave fellows in Kentucky were doing, and to help them if there was need. He took up his temporary abode at Harrodstown—visiting all the forts, however, and being much in the woods by himself,—and his commanding mind and daring, adventurous temper speedily made him, what for ten critical years he remained, the leader among all the bold "hunters

---

[1] Afterwards General William Ray. Butler, p. 37.

of Kentucky "—as the early settlers loved to call themselves.

He had advised against delegates to the convention being chosen, thinking that instead the Kentuckians should send accredited agents to treat with the Virginian government. If their terms were not agreed to, he declared that they ought to establish forthwith an independent state; an interesting example of how early the separatist spirit showed itself in Kentucky. But the rest of the people were unwilling to go quite as far. They elected two delegates, Clark of course being one. With them they sent a petition for admission as a separate county. They were primarily farmers, hunters, Indian fighters—not scholars; and their petition was couched in English that was at times a little crooked; but the idea at any rate was perfectly straight, and could not be misunderstood. They announced that if they were admitted they would cheerfully coöperate in every measure to secure the public peace and safety, and at the same time pointed out with marked emphasis " how impolitical it would be to suffer such a Respectable Body of Prime Riflemen to remain in a state of neutrality " during the then existing revolutionary struggle.[1]

Armed with this document and their credentials, Clark and his companion set off across the desolate and Indian-haunted mountains. They travelled very

Sent to Virginia as a Delegate.

[1] Petition of the committee of West Fincastle, dated June 20, 1776. It is printed in Col. John Mason Brown's " Battle of the Blue Licks " pamphlet.

fast, the season was extremely wet, and they did not dare to kindle fires for fear of the Indians; in consequence they suffered torments from cold, hunger, and especially from "scalded" feet. Yet they hurried on, and presented their petition to the Governor[1] and Council—the Legislature having adjourned. Clark also asked for five hundred-weight of gunpowder, of which the Kentucky settlement stood in sore and pressing need. This the Council at first refused to give; whereupon Clark informed them that if the country was not worth defending, it was not worth claiming, making it plain that if the request was not granted, and if Kentucky was forced to assume the burdens of independence, she would likewise assume its privileges. After this plain statement the Council yielded. Clark took the powder down the Ohio River, and got it safely through to Kentucky; though a party sent under John Todd to convey it overland from the Limestone Creek was met at the Licking and defeated by the Indians, Clark's fellow delegate being among the killed.

Before returning Clark had attended the fall meeting of the Virginia Legislature, and in spite of the opposition of Henderson, who was likewise present, he procured the admission of Kentucky as a separate county, with boundaries corresponding to those of the present State. Early in the ensuing year, 1777, the county was accordingly organized; Harrodstown, or Harrodsburg, as it was now beginning to be called, was made the county seat, having by this time sup-

He Procures the Erection of Kentucky County.

[1] Patrick Henry.

planted Boonsborough in importance. The court was composed of the six or eight men whom the governor of Virginia had commissioned as justices of the peace; they were empowered to meet monthly to transact necessary business, and had a sheriff and clerk.[1] These took care of the internal concerns of the settlers. To provide for their defence a county lieutenant was created, with the rank of colonel,[2] who forthwith organized a militia regiment, placing all the citizens, whether permanent residents or not, into companies and battalions. Finally, two burgesses were chosen to represent the county in the General Assembly of Virginia.[3] In later years Daniel Boon himself served as a Kentucky burgess in the Virginia Legislature[4]; a very different body from the little Transylvanian parliament in which he began his career as a law-maker. The old backwoods hero led a strange life: varying his long wanderings and explorations, his endless campaigns against savage men and savage beasts, by serving as road-maker, town-builder, and commonwealth-founder, sometimes organizing the frontiersmen for foreign war, and again doing his share in devising the laws under which they were to live and prosper.

[1] Among their number were John Todd (likewise chosen burgess—in these early days a man of mark often filled several distinct positions at the same time), Benj. Logan, Richard Calloway, John Bowman, and John Floyd; the latter was an educated Virginian, who was slain by the Indians before his fine natural qualities had time to give him the place he would otherwise assuredly have reached.

[2] The first colonel was John Bowman.

[3] John Dodd and Richard Calloway. See Diary of Geo. Rogers Clark, in 1776. Given by Morehead, p. 161.

[4] Butler, 166.

But the pioneers were speedily drawn into a life-and-death struggle which engrossed their whole attention to the exclusion of all merely War with civil matters; a struggle in which their the land became in truth what the Indians Indians. called it—a dark and bloody ground, a land with blood-stained rivers.[1]

It was impossible long to keep peace on the border between the ever-encroaching whites and their fickle and blood-thirsty foes. The hard, reckless, often brutalized frontiersmen, greedy of land and embittered by the memories of untold injuries, regarded all Indians with sullen enmity, and could not be persuaded to distinguish between the good and the bad.[2] The central government was as powerless to restrain as to protect these far-off and unruly citizens. On the other hand, the Indians were as treacherous as they were ferocious; Delawares, Shawnees, Wyandots, and all.[3] While deceiving the commandants of the posts by peaceful protestations, they would steadily continue their ravages and murders; and while it was easy to persuade a number of the chiefs and warriors of a tribe to enter into a treaty, it was impossible to make the remainder respect it.[4] The

[1] The Iroquois, as well as the Cherokees, used these expressions concerning portions of the Ohio valley. Heckewelder, 118.

[2] State Department MSS., No. 147, Vol. VI., March 15, 1781.

[3] As one instance among many see Haldimand MSS., letter of Lt. Col. Hamilton, August 17, 1778, where Girty reported, on behalf of the Delawares, the tribe least treacherous to the Americans, that even these Indians were only going in to Fort Pitt and keeping up friendly relations with its garrison so as to deceive the whites, and that as soon as their corn was ripe they would move off to the hostile tribes.

[4] State Department MSS., No. 150, Vol. I., p. 107. Letter of Captain John Doughty.

chiefs might be for peace, but the young braves were always for war, and could not be kept back.[1]

In July, 1776, the Delawares, Shawnees, and Mingo chiefs assembled at Fort Pitt and declared for

Double-Dealing of the Indians. neutrality[2]; the Iroquois ambassadors, who were likewise present, haughtily announced that their tribes would permit neither the British nor the Americans to march an army through their territory. They disclaimed any responsibility for what might be done by a few wayward young men; and requested the Delawares and Shawnees to do as they had promised, and to distribute the Iroquois "talk" among their people. After the Indian fashion, they emphasized each point which they wished kept in mind by the presentation of a string of wampum.[3]

Yet at this very time a party of Mingos tried to kill the American Indian agents, and were only prevented by Cornstalk, whose noble and faithful conduct was so soon to be rewarded by his own brutal murder. Moreover, while the Shawnee chief was doing this, some of his warriors journeyed down to the Cherokees and gave them the war belt, assuring them that the Wyandots and Mingos would support them, and that they themselves had been promised ammunition by the French traders of Detroit and the Illinois.[4] On their return home this party of Shawnees scalped two men in Kentucky near the Big Bone Lick, and captured a woman; but they

[1] State Department MSS., No. 150, Vol. I., p. 115. Examination of John Leith.   [2] " Am. Archives," 5th Series, Vol. I., p. 36.
[3] " The Olden Time," Neville B. Craig, II., p. 115.
[4] " Am. Archives," 5th Series, Vol. I., p. 111.

were pursued by the Kentucky settlers, two were killed and the woman retaken.[1]

Throughout the year the outlook continued to grow more and more threatening. Parties of young men kept making inroads on the settlements, especially in Kentucky; not only did the Shawnees, Wyandots, Mingos, and Iroquois [2] act thus, but they were even joined by bands of Ottawas, Pottawatomies, and Chippewas from the lakes, who thus attacked the white settlers long ere the latter had either the will or the chance to hurt them.

Until the spring of 1777 [3] the outbreak was not general, and it was supposed that only some three or four hundred warriors had taken up the tomahawk.[4] Yet the outlying settlers were **Their Ravages.** all the time obliged to keep as sharp a look-out as if engaged in open war. Throughout the summer of 1776 the Kentucky settlers were continually harassed. Small parties of Indians were constantly lurking round the forts, to shoot down the men as they hunted or worked in the fields, and to carry off the women. There was a constant and monotonous succession of unimportant forays and skirmishes.

[1] *Do.*, p. 137. [2] *Do.*, Vol. II., pp. 516, 1236.

[3] When Cornstalk was so foully murdered by the whites; although the outbreak was then already started.

[4] Madison MSS. But both the American statesmen and the Continental officers were so deceived by the treacherous misrepresentations of the Indians that they often greatly underestimated the numbers of the Indians on the war-path; curiously enough, their figures are frequently much more erroneous than those of the frontiersmen. Thus the Madison MSS. and State Department MSS. contain statements that only a few hundred northwestern warriors were in the field at the very time that two thousand had been fitted out at Detroit to act along the Ohio and Wabash; as we learn from De Peyster's letter to Haldimand of May 17, 1780 (in the Haldimand MSS.).

One band of painted marauders carried off Boon's daughter. She was in a canoe with two other girls on the river near Boonsborough when they were pounced on by five Indians.[1]   As soon as he heard the news Boon went in pursuit with a party of seven men from the fort, including the three lovers of the captured girls.   After following the trail all of one day and the greater part of two nights, the pursuers came up with the savages, and, rushing in, scattered or slew them before they could either make resistance or kill their captives. The rescuing party then returned in triumph to the fort.

[1] On July 14, 1776.   The names of the three girls were Betsy and Fanny Callaway and Jemima Boon ; See Boon's Narrative, and Butler, who gives the letter of July 21, 1776, written by Col. John Floyd, one of the pursuing party.

The names of the lovers, in their order, were Samuel Henderson (a brother of Richard), John Holder, and Flanders Callaway.   Three weeks after the return to the fort Squire Boon united in marriage the eldest pair of lovers, Samuel Henderson and Betsey Callaway.   It was the first wedding that ever took place in Kentucky.   Both the other couples were likewise married a year or two later.

The whole story reads like a page out of one of Cooper's novels.   The two younger girls gave way to despair when captured ; but Betsey Callaway was sure they would be followed and rescued.   To mark the line of their flight she broke off twigs from the bushes, and when threatened with the tomahawk for doing this, she tore off strips from her dress.   The Indians carefully covered their trail, compelling the girls to walk apart, as their captors did, in the thick cane, and to wade up and down the little brooks.

Boon started in pursuit the same evening.   All next day he followed the tangled trail like a bloodhound, and early the following morning came on the Indians, camped by a buffalo calf which they had just killed and were about to cook.   The rescue was managed very adroitly ; for had any warning been given the Indians would have instantly killed their captives, according to their invariable custom.   Boon and Floyd each shot one of the savages, and the remaining three escaped almost naked, without gun, tomahawk, or scalping-knife.   The girls were unharmed ; for the Indians rarely. molested their captives on the journey to the home towns, unless their strength gave out, when they were tomahawked without mercy.

Thus for two years the pioneers worked in the wilderness, harassed by unending individual warfare, but not threatened by any formidable attempt to oust them from the lands that they had won. During this breathing spell they established civil government, explored the country, planted crops, and built strongholds. Then came the inevitable struggle. When in 1777 the snows began to melt before the lengthening spring days, the riflemen who guarded the log forts were called on to make head against a series of resolute efforts to drive them from Kentucky.

APPENDICES.

APPENDICES

APPENDIX A—TO CHAPTER IV.

IT is greatly to be wished that some competent person would write a full and true history of our national dealings with the Indians. Undoubtedly the latter have often suffered terrible injustice at our hands. A number of instances, such as the conduct of the Georgians to the Cherokees in the early part of the present century, or the whole treatment of Chief Joseph and his Nez Perçés, might be mentioned, which are indelible blots on our fair fame ; and yet, in describing our dealings with the red men as a whole, historians do us much less than justice.

It was wholly impossible to avoid conflicts with the weaker race, unless we were willing to see the American continent fall into the hands of some other strong power ; and even had we adopted such a ludicrous policy, the Indians themselves would have made war upon us. It cannot be too often insisted that they did not own the land ; or, at least, that their ownership was merely such as that claimed often by our own white hunters. If the Indians really owned Kentucky in 1775, then in 1776 it was the property of Boon and his associates ; and to dispossess one party was as great a wrong as to dispossess the other. To recognize the Indian ownership of the limitless prairies and forests of this continent—that is, to consider the dozen squalid savages who hunted at long intervals over a territory of a thousand square miles as owning it outright— necessarily implies a similar recognition of the claims of every white hunter, squatter, horse-thief, or wandering cattle-man. Take as an example the country round the Little Missouri. When the cattle-men, the first actual settlers, came into this land in 1882, it was already scantily peopled by a few white hunters and trappers. The latter were extremely jealous of intrusion ; they had held their own in spite of the Indians, and, like the Indians, the inrush of settlers and the consequent destruction of the game meant their own undoing; also, again like the Indians, they felt that their having hunted over the soil gave them a vague prescriptive right to its sole occupation, and they did their best to keep actual settlers out. In some cases, to avoid difficulty, their nominal claims were bought up ; generally, and rightly, they were disregarded. Yet they certainly had as good a right to the Little Missouri country as the Sioux have to most of the land on their present reservations. In fact, the mere statement of the case is sufficient to show the absurdity of asserting that the land really belonged to the Indians. The different tribes have always been utterly unable to define their own boundaries. Thus the Delawares and Wyandots, in 1785, though entirely separate nations, claimed and, in a certain sense, occupied almost exactly the same territory.

Moreover, it was wholly impossible for our policy to be always consistent. Nowadays we undoubtedly ought to break up the great Indian reservations, disregard the tribal governments, allot the land in severalty (with, however, only a limited power of alienation), and treat the Indians as we do other citizens, with certain exceptions, for their sakes as well as ours. But this policy, which it would be wise to follow now, would have been wholly impracticable a century since. Our central government was then too weak either effectively to control its own members or adequately to punish aggressions made upon them ; and even if it had been strong, it would probably have proved impossible to keep entire order over such a vast, sparsely-peopled frontier, with such turbulent elements on both sides. The Indians could not be treated as individuals at that time. There was no possible alternative, therefore, to treating their tribes as nations, exactly as the French and English had done before us. Our difficulties were partly inherited from these, our predecessors, were partly caused by our own misdeeds, but were mainly the inevitable result of the conditions under which the problem had to be solved ; no human wisdom or virtue could have worked out a peaceable solution. As a nation, our Indian policy is to be blamed, because of the weakness it displayed, because of its shortsightedness, and its occasional leaning to the policy of the sentimental humanitarians ; and we have often promised what was impossible to perform ; but there has been little wilful wrong-doing. Our government almost always tried to act fairly by the tribes ; the governmental agents (some of whom have been dishonest, and others foolish, but who, as a class, have been greatly traduced), in their reports, are far more apt to be unjust to the whites than to the reds ; and the Federal authorities, though unable to prevent much of the injustice, still did check and control the white borderers very much more effectually than the Indian sachems and war-chiefs controlled their young braves. The tribes were warlike and bloodthirsty, jealous of each other and of the whites ; they claimed the land for their hunting grounds, but their claims all conflicted with one another ; their knowledge of their own boundaries was so indefinite that they were always willing, for inadequate compensation, to sell land to which they had merely the vaguest title ; and yet, when once they had received the goods, were generally reluctant to make over even what they could ; they coveted the goods and scalps of the whites, and the young warriors were always on the alert to commit outrages when they could do it with impunity. On the other hand, the evil-disposed whites regarded the Indians as fair game for robbery and violence of any kind ; and the far larger number of well-disposed men, who would not willingly wrong any Indian, were themselves maddened by the memories of hideous injuries received. They bitterly resented the action of the government, which, in their eyes, failed to properly protect them, and yet sought to keep them out of waste, uncultivated lands which they did not regard as being any more the property of the Indians than of their own hunters. With the best intentions, it was wholly impossible for any government to evolve order out of such a chaos without resort to the ultimate arbitrator—the sword.

The purely sentimental historians take no account of the difficulties under which we labored, nor of the countless wrongs and provocations we endured, while grossly magnifying the already lamentably large number of injuries for which we really deserve to be held responsible. To get a fair idea of the Indians of the present day, and of our dealings with them, we have fortunately one or two excellent books, notably "Hunting Grounds of the Great West," and "Our Wild Indians," by Col. Richard I. Dodge (Hartford, 1882), and "Massacres of the Mountains," by J. P. Dunn (New York, 1886). As types of the opposite class, which are worse than valueless, and which nevertheless might cause some hasty future historian, unacquainted with the facts, to fall into grievous error, I may mention, "A Century of Dishonor," by H. H. (Mrs. Helen Hunt Jackson), and "Our Indian Wards," (Geo. W. Manypenny). The latter is a mere spiteful diatribe against various army officers, and neither its manner nor its matter warrants more than an allusion. Mrs. Jackson's book is capable of doing more harm because it is written in good English, and because the author, who had lived a pure and noble life, was intensely in earnest in what she wrote, and had the most praiseworthy purpose—to prevent our committing any more injustice to the Indians. This was all most proper; every good man or woman should do whatever is possible to make the government treat the Indians of the present time in the fairest and most generous spirit, and to provide against any repetition of such outrages as were inflicted upon the Nez Percés and upon part of the Cheyennes, or the wrongs with which the civilized nations of the Indian territory are sometimes threatened. The purpose of the book is excellent, but the spirit in which it is written cannot be called even technically honest. As a polemic, it is possible that it did not do harm (though the effect of even a polemic is marred by hysterical indifference to facts.) As a history it would be beneath criticism, were it not that the high character of the author and her excellent literary work in other directions have given it a fictitious value and made it much quoted by the large class of amiable but maudlin fanatics concerning whom it may be said that the excellence of their intentions but indifferently atones for the invariable folly and ill effect of their actions. It is not too much to say that the book is thoroughly untrustworthy from cover to cover, and that not a single statement it contains should be accepted without independent proof ; for even those that are not absolutely false, are often as bad on account of so much of the truth having been suppressed. One effect of this is of course that the author's recitals of the many real wrongs of Indian tribes utterly fail to impress us, because she lays quite as much stress on those that are non-existent, and on the equally numerous cases where the wrong-doing was wholly the other way. To get an idea of the value of the work, it is only necessary to compare her statements about almost any tribe with the real facts, choosing at random ; for instance, compare her accounts of the Sioux and the plains tribes generally, with those given by Col. Dodge in his two books ; or her recital of the Sandy Creek massacre with the facts as stated by Mr. Dunn—who is apt, if any thing, to lean to the Indian's side.

These foolish sentimentalists not only write foul slanders about their own countrymen, but are themselves the worst possible advisers on any point touching Indian management. They would do well to heed General Sheridan's bitter words, written when many Easterners were clamoring against the army authorities because they took partial vengeance for a series of brutal outrages : " I do not know how far these humanitarians should be excused on account of their ignorance ; but surely it is the only excuse that can give a shadow of justification for aiding and abetting such horrid crimes."

APPENDIX B—TO CHAPTER V.

In Mr. Shaler's entertaining " History of Kentucky," there is an account of the population of the western frontiers, and Kentucky, interesting because it illustrates some of the popular delusions on the subject. He speaks (pp. 9, 11, 23) of Kentucky as containing " nearly pure English blood, mainly derived through the old Dominion, and altogether from districts that shared the Virginian conditions." As much of the blood was Pennsylvanian or North Carolinian, his last sentence means nothing, unless all the "districts" outside of New England are held to have shared the Virginian conditions. Turning to Marshall (I., 441) we see that in 1780 about half the people were from Virginia, Pennsylvania furnishing the next greatest number ; and of the Virginians most were from a population much more like that of Pennsylvania than like that of tide-water Virginia ; as we learn from twenty sources, such as Waddell's "Annals of Augusta County." Mr. Shaler speaks of the Huguenots and of the Scotch immigrants, who came over after 1745, but actually makes no mention of the Presbyterian Irish or Scotch Irish, much the most important element in all the west ; in fact, on p. 10, he impliedly excludes any such immigration at all. He greatly underestimates the German element, which was important in West Virginia. He sums up by stating that the Kentuckians come from the "truly British people," quite a different thing from his statement that they are "English."

The "truly British people" consists of a conglomerate of as distinct races as exist anywhere in Aryan Europe. The Erse, Welsh, and Gaelic immigrants to America are just as distinct from the English, just as "foreign" to them, as are the Scandinavians, Germans, Hollanders, and Huguenots—often more so. Such early families as the Welsh Shelbys, and Gaelic McAfees are no more English than are the Huguenot Seviers or the German Stoners. Even including merely the immigrants from the British Isles, the very fact that the Welsh, Irish, and Scotch, in a few generations, fuse with the English instead of each element remaining separate, makes the American population widely different from that of Britain ; exactly as a flask of water is different from two cans of hydrogen and oxygen gas. Mr. Shaler also seems inclined to look down a little on the Tennesseeans, and to consider their population as composed in part of inferior elements ; but in reality, though there are very marked differences between the two commonwealths of Kentucky and Tennessee, yet they resemble one another more closely, in blood and manners, than either does any other American State ; and both have too just cause for pride to make it necessary for either to sneer at the other, or indeed at any State of our mighty Federal Union. In their origin they were precisely alike ; but whereas the original pioneers, the hunters and Indian fighters, kept possession of Tennessee as long as they lived,—Jackson, at Sevier's death, taking the latter's place with even more than his power,—in Kentucky, on the other hand, after twenty years' rule, the first settlers were swamped by the great inrush of immigration, and with the defeat of Logan for governor the control passed into the hands of the same class of men that then ruled Virginia. After that date the "tide-water" stock assumed an importance in Kentucky it never had in Tennessee ; and of course the influence of the Scotch-Irish blood was greatly diminished.

Mr. Shaler's error is trivial compared to that made by another and even more brilliant writer. In the "History of the People of the United States," by Professor McMaster (New York, 1887), p. 70, there is a mistake so glaring that it would not need notice, were it not for the many excellencies and wide repute of Professor McMaster's book. He says that of the immigrants to Kentucky, most had come "from the neighboring States of Carolina and Georgia," and shows that this is not a mere slip of the pen, by elaborating the statement in the following paragraphs, again speaking of North and South Carolina and Georgia as furnishing the colonists to Kentucky. This shows a complete misapprehension not only of the feeding-grounds of the western emigration, but of the routes it followed, and of the conditions of the southern States. South Carolina furnished very few emigrants to Kentucky, and Georgia practically none ; combined they probably did not furnish as many as New Jersey or Maryland. Georgia was herself a frontier community ; she received instead of sending out immigrants. The bulk of the South Carolina emigration went to Georgia.

APPENDIX C—TO CHAPTER VI.

OFFICE OF THE SECRETARY OF STATE,
NASHVILLE, TENN., June 12, 1888.

Hon. THEODORE ROOSEVELT,
SAGAMORE HILL,
LONG ISLAND, N. Y.

DEAR SIR :

I was born, " raised," and have always lived in Washington County, E. Tenn. Was born on the " head-waters " of " Boone's Creek," in said county. I resided for several years in the " Boone's Creek Civil District," in Washington County (this some " twenty years ago "), within two miles of the historic tree in question, on which is carved, " D. Boon cilled bar &c."; have visited and examined the tree more than once. The tree is a beech, still standing, though fast decaying. It is located some eight miles northeast of Jonesboro, the county seat of Washington, on the " waters of Boone's Creek," which creek was named after Daniel Boone, and on which (creek) it is certain Daniel Boone " camped " during a winter or two. The tree stands about two miles from the spring, where it has always been understood Boone's camp was. More than twenty years ago, I have heard old gentlemen (living in the neighborhood of the tree), who were then from fifty to seventy years old, assert that the carving was on the tree when they were boys, and that the tradition in the community was that the inscription was on the tree when discovered by the first permanent settlers. The posture of the tree is " leaning," so that a " bar," or other animal could ascend it without difficulty.

While the letters could be clearly traced when I last looked at them, still because of the expansion of the bark, it was difficult, and I heard old gentlemen years ago remark upon the changed appearance of the inscription from what it was when they *first* knew it.

Boone certainly camped for a time under the tree ; the creek is named after him (has always been known as Boone's Creek) ; the Civil District is named after him, and the post-office also. True, the story as to the carving is traditionary, but a man had as well question in that community the authenticity of "Holy Writ," as the fact that Boone carved the inscription on that tree.

I am very respectfully

JOHN ALLISON.

APPENDIX D—TO CHAPTER VI.

The following copy of an original note of Boon's was sent me by Judge John N. Lea :

July the 20" 1786. Sir, The Land has Been Long Survayd and Not Knowing When the Money would be Rady Was the Reason of my not Returning the Works however the may be Returned when you pleas. But I must have Nother Copy of the Entry as I have lost that I had when I lost my plating instruments and only have the Short Field Notes. Just the Corse Distance and Corner trees pray send me Nother Copy that I may know how to give it the proper bounderry agreeable to the Location and I Will send the plat to the offis medetly if you chose it, the expense is as follows

Survayer's fees	.	.	.	.	£9	3	8
Ragesters fees	.	.	.	.	7	14	0
Chanman	.	.	.	.	8	0	0
purvisions of the tower		.	.	2	0	0
					£26	17	8

You will also Send a Copy of the agreement betwixt Mr. [illegible] overton and myself Where I Red the warrants.

I am, sir, your omble servant,

DANIEL BOONE.

APPENDIX E—TO CHAPTER VII.

Recently one or two histories of the times and careers of Robertson and Sevier have been published by " Edmund Kirke," Mr. James R. Gilmore. They are charmingly written, and are of real service as calling attention to a neglected portion of our history and making it interesting. But they entirely fail to discriminate between the provinces of history and fiction.

It is greatly to be regretted that Mr. Gilmore did not employ his powers in writing an avowed historical novel treating of the events he discusses; such a work from him would have a permanent value, like Robert L. Kennedy's " Horseshoe Robinson." In their present form his works cannot be accepted even as offering material on which to form a judgment, except in so far as they contain repetitions of statements given by Ramsey or Putnam. I say this with real reluctance, for my relations with Mr. Gilmore personally have been pleasant. I was at the outset prepossessed in favor of his books; but as soon as I came to study them I found that (except for what was drawn from the printed Tennessee State histories) they were extremely untrustworthy. Oral tradition has a certain value of its own, if used with great discretion and intelligence; but it is rather startling to find any one blandly accepting as gospel alleged oral traditions gathered one hundred and twenty-five years after the event, especially when they relate to such subjects as the losses and numbers of Indian war parties. No man with the slightest knowledge of frontiersmen or frontier life could commit such a mistake. If any one wishes to get at the value of oral tradition of an Indian fight a century old, let him go out west and collect the stories of Custer's battle, which took place only a dozen years ago. I think I have met or heard of fifty " solitary survivors " of Custer's defeat; and I could collect certainly a dozen complete accounts of both it and Reno's fight, each believed by a goodly number of men, and no two relating the story in an even approximately similar fashion. Mr. Gilmore apparently accepts all such accounts indiscriminately, and embodies them in his narrative without even a reference to his authorities. I particularize one or two out of very many instances in the chapters dealing with the Cherokee wars.

Books founded upon an indiscriminate acceptance of any and all such traditions or alleged traditions are a little absurd, unless, as already said, they are avowedly merely historic novels, when they may be both useful and interesting. I am obliged to say with genuine regret, after careful examination of Mr. Gilmore's books, that I cannot accept any single unsupported statement they contain as even requiring an examination into its probability. I would willingly pass them by without comment, did I not fear that my silence might be construed into an acceptance of their truth. Moreover, I notice that some writers, like the editors of the " Cyclopedia of American Biography," seem inclined to take the volumes seriously.

APPENDIX F—TO CHAPTER IX.

I.

(*Campbell MSS.;* this letter and the one following are from copies, and the spelling etc., may not be quite as in the originals).

CAMP OPPOSITE THE MOUTH OF THE GREAT KENAWAY.
October 16—1774.

DEAR UNCLE,

I gladly embrace this opportunity to acquaint you that we are all here yet alive through Gods mercies, & I sincerely wish that this may find you and your family in the station of health that we left you. I never had anything worth notice to acquaint you with since I left you till now—the express seems to be hurrying, that I cannot write you with the same coolness and deliberation as I would. We arrived at the mouth of the Canaway, thursday 6th. Octo. and encamped on a fine piece of ground, with an intent to wait for the Governor and his party but hearing that he was going another way we contented ourselves to stay there a few days to rest the troops, &c. where we looked upon ourselves to be in safety till Monday morning the 10th. instant when two of our company went out before day to hunt—to wit Val. Sevier and James Robinson and discovered a party of Indians. As I expect you will hear something of our battle before you get this, I have here stated the affair nearly to you :

For the satisfaction of the people in your parts in this they have a true state of the memorable battle fought at the mouth of the Great Canaway on the 10th. instant. Monday morning about half an hour before sunrise, two of Capt. Russells company discovered a large party of Indians about a mile from camp, one of which men was killed, the other made his escape & brought in his intelligence. In two or three minutes after, two of Capt. Shelby's Company came in & confirmed the account, Col. Andrew Lewis being informed thereof immediately ordered Col. Charles Lewis to take the command of 150 men from Augusta and with him went Capt. Dickison, Capt. Harrison, Capt. Wilson, Capt. John Lewis, from Augusta and Capt. Sockridge which made the first division. Col. Fleming was also ordered to take the command of one hundred and fifty more, consisting of Battertout, Fincastle & Bedford troops, —viz., Capt, Buford of Bedford, Capt. Lewis of Battertout, Capt. Shelby & Capt. Russell of Fincastle which made the second division. Col. Lewis marched with his division to the right some distance from the Ohio. Col. Fleming with his division up the bank of the Ohio to the left. Col. Lewis' division had not marched little more than a quarter of a mile from camp when about sunrise, an attack was made on the front of his division in a most vigorous manner by the united tribes Indians,—Shawnees, Delawares, Mingoes, Taways, and of several other nations, in number not less than eight hundred, and by many thought to be a thousand. In this heavy attack Col. Charles Lewis received a wound which soon after caused his death, and several of his men fell on the spot, —in fact the Augusta division was forced to give way to the heavy fire of the enemy. In about the second of a minute after the attack on Col. Lewis' division, the enemy engaged of Col. Fleming's division on the ohio and in a short time Col. Fleming received two balls thro' his left arm and one thro' his breast ; and after animating the Captains & soldiers in a calm manner to the pursuit of victory returned to the camp. The loss of the brave Col's was severely felt by the officers in particular. But the Augusta troops being shortly reinforced from camp by Col. Field with his company, together with Capt. M'Dowers, Capt. Matthew's and Capt. Stewart's from Augusta ; Capt. John Lewis, Capt. Paulins, Capt. Arbuckle's, and Capt. M'Clannahan's from Battertout. The enemy no longer able to maintain their ground was forced to give way till they were in a line with the troops left in action on branches of ohio by Col. Fleming. In this precipitate retreat Col. Field was killed ; after which Capt. Shelby was ordered to take the command. During this time which was till after twelve of the clock, the action continued extremely hot, the close underwood, many steep banks and logs greatly favored their retreat, and the bravest of their men made the *best* use of themselves, while others were throwing their dead into the ohio, and carrying off the wounded   After twelve the action in a small degree abated, but continued sharp enough till after one o'clock.   Their long retreat gave them a most advantageous spot of ground ; from which it appeared to the officers so difficult to dislodge them, that it was thought most advisable, to stand as the line was then formed, which was about a mile and a quarter in length, and had till then sustained a constant and equal weight of fire from wing to wing. It was till half an hour of sunset they continued firing on us, which we returned to their disadvantage, at length night coming on they found a safe retreat.   They had not the satisfaction of scalping any of our men save one or two straglers, whom they killed before the engagement.   Many of their dead they scalped rather than we should have them, but our troops scalped upwards of twenty of those who were first killed.   Its beyond a doubt, their loss in numbers far exceeds ours which is considerable.

Field officers killed—Col. Charles Lewis, & Col. John Fields.   Field officers wounded—Col. William Fleming ;— Capts. killed, John Murray, Capt. Samuel Wilson, Capt. Robert M'Clannahan, Capt. James Ward.   Capts. wounded —Thomas Buford, John Dickison & John Scidmore.   Subalterns killed, Lieutenant Hugh Allen, Ensign Matthew Brackin & Ensign Cundiff ; Subalterns wounded, Lieut. Lane, Lieut. Vance, Lieut. Goldman, Lieut. James Robertson ; and about 46 killed and 60 wounded.   From this sir you may judge that we had a very hard day ; its really impossible for me to express or you to conceive the acclamations that we were under,— sometimes the hideous cries of the enemy, and the groans of our wounded men lying around, was enough to shudder the stoutest heart.   Its the general opinion of the officers that we shall soon have another engagement, as we have now got over into the enemy's country. We expect to meet the Governor about forty or fifty miles from here. Nothing will save us from another battle, unless they attack the Governors party. Five men that came in dadys (daddy's) company were killed, I don't know that you were acquainted with any of them, except Mark Williams who lived with Roger Top. Acquaint Mr. Carmack that his son was slightly wounded through the shoulder and arm and that he is in a likely way of recovery. We leave him at the mouth of the Canaway and one very careful hand to take care of him. There is a garrison and three hundred men left at that place, with a surgeon to heal the wounded. We expect to return to the garrison in about 16 days from the Shawny towns.

I have nothing more particular to acquaint you with concerning the battle. As to the country I cannot say much in praise of any that I have yet seen. Dady intended writing you, but did not know of the express until the time was too short. I have wrote to mammy tho' not so fully to you, as I then expected the express was just going. We seem to be all in a moving posture, just going from this place, so that I must conclude, wishing you health and prosperity until I see you and your family. In the meantime I am your truly affectionate friend and humble servant,

ISAAC SHELBY.

To MR. JOHN SHELBY,
         Holston River,
                  Fincastle County.
Favd. by Mr. Benj. Gray.

II.

(*Campbell MSS.*)

October ye 31st. 1774.

DEAR SIR,

Being on my way home to Fincastle court, was overtaken this evening by letters from Colo. Christian and other gentlemen on the expedition, giving an account of a battle which was fought between our troops & the enemy Indians, on the 10th instant, in the Fork of the Ohio & the Great Kanhawa.

The particulars of the action, drawn up by Colo. Andr. Lewis I have sent you enclosed, also a return of the killed and wounded, by which you will see that we have lost many brave and valiant officers & soldiers, whose loss to their families, as well as to the community, is very great.

Colo. Christian with the Fincastle troops, (except the companies commanded by Capts. Russell & Shelby, who were in the action) were on their march ; and on the evening of that day, about 15 miles from field of battle, heard that the action began in the morning. They marched hard, and got to the camp about midnight. The cries of the wounded, without any persons of skill or any thing to nourish people in their unhappy situation, was striking. The Indians had crossed the river on rafts, 6 or 8 miles above the Forks, in the night, and it is believed, intended to attack the camp, had they not been prevented by our men marching to meet them at the distance of half a mile. It is said the enemy behaved with bravery and great caution, that they frequently damned our men for white sons of bitches. Why did they not whistle now ? (alluding to the fifes) & that they would learn them to shoot.

The Governor was then at Hockhocking, about 12 or 15 miles below the mouth of the Little Kanhawa, from whence he intended to march his party to a place called Chillicoffee, about 20 miles farther than the towns where it was said the Shawneese had assembled with their families and allies, to make a stand, as they had good houses and plenty of ammunition & provisions & had cleared the woods to a great distance from the place. His party who were to march from the camp was about 1200, and to join Colo. Lewis' party about 28 miles from Chillicoffee. But whether the action above mentioned would disconcert this plan or not, I think appears a little uncertain, as there is a probability that his excellency on hearing the news might, with his party, fall down the river and join Colo. Lewis' party and march together against the enemy.

They were about building a breastwork at the Forks, & after leaving a proper party to take care of the wounded & the provisions there, that Colo. Lewis could march upwards of a thousand men to join his Lordship, so that the whole when they meet will be about 2200 choice men. What may be their success God only knows, but it is highly probable the matter is decided before this time.

Colo. Christian says, from the accounts he had the enemy behaved with inconceivable bravery. The head men walked about in the time of action, exhorting their men " to be close, shoot well, be strong of fight." They had parties planted on the opposite side of both rivers to shoot our men as they swam over, not doubting, as is supposed, but they would gain a complete victory. In the evening late they called to our men "that they had 2000 men for them to-morrow, and that they had 1100 men now as well as they." They also made very merry about a treaty.

Poor Colo. Charles Lewis was shot on a clear piece of ground, as he had not taken a tree, encouraging his men to advance. On being wounded he handed his gun to a person nigh him and retired to the camp, telling his men as he passed "I am wounded but go on and be brave." If the loss of a good man a sincere friend, and a brave officer, claims a tear, he certainly is entitled to it.

Colo. Fields was shot at a great tree by two Indians on his right, while one on his left was amusing him with talk and the Colo. Endeavoring to get a shot at him.

Besides the loss the troops met with in action by Colo. Fleming who was obliged to retire from the field, which was very great, the wounded met with the most irreparable loss in an able and skillful surgeon. Colo. Christian says that his (Flemings) lungs or part of them came out of the wound in his breast but were pushed back ; and by the last part of his letter, which was dated the 16th. instant, he has some hopes of his recovery.

Thus, sir, I have given you an account of the action from the several letters I recd., and have only to add, that Colo. Christian desires me to inform Mrs. Christian of his welfare, which with great pleasure I do through this channel, and should any further news come, which I much expect soon, I shall take the earliest oppy. of communicating the same to you. It is believed the troops will surely return in Nov.

I write in a hurry and amidst a crowd of inquisitive people, therefore hope you will excuse the inaccuracy of, D'r. Sir,

Your sincere well wisher & most obedt. Servt.,

WM. PRESTON.

P. S. If you please you may give Mr. Purdie a copy of the enclosed papers, & anything else you may think worthy the notice of the Public.

III.

LOGAN'S SPEECH.

There has been much controversy over the genuineness of Logan's speech ; but those who have questioned it have done so with singularly little reason. In fact its authenticity would never have been impugned at all had it not (wrongly) blamed Cresap with killing Logan's family. Cresap's defenders, with curious folly, have in consequence thought it necessary to show, not that Logan was mistaken, but that he never delivered the speech at all.

The truth seems to be that Cresap, without provocation, but after being incited to war by Conolly's letter, murdered some peaceful Indians, among whom there were certainly some friends and possibly some relations of Logan (see testimony of Col. Ebenezer Zane, in Jefferson's Notes, and " American Pioneer," I., 12 ; also Clark's letter in the Jefferson Papers) ; but that he had no share in the massacre of Logan's family at Yellow Creek by Greathouse and his crew two or three days afterwards. The two massacres occurring so near together, however, produced the impression not only among the Indians but among many whites (as shown in the body of this work), that Cresap had been guilty of both ; and this Logan undoubtedly believed, as can be seen by the letter he wrote and left tied to a war club in a murdered settler's house. This was an injustice to Cresap ; but it was a very natural mistake on Logan's part.

After the speech was recited it attracted much attention ; was published in newspapers, periodicals, etc., and was extensively quoted. Jefferson, as we learn from his Papers at Washington, took it down in 1775, getting it from Lord Dunmore's officers, and published it in his "Notes," in 1784 ; unfortunately he took for granted that its allegations as regards Cresap were true, and accordingly prefaced it by a very unjust attack on the reputed murderer. Until thirteen years after this publication, and until twenty-three years after the speech had been published for the first time, no one thought of questioning it. Then Luther Martin, of Maryland, attacked its authenticity, partly because he was Cresap's son-in-law, and partly because he was a Federalist and a bitter opponent of Jefferson. Like all of his successors in the same line, he confused two entirely distinct things, viz., the justice of the charge against Cresap, and the authenticity of Logan's speech. His controversy with Jefferson grew very bitter. He succeeded in showing clearly that Cresap was wrongly accused by Logan ; he utterly failed to impugn the authenticity of the latter's speech. Jefferson, thanks to a letter he received from Clark, must have known that Cresap had been accused wrongly ; but he was irritated by the controversy, and characteristically refrained in any of his publications from doing justice to the slandered man's memory.

A Mr. Jacobs soon afterwards wrote a life of Cresap, in which he attempted both of the feats aimed at by Martin ; it is quite an interesting production, but exceedingly weak in its arguments. Neville B. Craig, in the February, 1847, number of *The Olden Time*, a historical magazine, followed on the same lines. Finally, Brantz Mayer, in his very interesting little book, " Logan and Cresap," went over the whole matter in a much fairer manner than his predecessors, but still distinctly as an advocate ; for though he collected with great industry and gave impartially all the original facts (so that from what he gives alone it is quite possible to prove that the speech is certainly genuine), yet his own conclusions show great bias. Thus he severely rules out any testimony against Cresap that is not absolutely unquestioned ; but admits without hesitation any and every sort of evidence leaning against poor Logan's character or the authenticity of his speech. He even goes so far (pp. 122, 123) as to say it is not a "speech" at all,—although it would puzzle a man to know what else to call it, as he also declares it is not a message,—and shows the animus of his work by making the gratuitous suggestion that if Logan made it at all he was probably at the time excited "as well by the cruelties he had committed as by liquor."

It is necessary, therefore, to give a brief summary of a portion of the evidence in its favor, as well as of all the evidence against it. Jefferson's Notes and Mr. Mayer's book go fully into the matter.

The evidence in its favor is as follows :

(1.) Gibson's statement. This is the keystone of the arch. John Gibson was a man of note and of unblemished character ; he was made a general by Washington, and held high appointive positions under Madison and Jefferson ; he was also an Associate Judge of the Court of Common Pleas in Pennsylvania. Throughout his life he bore a reputation for absolute truthfulness. He was the messenger who went to Logan, heard the speech, took it down, and gave it to Lord Dunmore. We have his deposition, delivered under oath, that "Logan delivered to him the speech nearly as related by Mr. Jefferson in his Notes," when the two were alone together, and that he "on his return to camp delivered the speech to Lord Dunmore," and that he also at the time told Logan he was mistaken about Cresap. Brantz Mayer, who accepts his statement as substantially true, thinks that he probably only reported the *substance* of Logan's speech, or so much of it as he could recollect ; but in the State Department at Washington, among the Jefferson Papers (5–1–4), is a statement by John Anderson, a merchant in Fredericksburg, who was an Indian trader at Pittsburg in 1774 ; he says that he questioned Gibson as to whether he had not himself added something to the speech, to which Gibson replied that he had not changed it in any way, but had translated it literally, as well as he could, though he was unable to come up to the force of the expressions in the original.

This evidence itself is absolutely conclusive, except on the supposition that Gibson was a malicious and infamous liar. The men who argue that the speech was fictitious are also obliged to explain what motive there could possibly have been for the deception; they accordingly advance the theory that it was part of Dunmore's (imaginary) treacherous conduct, as he wished to discredit Cresap, because he knew—apparently by divination—that the latter was going to be a whig. Even granting the Earl corrupt motives and a prophetic soul, it remains to be explained why he should wish to injure an obscure borderer, whom nobody has ever heard of except in connection with Logan; it would have served the purpose quite as well to have used the equally unknown name of the real offender, Greathouse. The fabrication of the speech would have been an absolutely motiveless and foolish transaction; to which Gibson, a pronounced whig, must needs have been a party. This last fact shows that there could have been no intention of using the speech in the British interest.

(2) The statement of General George Rogers Clark. (Like the preceding, this can be seen in the Jefferson Papers.) Clark was present in Dunmore's camp at the time. He says: "Logan's speech to Dunmore now came forward as related by Mr. Jefferson and was generally believed and indeed not doubted to have been genuine and dictated by Logan—The Army knew it was wrong so far as it respected Cresap, and afforded an opportunity of rallying that Gentleman on the subject—I discovered that Cresap was displeased and told him that he must be a very great Man, that the Indians shouldered him with every thing that had happened. . . . Logan is the author of the speech as related by Mr. Jefferson." Clark's remembrance of his rallying Cresap shows that the speech contained Cresap's name and that it was read before the army; several other witnesses, whose names are not necessary to mention, simply corroborate Clark's statements, and a large amount of indirect evidence to the same effect could be produced, were there the least necessity. (See Jefferson's Notes, "The American Pioneer," etc., etc.)

The evidence against the authenticity of the speech, outside of mere conjectures and inuendoes, is as follows:

(1) Logan called Cresap a colonel when he was really a captain. This inability of an Indian to discriminate accurately between these two titles of frontier militia officers is actually solemnly brought forward as telling against the speech.

(2) Logan accused Cresap of committing a murder which he had not committed. But, as we have already seen, Logan had made the same accusation in his unquestionably authentic letter, written previously ; and many whites, as well as Indians, thought as Logan did.

(3) A Col. Benj. Wilson, who was with Dunmore's army, says that "he did not hear the charge preferred in Logan's speech against Captain Cresap." This is mere negative evidence, valueless in any event, and doubly so in view of Clark's statement.

(4) Mr. Neville B. Craig, in *Olden Time*, says in 1847 that "many years before a Mr. James McKee, the brother of Mr. William Johnson's deputy, had told him that he had seen the speech in the handwriting of one of the Johnsons . . . before it was seen by Logan." This is a hearsay statement delivered just seventy-three years after the event, and it is on its face so wildly improbable as not to need further comment, at least until there is some explanation as to why the Johnsons should have written the speech, how they could possibly have gotten it to Logan, and why Gibson should have entered into the conspiracy.

(5) A Benjamin Tomlinson testifies that he believes that the speech was fabricated by Gibson ; he hints, but does not frankly assert, that Gibson was not sent after Logan, but that Girty was ; and swears that he heard the speech read three times and that the name of Cresap was not mentioned in it.

He was said in later life to bear a good reputation ; but in his deposition he admits under oath that he was present at the Yellow Creek murder (*Olden Time*, II., 61 ; the editor, by the way, seems to call him alternately Joseph and Benjamin) ; and he was therefore an unconvicted criminal, who connived at or participated in one of the most brutal and cowardly deeds ever done on the frontier. His statement as against Gibson's would be worthless anyhow ; fortunately his testimony as to the omission of Cresap's name from the speech is also flatly contradicted by Clark. With the words of two such men against his, and bearing in mind that all that he says against the authenticity of the speech itself is confessedly mere supposition on his part, his statement must be promptly set aside as worthless. If true, by the way, it would conflict with (4) Craig's statement.

This is literally all the "evidence" against the speech. It scarcely needs serious discussion; it may be divided into two parts — one containing allegations that are silly, and the other those that are discredited.

There is probably very little additional evidence to be obtained, on one side or the other; it is all in, and Logan's speech can be unhesitatingly pronounced authentic. Doubtless there have been verbal alterations in it; there is not extant a report of any famous speech which does not probably differ in some way from the words as they were actually spoken. There is also a good deal of confusion as to whether the council took place in the Indian town, or in Dunmore's camp; whether Logan was sought out alone in his hut by Gibson, or came up and drew the latter aside while he was at the council, etc. In the same way, we have excellent authority for stating that, prior to the battle of the Great Kanawha, Lewis reached the mouth of that river on October 1st, and that he reached it on October 6th; that on the day of the attack the troops marched from camp a quarter of a mile, and that they marched three quarters; that the Indians lost more men than the whites, and that they lost fewer; that Lewis behaved well, and that he behaved badly; that the whites lost 140 men, and that they lost 215, etc., etc. The conflict of evidence as to the dates and accessory details of Logan's speech is no greater than it is as to the dates and accessory details of the murder by Greathouse, or as to all the preliminaries of the main battle of the campaign. Coming from backwoods sources, it is inevitable that we should have confusion on points of detail; but as to the main question there seems almost as little reason for doubting the authenticity of Logan's speech, as for doubting the reality of the battle of the Great Kanawha.

END OF VOL. I.

All Four Volumes Available in Bison Book Editions

THE WINNING OF THE WEST.

By THEODORE ROOSEVELT.